QUICK CLICKS

40 Fast and Fun Behaviors to Train with a Clicker

MANDY BOOK / CHERYL S. SMITH

the art of dog training

Legacy By Mail   Carlsborg, Washington

Cover Design and Illustrations by Judy Winthrop
Book Design by Olympic Graphic Arts, Inc.

ISBN 0-9674796-4-9

Published by
LEGACY BY MAIL
PO Box 697
Carlsborg, WA 98382

360-683-9646   (fax) 360-683-5755
clicks@legacybymail.com

DEDICATION

For "the girls" – who taught me to be patient, to observe, and to understand, so that I could teach others.
Mandy Book

For the dogs who suffered through my "training" before I saw the light.
Cheryl S. Smith

ILLUSTRATIONS

Illustrations by Judith L. Winthrop

PHOTOGRAPHS

Contents

LIST OF CLICK TRICKS

Chapter 7

CHAPTER 1
A Click and a Promise

WHY CLICKER TRAINING?

If you've ever been to a seaquarium and watched the dolphin or killer whale show, you've seen the principles of clicker training in action. The trainers of these and other marine mammals can't just put a choke collar on their animal and jerk it around the pool. They have to work another way. What they use is a "marker" — a unique sound such as a whistle, click, or word – to select out the behavior that they want and let the animal know it will be rewarded. It's like taking a snapshot of the behavior that will get the treat. Over time, trainers realized that this hands-off training technique works equally well with a variety of animals. . . including dogs and other pets.

Clicker training can be used to teach simple behaviors such as sit, down, and stay, as well as more complicated behaviors like tricks and advanced obedience. It's very useful for breaking through problems in teaching, and increasing attention. Because clicker training is "no-force" training, it's an excellent method to use with fearful dogs, and can be managed by both children and seniors, even with large-breed dogs. For anyone who doesn't

1

like or can't manage the jerking and pulling at the dog required by traditional training, clicker training is the answer.

Not only is it easily managed by any person, it's great for any dog. You can start with a dog of any age, whether or not the dog has had any other type of training. Eight-week-old puppies or eight-year-old adults, big or small, shy or self-assured, clicker training works with them all. Even deaf and disabled dogs can be trained with this method (using a light instead of a click for deaf dogs).

In short, clicker training is fast, effective, easy, not physically demanding for the trainer, and lots of fun for the dog!

SITS HAPPEN

All sorts of good things happen with clicker training. The clicker isn't magic, but sometimes it sure seems to be! The magic is that it delivers specific and useful information to the dog in a timely fashion. It actually makes it easier for the dog to learn. Because the sound of the clicker is unique, unlike anything they might have heard before, dogs pay attention to it. Pairing the click sound with a treat teaches the dog that the click means "treat coming." Once the dog makes this connection, you can use the clicker to pinpoint for the dog the exact behavior that earns the treat. The dog repeats the behavior because he's interested in getting more treats, and the click provides information to the dog on what exactly he is doing that is making you give up those treats. It's like saying "good dog," only better.

Timing can be very bad with verbal praise, very slow. Just try saying "good dog" while someone else clicks the clicker that came with this book. There's no contest. Not to mention the fact that what we say very often has few implications for the dog.   Any quick, distinct sound (including a word) will work, but the clicker is convenient to carry around, readily available and leaves your hands nearly free.

But it isn't just the correct timing, though that's certainly important. Unlike traditional training, clicker training lets you reward the rough beginning "outline" of a behavior and work up step by step to the final picture. It also allows the dog to participate in the learning process, encouraging him to offer behaviors to see if they will be rewarded.

With traditional training, you can only reward the final complete behavior, and you often have to show the dog what you want over and over again. Finally, at some point, you just have to let the dog try it on his or her own, without any help. Often, the dog will give up in frustration if he or she isn't sure what you want.

For any of you who have read other training literature, and find the term "reward" imprecise, Chapter 7 and the definitions at the end of this chapter cover some of the basic scientific terminology of "operant conditioning," as clicker training is formally called. Until then, we are going to try and avoid technical terms as much as possible, in an effort to simplify your learning process. We should note, however, that a reward is not exactly the same as a reinforcer (a scientific term), although they are often used interchangeably. In the text, what we mean by reward is something the dog will work for.

As an example, if you've ever taught a dog to sit, you probably either did something like pulling up on the leash and pushing down on the butt, or used a food treat as a lure to maneuver the dog into a sit. In either case, you showed the dog how to do it and the payoff for the dog was delivered when he completed the behavior - the dog got the treat, or the pressure on the choke collar was released.

With clicker training, one way to teach the sit is to wait for it to happen. As soon as the dog's butt hits the ground, you click and treat. The dog, who wants you to keep clicking and treating, wonders what it was that got the click and tries to repeat the behavior. Very quickly you will have a dog who's a sitting fool, trying to get you to click and deliver treats! Instead of having training done TO him or her, the dog participates actively and enthusiastically.

GETTING IN SHAPE

While we will do our best to avoid a technical vocabulary throughout this book, "shaping" is a term that's too good not to use. It beautifully describes breaking a behavior down into a series of small steps that look increasingly like the end behavior and gradually putting them together, "shaping" them into a final picture of the behavior for the dog. Each small step toward the final picture is rewarded with MANY clicks and treats.

With a little patience, skilled shaping, and a lot of clicks and treats, many complicated behaviors can be taught this way. It's crucial to break the behavior down into many, MANY steps. Think about it and write the steps down to help keep you on track. Problems will occur if you try to take steps that are bigger than the dog can understand. Picture yourself trying to climb to the top of the Empire State Building. If you take your time, rest when you have to, and don't care if the trip takes all day, you'll probably make it. But if you try to sprint to the top, skipping every other stair, unless you're a really well-conditioned athlete, you'll probably collapse and give up. It's the same with shaping. Trying to take steps that are too big too quickly will ultimately result in failure.

Plentiful rewards are also essential. Monty Roberts, one of those people now being called "horse whisperers," has said that he was once told that if the learning process is a range from zero to ten, then the most important part is the stage from zero to one. Reward early and often.

FIRST THINGS FIRST

In order to be successful at clicker training, you, the trainer, will need some basic skills under your belt. Three things will impact your success as a trainer: your timing, how generous you are with treats (scientifically called the "rate of reinforcement"), and how well you are able to break down behaviors into tiny steps for shaping. Understand that these aren't just skills that are useful for clicker training - your mastery of them will impact any type of training method you intend to use. So, we're going to train you first, before you get to train the dog.

We'll start with some experience on breaking behaviors down into small steps. For a practice behavior, let's use spin in a circle to the left, broken into 10 steps. (Note: We wouldn't use this as an early behavior in your clicker training because it offers a lot of variety on how it could be completed and what each step could be. But for shaping practice – since we're not actually working the dog – it will do very nicely!)

We'll provide some answers for you as work through this. But keep in mind this isn't the only way to shape this behavior! Your dog, for example, might need even more than 10 steps, or might do it in as few as 5. The idea here is to gain skill in breaking things down. The better you are at this skill, the better and easier your shaping will be.

What is the end behavior? 10. Dog spins in a circle to the left
What is the first step? 1. _____
What is a middle step? _____

Now, add another step between the first step and the middle step:
1.   Eye flick to the left (you probably didn't realize you could – or might need to — start with such a small step!)

4

4. _____

6. Dog turns his body 1/2 way to the left until he is facing the opposite direction

(We intentionally left more room to break steps smaller at the beginning. This is usually the most critical part of getting the behavior.)

And between the middle and end:

6. Dog turns his body 1/2 way to the left until he is facing the opposite direction

8. _____

10. Dog spins in a circle to the left

Now continue filling in between these steps:

1. Eye flick to the left
2. _____
3. _____
4. 1/4 turn to the left
5. _____
6. Dog turns his body 1/2 way to the left until he is facing the opposite direction
7. _____
8. Dog turns 3/4 of the way to the left
9. _____
10. Dog spins in a circle to the left

Here are 10 likely steps to getting this behavior:

1. Eye flick to the left
2. Head turn to the left
3. One step to the left
4. 1/4 turn to the left
5. Halfway between 1/4 turn and 1/2 turn to left
6. Dog turns his body 1/2 way to the left until he is facing the opposite direction
7. Halfway between 1/2 turn and 3/4 turn to the left
8. Dog turns 3/4 of the way to the left
9. Dog turns most of the way in a circle to the left
10. Dog completes spinning in a circle to the left

Note that the steps between 1 and 4 are broken down much more finely than those between 4 and 8. Remember that the first few steps are the most important part of the behavior.

If this seems really detailed and time-consuming, don't worry. Each step will take less than 30 seconds to complete, since you will only be clicking the dog 3 to 5 times at that step before requiring that the dog do more to get clicked and treated. This is referred to as changing the criteria or "upping the ante." So the process with the dog would look like this: The dog is standing in front of you. You are waiting patiently with your clicker and treats. The dog gets bored waiting, and glances away, you click and treat. He wonders why you clicked, stares at you again, then gives up and glances away again, you click and treat. He does it a third time, you click and treat. And a fourth time, click and treat. And a fifth time, click and treat. Take a 10 second break to reload your hand with treats.

This time, you are not going to click the glance, you are going to wait for something more (upping the ante), such as a slight head turn. Click and treat the new step 3 to 5 times (5 or even a couple more repetitions is a good number for novice dogs and trainers, but do not repeat more than 10 times at the same level). Take a 10 second break, and up your criteria again to the next step you have written down. Work through 3 to 5 steps, then stop training for a while (you and the dog will both need a break). When you come back, start at the last step you left off at (you made a note to yourself about that, didn't you?) and continue working through the next couple of steps. Repeat these brief training sessions until you have the complete behavior.

But what if the dog never flicks his eyes to the left, even though you were staring at each other for five minutes? You have a couple of options — you can break your steps even finer between 0 and 1, such as clicking and treating ANY eye movement 5 times, then eye movement only to the left 5 times. (Be sure to break down your other steps further, as well.) It NEVER hurts your shaping to have smaller steps — EVER. If the dog doesn't need them you can always skip some (although that won't happen much in the beginning.) In fact, steps that are too big is the most common reason for lack of success in your training. You'll see that in the form of barking or other signs that the dog is shutting down (leaving the area, lying down, acting silly, doing something else). Steps that are too big can even cause you to train something different than you intended to.

Another option is to click and treat doing anything besides staring at you, choosing something different for each click. The warm-up exercises in this chapter will help the dog learn that he'll be clicked for doing something, not waiting for instruction from you. They will also help you learn to be more observant – maybe after some practice, you'll realize you were missing small eye movements your dog was making.

Now, work on this on your own. Take the first 5 steps above and break them into at least 10 steps, layering another step or two between each of the ones we indicated earlier. Take another behavior and see how finely you can break it down. The more you do this, the better you'll get at it.

CLICK TRICKS

By the way, people who tend to break behaviors into steps that are too large are called "lumpers." Those who are able to break them into minute steps are called "splitters." You don't want to be a lumper, do you?

THE SPIRIT OF GENEROSITY

Another skill you'll need to master is how, and how often, to give treats. Clicker training uses a lot of treats - there's no way around it. Treats are easy to dispense, take little time to consume (allowing you to train quickly), and are something most dogs will work for. There are other types of rewards you can use, which we'll cover in later chapters, but first we want you to get some experience with delivering treats quickly and frequently. If you're concerned about loading the dog up with calories, you can use some of his regular dog kibble mixed in with treats. We use a "click mix" of a couple of cups of a variety of bite-sized treats with a scoop or two of dog food (for information on where to get suitable treats, see the Resources at the end of the book), which lasts a week or two, depending on how much training you're doing daily.

Store it in a container out of the dog's reach, and don't forget to subtract the equal quantity being used as training treats from the dog's normal amount of dinner, to prevent him from becoming a pudgy pooch.

This practice session will involve the dog. We're going to show you first how effectively rewards change your dog's behavior — without even using the clicker. Let's start with something you would like the dog to do in many cases — sit. Your dog, by the way, does not have to do this behavior on command in order for you to work on this. In fact, if he doesn't, you'll be even more impressed at the results. We mentioned earlier that in clicker training, you wait for the sit to happen (rather than showing the dog what you want). You could also shape a sit by breaking it down into steps fairly easily, just like we did with the spin. But most dogs, even very young puppies, will sit on their own often enough that you don't have to bother shaping it. In this case, since we aren't practicing shaping right now, we're going to wait for the sit to happen, then treat it.

You'll need a pencil and paper, a stop watch, timer or clock with a second hand, and tasty treats your dog likes. Set your timer for 30 seconds. Don't give any treats yet, or even show the dog you have them. Observe your dog for 30 seconds and count how many times the dog sits during that time (don't tell him to sit, just see how many times he does it on his own). Every time he sits, have him get up again (move or release him). Write down the number of sits you saw during that time. This is going to be your baseline - what the behavior looks like before you start working on it.

Now get a handful of treats, set your timer for 30 seconds and give the dog a treat each time he sits. Try to time your treat delivery so that he gets the treat while his butt is still on the floor. Also concentrate on being perfectly still until the dog actually sits – do not say anything to the dog or move around. We don't want him thinking there is some kind of signal from you to sit (not yet, anyway — we'll add that later!).

Move or release the dog after every sit. Now write down the number of sits the dog did during the 30 second session. How does it compare to your baseline? Get another handful of treats, and do another 30 second training session (yes, you're training, even though you're not saying anything to the dog!) Continue to work in 30 second sessions, giving a treat each time the dog sits and counting how many sits you get in each 30 second session. Remember, you're not saying anything to the dog at all, just waiting for a sit and treating it. Do this until you have done 10 sessions, each 30 seconds long. This should take no longer than 10 minutes. Give the dog a break to get a drink and go to the bathroom and then take a look at what you've recorded. How did your 10th session compare with your baseline?

What you should see is an increase from the number of sits your dog did in the baseline session. If the number of sits actually DECREASED, then A) you weren't rewarding a sit, you were rewarding something else (a timing problem) or B) what you're using for a treat isn't considered a reward by the dog. Change treats to something more tasty that the dog gobbles quickly. Try a couple of 30 second sessions and see if the number of sits increases. If you suspect the problem is your timing, have someone watch a session. Don't tell the person what you are giving treats for — ask them what they THINK you're giving treats for. If it isn't clear to them, it won't be clear to the dog either. If the problem is timing, there's help for you in the next section.

Now try this variation. Do another 30 second baseline timing how much the dog is standing vs sitting (no treats, just observing and counting the number of seconds he is standing during your 30 second time period). If the dog hardly ever stands up during the 30 seconds, pat yourself on the back, because you did an excellent job training that sit!

You're not going to give treats for sits any more though. Instead, every time the dog stands up, give him a treat. If he stands for more than one second, give him another treat for each second he stands. Ignore the sits. Repeat for 10 sessions, giving the dog a 10-15 second break between each session. Now compare the amount of time the dog stood during your baseline with how much he's standing in the last session. You just untrained your sit (see how easy it is to do?) It probably progressed a little slower than training the sit, because you rewarded that first and heavily, but you still saw a decrease in the amount of sitting the dog was doing. Now think about how many rewards your dog gets for not sitting, when you really want him to sit, rewards such as someone looking at him, talking to him (including yelling), touching or petting him (including shoving him off). Are you getting a better picture of why your dog doesn't sit very much?

Try this variation: Give the dog a treat every 2 seconds during your 30 second time, regardless of what the dog is doing. Repeat for 2 or 3 sessions. What happens to the dog's sit behavior? What happens to his interest level? You'll see that his interest in remaining with you increases, while the sit behavior probably falls apart. What this demonstrates is the importance of being generous with your treats. The more freely you dispense them, the greater will be the dog's interest in continuing to work. But you'll also want to deliver them specifically for a behavior. That's where the importance of breaking down your behavior into many small pieces comes in. You want the dog to be rewarded frequently enough that he continues to work, but is always working toward your specific goal. The smaller the steps, the easier that will be to accomplish.

Here are other variations you can try. Each time the dog sits, drop the treat on the floor next to you. What happens to your sit after 2 or 3 sessions of 30 seconds each? Does it increase or decrease in frequency? Does the dog sit closer or farther away from you? Now toss the treat away from you each time the dog sits, to the same spot on the floor each time. Repeat for 2 or 3 sessions. How many sits is the dog doing? Where is he sitting in relation to where you're throwing the treats? Both these variations will give you information about how WHERE the treat is delivered can impact your training. Take notes, because you'll be using this information in later training. There will be training sessions where you'll want the dog to restart a behavior from the beginning (such as stepping on a skateboard) so you'll toss the treat or have the dog come get it. But that impacts how many repetitions you can do in the same amount of time. In other cases, you'll want the dog to remain in place, so you'll bring the treat to him or be standing next to him when you click. It all depends on what your end goal is.

Another good example of how where you deliver treats impacts what the dog does can be experienced by practicing a bit of "heeling" with the dog. Take a handful of treats and start walking around the room. When the dog comes up next to you beside your leg, hand him a treat, but deliver it behind your back. After a few sessions of this, where is the dog hanging out? Can you see how something as simple as where you give the treat can greatly impact the end behavior you are looking for?

CLICK TRICKS

While training chickens, you quickly learn the importance of treat delivery. Mandy was trying to teach her chicken to stay on the table (the chicken had never been on a table before and had to learn that skill first before doing anything else). Mandy started clicking and treating the chicken for being on the table, but noticed the chicken was gradually getting closer to the edge and "hanging out" there (sometimes flying off the table). When Mandy readjusted the treat delivery, always giving the feed pellets in the middle of the table instead of close to the edge, the chicken stopped coming to the edge of the table.

Okay, let's practice delivering treats and see what happens (believe it or not, you need to practice this!) Put the dog away for the moment and get someone to help you with this exercise (tell them there's food involved and you should quickly get a volunteer). Count out 10 M&M's™ or small jelly beans, hold them in one hand, and put your clicker in the other hand. Set your timer for 10 seconds. Rest both hands by your side, click the clicker and give a candy to your helper (if you don't have a helper, just put the candy in a small dish set on a counter). Put your hand down by your side again, click the clicker, deliver a candy. How many candies can you get rid of in 10 seconds? Make sure you click first, then deliver the candy — don't do it at the same time (that's cheating!) Have your helper tell you if you are moving your candy-delivering hand before you click (or videotape it so you can see what you're doing). You won't want the dog to know he's getting the treat before you actually click so it's important that your hand not move (and that your body remains still) until the click happens. Can you speed it up until you can click and deliver 20 candies in 10 seconds, without dropping any or giving more than one candy at a time? Try using a variety of different size and shape candies and see how that impacts your speed. You won't need much practice with this before you get a smooth rhythm going.

IMPROVING YOUR TIMING

The first dogs we ever trained with a clicker learned to subtract time from our very slow clicks to figure out what they needed to do. As our timing improved, the dogs had to adjust to the time difference! The better your timing is at the outset, the easier it is for the dog to learn. Following are some exercises that will help you be a pro clicker. Practice these exercises for 3 to 5 minutes at a time. Try to involve someone else to help you and give you feedback on whether you are timing your click correctly.

1. Click when a tennis ball bounces on the floor, then try clicking at the highest point of a toss (have someone else do the bouncing and tossing if you want to challenge yourself a bit more).
2. Have a friend touch their arm at random intervals and give you feedback on whether the click was well-timed. (You'll also get some practice in being random rather than falling into a pattern if you switch places!)

3. Have a helper walk randomly around your living room, changing direction and speed often. Click for their left heel touching the ground. Then try clicking just for the front of the toe touching the ground.
4. While you watch a videotape, pick a character and a behavior to "click." Stop the tape when the character does the behavior — can you still see it on the screen? If not, you're too slow! Try behaviors of varying difficulty (such as glancing in a particular direction or saying a specific word) and see if you can actually anticipate when the character will do them.
5. If you have a cooperative friend with a clicker-savvy dog, ask if you can experiment! You'll very quickly find out if your clicks are well-timed, because the dog will only get the behavior if they are. You'll also learn to be faster with your clicking so you can keep up with how fast the dog is working.

CLICK AND TREAT - IT'S THAT EASY!

Time to charge up the clicker! Your dog won't know what this new sound means until you teach that to him.

Click, then toss or hand a treat or a piece of kibble to the dog. Always click first, then give the treat. Don't say anything to the dog – right now you want him to be focused on the click. Repeat this click and treat twenty or thirty times, a couple of times a day, for a few days. It sounds like a lot of work, but it goes very quickly, taking only a matter of minutes for each session, using tiny bits of treats. You can start while you read the rest of this chapter. You don't have to be watching the dog while you randomly click and treat. . . in fact, it's better if you don't watch because you don't want to accidentally reward any particular behavior at this point.

It's not important right now whether you hand the treat to the dog or drop it on the ground. The only rule is not to go to the dog, but make him come to you. If your dog is "grabby" and snatches at food, it's probably better to drop the treat (and see Chapter 2 for suggestions on how to solve this problem). Otherwise, vary it, sometimes handing it over, sometimes dropping it.

When the dog "startles" at the sound of the clicker, or immediately looks at the floor for the treat he's come to expect, you've made the clicker connection. You're ready to do some warm-up exercises with the dog and work on your first clicker trained behavior. The behavior we've chosen is a handy one you'll probably use a lot - a hand touch (more detailed instructions are in Chapter 2). It's also an easy one to help you with the timing of the click. Don't get too frustrated when things don't go as planned. These are nothing more than training exercises to get you and your dog used to using the clicker. Don't get hung up on looking for perfection. If you mess up, you'll be able to fix it later quite easily.

CLICK TRICKS

Clickers are small things, easily misplaced. We admit that we've lost our fair share over the years. So we offer some strategies to keep from losing yours.

You'll note that our Quick Clicks clickers have a tab at one end. This allows you to attach them to things. Here are some suggestions:

o Take a large safety pin, slide the clicker onto it, and pin it to your bait bag or shirt.

o Get a piece of string (or buy a length of hemp from a crafts or bead store if you want to be fancier), slide the clicker onto it, tie the ends together, and wear it as a necklace.

o Slide the clicker onto a clip – there are various kinds, including hinged circles, screw-tight carabiners, even a clip attached to a tiny retractable reel – and fasten it onto a jeans belt loop. (It will survive a trip through the washer and dryer, if you forget to unfasten it.)

o Put it on a key ring. Depending on the size and style of key ring, you can slip it onto a finger as a ring, attach it to a belt loop or buttonhole, or hang it from a jacket zipper.

o Have a central location to which you always return your clicker. If you get into the habit right from the start, you'll always know where to find it.

o Buy extra clickers – they don't cost much – and have them scattered everywhere throughout the house — next to your keys, near your jacket, in every room, in pockets, and in the car – wherever you might need to grab one.

If you lose one or two, or three or four, don't worry – you're not alone.

WARM-UP EXERCISES

The first thing we need to teach the dog is to try different things rather than standing around waiting to be told what to do. If your dog has been involved in a lot of traditional training, this is especially important because the dog has learned to wait for direction from you.

Show the dog that you have a treat. Wait (patiently) for the dog to do something. . . anything! Impatient for the treat to be given, the dog may back up, lift a paw, stand up, or any of a dozen other actions. Click and treat the dog for ANY action.

CLICK TRICKS
Try to avoid clicking and treating a down, sit, or looking at you (which may be the first things the dog offers). Too much time early on spent rewarding these "stationary" behaviors will cause you difficulty when you later want movement from the dog.

Now wait again, but this time click and treat for a DIFFERENT action. Repeat this another four or five times, rewarding a different action each time. Take a break and repeat at a later time. Do this exercise as often as you like to keep the dog offering fresh responses when you take out the clicker.

Another fun (and funny) warm-up exercise is to clicker train a silly behavior using a canvas bag. (If you don't have such a bag, use a blanket, a towel, whatever you have available.) Put the bag in the middle of the room. Click the first ten behaviors the dog does with the bag, regardless of what they are. Take a 5-minute break. Try it again — you want the dog to get the idea that "fooling around," offering different behaviors, gets rewarded. Repeat as often as you like.

Now think about a behavior you might want to shape using the bag. Some examples might be pawing the bag, sticking his head in the bag, putting his mouth on the bag. Consider the end result you would want and how small your steps would need to be to get there, and write down your plan for shaping a silly behavior. Shape a different behavior each time you get the bag out. Try at least 5 sessions, each no more than 1-2 minutes long, writing down your progress for each behavior. Come back to the canvas bag exercises after you've been clicker training for a few months, and see how the dog's responses differ, and how differently you might think about shaping those same behaviors.

HAND TOUCH

Now let's teach the dog to touch the palm of your hand with his nose. This is called a "target" behavior, because you're using your hand as a target for the dog (more on that later). You'll need your dog, clicker, and treats. Before you start, write down the steps you would need to get the dog from where he is today (no interest in your hand) to your end goal of touching the palm of your hand, or even following the hand as it's moving.

Here are the first few steps:
1. Click and treat the dog for looking at the hand.
2. Click and treat the dog for leaning forward toward the hand.
3. Click and treat the dog for touching anywhere on your hand.

Can you fill in the rest? What might be a step between 1 and 2 if the dog needs smaller shaping steps? Try to add at least 5 more steps to the ones we've indicated.

Okay, let's begin the training. Remember that this is for practice — don't worry about results so much as the learning process. Bring your dog into a room where he's unlikely to get distracted (such as a kitchen). Gather 5 treats together (either in a bowl on the counter or a shirt pocket). Hold the clicker in one hand, and put your other hand out at the dog's nose level with your palm facing the dog, about 1 foot in front of his nose. Click and treat when he looks at the hand, then put the hand down. Lift it again in front of the dog's nose at the same distance, click and treat when he looks at the hand, put the hand down. Repeat 5 times total (no more, or the dog will think this is all he needs to do).

Remember, you are working on your timing and learning how to shape. Try to get that click exactly when the dog looks at the hand. If he touches the hand, your click was TOO SLOW (but you'll still give the dog a treat when you click - he shouldn't suffer for your error). It won't matter too much for this behavior, but it will for others later on. Practice your timing! Don't forget — don't reach for a treat until after you have clicked.

It's time to "up the ante." Just looking at the hand won't work any more...the dog has to try harder to get his click and treat. Working in the same room, reload your treats. Now offer your hand in exactly the same place in front of the dog's nose, but don't click when he looks at it. Wait patiently until he moves his head forward a bit, then click and treat. Repeat up to 5 times, removing the target hand each time after you've clicked. Time the click with the forward movement of the dog's head — if you're slow, he might think he's supposed to be touching the hand or that he's supposed to be moving his head away from it.

Working in the same room, reload your treats. Offer your hand, but wait for the dog to actually touch it with his nose, anywhere on the hand. Click and treat the touch, repeating up to 5 times. Time your click so that you click exactly when you feel the wetness of his nose on your hand. If you can anticipate, and be READY to click when the dog touches, even better — then your timing will be dead on. If you're slow clicking, the dog may think he is supposed to pull his head away from the hand.

Congratulations! You have experienced clicker training your first behavior. Take a break and evaluate how the dog did. Would you need additional steps for your dog (in other words, did he follow along with the book)? Could you have clicked and treated only 3 times at each level instead of 5? Did the dog immediately touch the hand when it was offered, skipping the first two steps? Did he wander off or look at a bug on the floor because your steps were too big and he wasn't getting clicked very much? Remember our earlier exercise on keeping the dog working. Revise your shaping plan for the next few steps, if necessary. Chapter 2 outlines additional steps to continue this behavior, if you would like to go on. For now, we want to point out some important things for you to be keeping in mind while shaping:

- Before you start, decide what the behavior is and have a rough idea of how many steps you'll take to shape it. Work at a step until the dog does 3 to 10 correct repetitions, getting a click and a treat every time — this will probably take about one to two minutes. Take a short break (ten seconds) between each step.
- Have in mind at the start of each step exactly what you will click for. Don't change what you are clicking for in the middle of the step, even if the dog seems ready to work at a higher level than you anticipated. Reward, even jackpot (see definitions) better-than-anticipated performance, but do not then demand that new level of performance for the rest of the clicking at that step. Continue rewarding at the level you decided on before you began until the dog has made 3 to 10 correct repetitions and you are ready to step up. Re-evaluate between steps if you would be able to step up more quickly.
- Remember, wait for the DOG to do something you can click. Allow the dog to LEARN what to do instead of trying to TEACH him. Give him time

to work things out for himself. The dog needs to practice offering behavior to get good at it. The hand touch we outlined above is pure shaping, though when we get to actual behaviors we want to train, we'll often use lures or whatever it takes to get the behavior.

- On the other hand, make sure you are clicking and treating frequently enough to keep the dog working. You should be clicking and treating at least every 3-5 seconds, or your shaping plan needs rethinking. Make your steps smaller, if you need to.
- Resist the urge to give the dog any help, cues, signals, or "encouragement" for now. Keep your mouth and your body still. Imagine trying to take a quiz while the teacher walks around the room talking and slapping people on the back. It's impossible for your dog to concentrate if you play the part of cheerleader babbling on beside him or constantly moving around.
- As a rule, you can step up to a new level after three to ten correct repetitions at the old level. Your dog may work best with only three repetitions, or he may need all ten. You'll have to experiment a bit to figure out what works best for your particular dog.
- Periodically stop and evaluate how the steps are going and whether you need to make adjustments in your shaping plan.
- Write down your progress (keep records! It's one of the most neglected areas of training, but it helps tremendously with the process, and you'll enjoy being able to look back and remember where you came from!) so you know where to start the next day and how the behavior is progressing.

PROBLEM SOLVING

When you're both just starting in clicker training, there are bound to be problems. That's normal, and most are easily solved.

If you get out the clicker and the dog immediately starts doing all kinds of things, rejoice! The dog is learning the game. You will have a lot to work with, and just have to help with focus.

But what if the dog doesn't do anything? If he's staring at you intently, it's an indication that he wants to work but doesn't know how. Repeat the Warm-Up Exercises for a couple of days to get him moving and help him learn to keep trying new things. If it doesn't seem to help, stop the session and try again when you are both fresh.

If the dog seems confused or frustrated (he's barking or sniffing, has stopped working or laid down, left the area or looked for something else to do), your last step was probably too big. Try again at the previous step for a few click and treat repetitions. Break your next intended step into at least 2 smaller steps (more would probably not hurt). When you're ready, take a smaller step to the next level. Or take a break from training and come back to it later — the dog may just be getting tired. Try changing to a less distracting environment. Clicker training takes a lot of concentration for both of you.

Some dogs like to bark when they're excited or frustrated, and clicker training can lead to both excitement and frustration. If your dog starts barking, or pawing at you, try turning your back on him until he quiets down. You can't click and treat if you aren't watching what he's doing, and the barking and pawing usually will taper off. In other words, he won't be rewarded for the barking because all training stops. When he's been quiet for 5-10 seconds, turn back and tell him what a good boy he is, then review your training techniques. Are your steps too big? Is your timing so slow you're clicking the wrong thing? Are you being stingy with your clicks and treats? If you're not clicking every three to five seconds, you're being too picky about what behaviors to reward. Your dog is going to get frustrated and stop working if he can't figure out what makes you click. Make your steps small enough that the clicks and treats are frequent. Remember, we don't want to wait for the whole behavior to happen before clicking!

If your dog wanders away or leaves the room, either your treats are boring, not being delivered frequently enough, or the dog is just not ready to work yet. Change treats and see if that helps. Try clicking and treating twice as often as you were (in other words, review your shaping steps). Work on a simpler behavior that the dog can get more clicks and treats for, or just put everything away and come back to it later. Perhaps you both need a break right now. Don't be discouraged by an initial lack of response — you are both learning how to do this, and the training will progress quickly as you both get better at it.

Some dogs are not treat hounds. You may have to use another reward. Click and toss a toy, click and play a game, click and take a walk. Although training will go more slowly at the start, it will still progress. Work on easy behaviors such as those in the first chapter until the dog approaches training with enthusiasm. Whatever your reward ends up being, stop each session well before the dog slows or stops working.

One final problem — some dogs are afraid of the clicker! If your dog seems frightened, try putting the clicker in your pocket when you click, or muffling it with tape over the metal part. Or you can try a different sound-making device, such as a frog clicker (available from Legacy By Mail, listed in Chapter 7 Resources), a Snapple™ tea bottle cap, a ballpoint pen, finger snap, click with tongue, or buzz, bell, or beep sound or a bridge word such as Yes! (see Chapter 7 for more information on introducing a bridge word). Whichever you choose to try, spend an extra fourteen sessions (two weeks) working on associating the sound with a really exciting treat before you try to train any new behaviors.

CLICK TRICKS

One of the dogs in our group classes hated the clicker. Yet when switched to a bridge word, the dog was eager to work. She eventually did learn to accept the clicker, as she began to learn what happened when she heard a novel sound (cookies!).

ANOTHER SHAPED BEHAVIOR

The first behaviors learned through clicker training tend to have a lot of staying power for the dog. Often, when you start a training session and the dog doesn't yet know what you're looking for, he will offer one of the first few clicker-trained behaviors. So it's important to think about how these behaviors will impact your future training. For example, a down-stay is an easy behavior to train with a clicker, but do you really want your dog to do a down-stay every time he can't figure out what you're trying to teach him? There's no way you can click him for a new behavior if all he's doing is lying down! Here's a useful behavior that usually doesn't interfere with other training — attention.

Put a bunch of treats in your hand. Hold this hand out to the side, perpendicular to your body, and put your clicker in the other hand. Your dog will probably stare at your treat hand, waiting for a click and treat (or maybe just waiting for the treat!) He may start drooling or pawing at you. Watch for the dog's eyes to leave your hand. Even if he looks at your knee or your foot or your elbow or the floor, click and treat the instant he looks away from your treat-laden hand. That was your first repetition — a single click and treat. Repeat that three times, clicking and treating when the dog looks away from your hand each time. Take a break, and write down all the steps you think you will need to eventually get the dog looking at your face. (Hint: You'll need a lot fewer steps if the first couple of glances were in that general direction than at the floor!) You will now work, step by step, to shape eye contact. You should be starting to get the idea of how to do this by now. . . Click and treat for looking at your knee (or foot, or wherever the dog first shifted his gaze) until the dog has made his three to five correct repetitions (don't do more than 10 maximum). Then work up your body slowly, clicking and treating for looking at your thigh, your hip, your elbow, your shoulder. . . your face.

Your dog has just learned an important lesson — the food still gets delivered even if he's not staring at it! In other words, he's learned he has to DO something to get the treat, you're not going to do something TO HIM. Training this behavior will encourage the dog's focus on the work involved rather than the treat. This is especially important if your dog is highly motivated by food. Once the dog looks at your face immediately instead of at the hand full of treats, you need to give this behavior a name (Watch or Look are good choices). We'll tell you how later in the chapter, in Name That Touch.

ANOTHER WAY TO GET A BEHAVIOR

If you went to a puppy kindergarten class, you probably taught your pup to sit by using a food treat (a "lure") held over his head to get him to look up and put his butt on the ground. This process is called "lure training" or "luring." You may have found it really easy, and might be wondering why we haven't suggested it till now. We wanted you to start with a little "pure" shaping to experience how the dog can learn on his own. All the exercises you've done thus far have been shaping because you waited for the dog to attempt something before he got his click and treat, rather than helping him. But using a lure to "give the dog a clue" can often help get the dog jump started on the first step to a behavior. Some behaviorists insist that you should never use a lure to get a behavior. Practical dog owners will probably find many situations where using a lure is helpful.

Another way to lure behaviors (called targeting) is using a hand touch, target stick or contact disk to get another behavior, then getting rid of the target. (Chapter 3 covers information on how to teach these useful targets.)

Targets can be used very effectively but they will eventually need to be faded. Fading involves gradually making the item less and less obvious to the dog, a little bit at a time, such as by making it smaller (cutting it or using a smaller version), changing the color gradually from opaque to clear, or moving it farther away. (Fading is explained in more detail in Chapter 7.)

There will be times when pure shaping will work better and other times when luring will be preferable. In general, luring is best when you know it is unlikely the dog will start the behavior on his own, or if you are having trouble getting started on the first step. If you wanted to shape "drinking water," for example, you might have to wait a very long time for the dog to approach the water bowl. And you would probably only be able to click it once before the dog stopped doing it. But by dropping a treat in the water bowl, you will quickly get some drinking behavior, which can be clicked and treated.

Luring is also good for shy or sensitive dogs, who tend to shut down and give up if they are not quickly successful. Some initial lure training will help to build their confidence.

But using a lure has two major disadvantages. For many behaviors, you'll want to eventually get rid of the lure. After all, you want the dog to sit or come whether or not you happen to be carrying any treats. Because luring is easy, people tend to hold on to the lures for way too long, making the process of fading or weaning off the lure difficult. Second, using a lure will keep your dog in the mode of waiting for you to show him what you want. It will be a crutch. If you really want your dog to start thinking and participating in the training process, avoid using a lot of lures in your training in the early stages.

There are a couple of key things to keep in mind for using luring effectively in your training program:

- Don't tease the dog with the lure. If you use a food treat or toy to lure, the dog needs to get it when he does the behavior or piece of behavior you're looking for.
- Food lures and toys should be used sparingly, usually in the beginning stages of a behavior. A good rule of thumb is to use these lures 3 to 5 times, then wait and see what the dog does without them.
- You will still be clicking and treating, even if you are using a lure. The lure just gets you the behavior, you still have to mark the behavior and reward the animal for doing it.
- If you are using a target, such as a hand, stick or plastic disk, for your lure, it will need to be faded eventually. The sooner, the better.
- If the lure seems to be interfering with the behavior, try shaping it instead.

Shaping may sometimes start more slowly than luring a behavior — but not always. Some simple behaviors, such as shaking hands, can be shaped very quickly. Even if you do find shaping slower initially, you won't have to spend time later getting rid of a lure. For a treat-focused dog easily distracted by a piece of food waving in front of him, shaping is definitely the better choice for most behaviors. And you will learn a lot more about the clicker training process.

If you're interested in experiencing the difference between shaping and luring, try this experiment. Put your canvas bag back in the middle of the room and choose a new behavior to teach, say, putting one foot on the bag. Use a lure to teach the behavior, then try to get rid of the lure. Did you find this easier or harder than shaping the hand touch or attention? If you weren't going to use a lure, how would you go about shaping this same behavior?

In our instructions, we sometimes start with luring and sometimes shape from the very beginning of a behavior. Mostly we'll start with shaping when it's an easy behavior for a beginner to shape. If the shaping isn't working for you, try luring the behavior a few times. If we suggest a lure, and you find that it isn't working (the lure is too distracting, or the dog seems to be dependent on it), shape the behavior instead. Above all, remember that our instructions are just ONE way to get a behavior, not the only way. While we believe that shaping is an excellent skill for you to master and encourage you to learn how to do it well, we also recognize that in the meantime, the dog has to be trained!

RULES TO REMEMBER WHEN SHAPING

- Never click without giving a treat — you will "discharge" the clicker and make it meaningless for the dog
- Work in short steps . . . a MAXIMUM of three minutes.
- Quit the lesson before you or the dog get tired or bored.
- Remember our little tale about climbing the Empire State Building — steps can go up or down (you might experience a brief spurt of worse-than-anticipated behavior) and you can rest on a step for a little while if you run into problems. It's all okay — you'll be back on your way to the top in no time.
- If you hit a "learning plateau" (the dog doesn't seem to be progressing over the course of several sessions), your first line of defense — always

— is to review your shaping steps to make sure they are small enough and the dog is getting frequent clicks and treats, at least every 3-5 seconds. If you're waiting longer than that to click, your step is too big.

- When just starting out, work before meals, when the dog is most likely to be attentive. Once the dog has some experience with shaping, you'll be able to work any time.

- If you and your dog are new to clicker training, work on only one behavior until you have finished and named it (see section Name That Touch! for more on naming a behavior). As you both get better at this, you can work on multiple behaviors, but only one in each session.

- Keep in mind that the dog must be physically capable of performing the behavior you want to teach. No amount of training will help a dog learn to open a jar because you need opposable thumbs for that.

- Decide, before you start working, what the end behavior (the "final picture") is going to look like and what the first behavior you will click and treat will be. Have in mind how the steps will progress for at least the first part of the behavior (even better to plan it all, write it all down and adjust as needed!)

- Make sure that your steps are small enough so that your dog gets rewarded often. If you're concerned about filling him up with treats, use some kibble from his regular meals (deduct that amount from his bowl) for your at-home training sessions. You may need something more enticing in group classes or other more distracting locations.

- Have an idea of what the next three steps in your shaping will be, in case your dog decides to skip a few of the in-between steps!

- Realize that as your dog gets more clicker savvy, you may not stay at one step for very long, maybe only those three consecutive successful repetitions, before you get something better that you can click. It's best not to linger too long at any one step if the dog is doing well, or you might get stuck there.

- But also remember that we humans generally want to get where we're going in an awful hurry. Clicker training works in steps. Resist "final-picture-itis." If you find that your dog just isn't getting the hang of clicker training, take a close look at how much you're expecting in the initial sessions. Are you trying to teach the dog too much in too short a time? Are you trying to work on multiple behaviors at once? Are your steps

CLICK TRICKS

A boxer learning to retrieve came to our training classes. His owner said she couldn't get the dog to pick the dumbbell up off the floor. When asked to demonstrate what the dog was doing, she put the dumbbell down and the dog promptly grabbed it and held on as if his life depended on it...with the dumbbell still firmly on the floor, looking as if it had been glued down. It was obviously clear in the dog's mind that he was supposed to grab the dumbbell, but he had no idea that he was supposed to be picking it up. Asked how long she had stayed at the step, the dog's owner said one week. She had clicked and treated this step so much that the dog was convinced it was the final behavior and he wasn't supposed to do anything else! The trainers solved the problem by clicking the dog when he accidentally pushed the dumbbell forward as he grabbed it, but not if it stayed still. A few steps later he was successfully picking it up off the floor.

small enough to ensure that the dog is successful? You should be able to break ANY behavior into a minimum of ten steps. Write them down if you have a tendency to skip ahead without waiting for the dog.

- Periodically review your plan to make any adjustments for the dog's progress — either faster or slower than you anticipated.
- If you're training more than one dog, put the others in another room so you can focus on the dog you're working with. As you and the dogs get used to clicker training, you can train a down-stay with the others while you work with one.
- Encourage everyone in the family to get involved. Each person should work on his or her own behavior. Natural inconsistencies between trainers will confuse the dog if more than one person teaches the same behavior. Children (or adults) who aren't skilled with timing the clicker correctly can just practice giving the dog food for the correct behavior without clicking (remember our earlier practice on the sit).
- Don't interrupt a session to do something else — answer the door or chat on the phone — while the dog is working. Most dogs will see this as punishment. (However, this can be used as a nifty way to correct a dog who is easily distracted. See Chapter 7 for more on this.)
- If what you're doing isn't working, try some other shaping plan. Ask family and friends for ideas. The ideas we give you in this book have worked for

the dogs trained to do these behaviors, but that doesn't mean there aren't other (better, faster, easier even!) ways to arrive at the same final behavior.

- Vary the time of day, the length of a session, and the rewards you use as the dog starts to understand how to play the "game." As the behavior becomes stronger, you will also work in other locations, gradually increasing the amount of distractions for the dog. (More in Chapter 7.)

- If your dog seems to go blank and lose all sense of what you're working on, don't panic. Go back to the previous step for a few clicks and treats, then try stepping up again, or just stop the lesson, regroup your thoughts and rethink your shaping plan. It's perfectly okay for the dog to take a break (some will stop to get a drink. . . this stuff is hard work!). But if he stops working completely (lies down or leaves the area), seems confused, or exhibits stress (see the final section of this chapter, Stress Signals, for how to recognize stress), go back to something easy so you can end the lesson on a successful note.

- If your dog makes the same mistake over and over, it means your shaping step was too big or you are clicking something different from what you intend to. Review your shaping steps, and at the next training session, do a short review at a lower level and take smaller steps when you advance. Have someone watch you and tell you what they think you're clicking for.

- In fact, at the beginning of each session, go back a bit and briefly review with the dog what was learned at the end of the previous session.

- Don't try to shape two different dimensions of a behavior at the same time. Behaviors can be improved in terms of intensity (how hard they are), speed of performance, or duration of the behavior. For our behavior of a hand touch, intensity would be an extremely hard nose bump on your hand, speed would be a rapid bump or multiple bumps one after another, and duration would be a touch on your hand for an extended period. Think of the different dimensions of a behavior as sides of a triangle laid out with string. If one side changes, another will change as well. If you are going to try to get really fast hand touches, you need to ease up on how hard they are and how long the dog keeps his nose on your hand, even though the dog may have worked at higher levels on these dimensions in a previous session. If you try to work on more than one dimension at a time, both you and the dog will get confused. See Chapter 7 for more information.

- The click sound, and sometimes the taught behavior as well, can become self-rewarding to the dog. Launching a tennis ball from a dog-a-polt may be more fun than eating the treat you are offering. (If you've ever played a computer game, you know that getting to the next level of the game can be really rewarding, maybe even more than a prize you might get at the end of the game.) If the dog is still working but doesn't come to get the treat when you click, don't fret — it just means the behavior is self-rewarding. You may get more interest in the treat at a different session or in a different environment.

- The click sound may stop the shaping temporarily as the dog comes back to you to get "paid." This is normal, and the dog will return to his task once he collects the reward. You might even want to test to see if the dog really understands the behavior by making him come to collect a treat, then waiting to see if he repeats the behavior. Or, give the dog a treat while he's "in position" so he doesn't have to interrupt the behavior to collect. This can be really effective for behaviors such as heel.
- Keep track of what you and your dog are learning at each session.
- Keep it fun! Remember that dogs are individuals and learn at different rates, the same as humans. Be patient. Be positive!

JACKPOT!

Jackpots are large unexpected rewards, like the coins suddenly pouring out of a slot machine. They can take the form of multiple treats for one performance, an extra special treat (such as steak), a completely different and highly valued reward (such as a walk or play with another dog), or a combination of different types of rewards. Jackpots are useful for making an impression on the dog when he does something particularly well, takes a leap of several steps, or can be used in stressful situations to refocus the dog on the reward rather than what's causing him stress. For example, if your dog is stressed when a strange dog approaches, start by being far enough away that your dog is not stressed, click and give a jackpot for being calm. Gradually decrease the distance, shaping an "approach." (For more information on how to teach this behavior, see Chapter 6.)

While not everyone agrees that jackpots actually have an impact on the training process, we have found in our training classes that more people tend to be stingy than overly generous with treats. By encouraging you to use jackpots from time to time, we hope to help you learn that rewarding the dog frequently and well is a GOOD thing and will make your training progress more smoothly.

NAME THAT TOUCH!

Before you can move on to a new behavior, you need to name the one you've already taught. Naming teaches the dog to discriminate between different behaviors, and gives you control over behaviors so that the dog only does them when he's told. (Some dogs will try offering unrequested behaviors, but if they go unrewarded, the dog will generally settle down.) Without the naming of behaviors, you will end up with a dog who performs an amazing array of useless actions, in no particular order, whenever you bring out your clicker.

So let's return to your first real behavior, the hand touch. Is it at a level that you like — as far forward, as fast, and as sustained as you want it to be? Will the dog touch your hand regardless of how you orient it? Can you predict when the dog will do it? If the answer to these questions is yes, you're ready to name the hand touch behavior. Get out your clicker and treats. Now, just before the dog touches your hand, say "touch" (or whatever command tickles your fancy). Click and treat when he does it. Repeat the sequence of command-behavior-click-treat about 30 to 50 times over a period of several days. Every tenth time or so, DON'T say "touch" when you put your hand out, and don't click the dog if he touches. At first the dog won't be paying much attention to what you're saying. But gradually he'll figure out that if you say something just before he touches and he does it, he gets a click and treat. Your verbalization starts to become meaningful when the dog realizes that it predicts a click and treat.

When you start to see that the dog does nothing when you say nothing, but touches when you say "touch" you'll know he's starting to understand that the command tells him to do something specific. Now you can say the command gradually earlier and earlier, so that it's not just being said directly before you think he'll do the behavior, but far enough in advance that the dog does it BECAUSE you said the command.

At this point, you can alternate your command "touch" with another command that the dog knows well (like "sit") and with not giving any command at all. Click and treat only when the dog performs a behavior that matches a command you have given. Don't click if he offers a hand touch or sit when you have not given the appropriate command, or if he does something else.

If you're wondering why we don't just use a command from the start of training (as much traditional training does), there are several good reasons.

27

First, we don't have a focused "final picture" of a behavior for the dog when we start training. While our hand touch only took a few sessions to complete, a more complicated behavior such as a retrieve could take several weeks of working step by step to get a final picture (less time, by the way, than teaching it traditionally). We want the dog to associate the name or command only with the final, perfect behavior.

Second, verbal information is more meaningful to the dog if you have been quiet throughout the initial training. He will be naturally more inclined to pay more attention when you do say something. It will be easier to associate a specific word (or words) with a particular behavior.

Finally, telling the dog the command does not help him learn how to do it. Telling you to "perform open heart surgery" isn't going to let you actually do it without some serious training. And you probably consider yourself smarter than your dog.

This same idea applies to physical information you may be giving to the dog. If you are moving around a lot during your training, the dog may inadvertently think that your movement is relevant to the behavior he is supposed to do. It's helpful to have someone watch you to make sure you aren't, for example, reaching for a treat before you click, or pointing at something you want the dog to touch, without being aware of it. This unintentional body language can interfere with the dog's learning, or even prevent him from learning an appropriate signal for the behavior.

You can use the same principle to change the name of a behavior the dog is already doing. Say you've already trained the dog to "sit" when told, but now you want to say "zucchini" rather than "sit." Proceed in this order: NEW command - OLD command - behavior - reward. Just remember that New comes before Old just as N comes before O. So your sit sequence would now be "Zucchini" - "Sit" - dog sits - click – dog is rewarded. The dog soon realizes that you tell him "Zucchini" just before you tell him "sit." Eager for his reward, he anticipates the sit when he hears "Zucchini." Now you don't have to say "sit" any more. You have renamed the behavior. Use the same procedure to add a hand signal to a verbal command or vice versa.

STRESS SIGNALS

Learning something new is always stressful, and your job is to keep your dog's stress at a manageable level and not let it overwhelm the training process. Stress signals vary from dog to dog, and you need to learn to recognize your dog's. A stressed dog may yawn, freeze in place, avoid eye contact, pant, lick his lips, scratch, move more slowly, seem inattentive or hyperactive, bark, jump around, or whine. Making play part of your lesson may help relieve stress. Make sure your rewards are frequent and generous. Don't ask for too much at a time, especially when in a new environment. Add distractions to the training process very slowly. Build on each small success to instill confidence in the dog. Using jackpots BEFORE you start seeing stress signs (at a level where the dog is not yet stressed) can help get the dog past the stressful situation.

With more active stress signs — the barking and jumping around — be calm yourself. Keep your physical movements deliberate and low-key. Play relaxing music during training sessions. Yawn, breathe, and smile!

You now have the basic ideas behind clicker training. The chapters following this will help you work through a variety of training projects. Come back and review the basics if you find yourself having problems along the way.

Chapter Definitions - read more about them in Chapter 7

Behavior - anything the dog does is a behavior, breathing included. Therefore, anything that the dog does can be impacted by giving or taking away rewards.

Jackpot - A large unexpected reward, delivered in stressful situations or for particularly excellent performance, used most effectively for large physical energy outputs by the dog.

Rate of Reinforcement - how frequently the dog is getting treats or other rewards.

Reinforcement - Giving the dog something he likes or stopping something that he doesn't like. Reinforcement increases (reinforces) the amount of a behavior the dog is doing. Clicker training uses positive reinforcement (rewards of any type that the dog will work for) to teach behaviors.

Repetition - A single click and treat for some level of behavior. Also called a trial.

Reward - Something the dog likes, such as treats, toys, activities, petting, or praise and will work for. Note that it is not something you think the dog should like, but something he actually values.

Session - A series of steps, with brief breaks between each step, generally lasting less than ten minutes total.

Step - A series of clicks and treats at one level of performance, generally lasting one to two minutes, until three to ten consecutive successful repetitions are achieved.

Shaping - Teaching a behavior by breaking it down into a series of small steps which look increasingly like the end behavior. Each movement from step to step results in behavior more closely resembling the final desired picture of the behavior for the dog.

Road Map

From here on, we will be showing you some of the many ways you can use clicker training. For each behavior or command, we will use the same sequence. Not every command will use every subheading, but the flow will be generally as follows:

The Final Picture: exactly what it is we're going to be working on accomplishing

Uses: other behaviors/commands that can be built on this one (with reference to where to find these further commands in the book), or ways you'll find this command useful

Preparation and Props: background work to do before you begin training, or materials you will need in training

What's in it for the Dog?: you won't encounter these until Chapter 6, when we're working on changing the dog's basic behavioral responses to people, other dogs, and other things in his environment

The Steps Along the Way: step-by-step instructions for training the behavior

Early Steps: more detailed instructions for starting training

Problem Solving Tips: the most likely glitches, and how to get past them

Suggested Commands: the best command word(s) to use, based on our experience

Suggested Signals: suggestions for some body cues you can use for the behavior

Variations: ways you can make the behavior more complex for yourself and your dog, or use it for other purposes

Also scattered throughout the chapters will be "Slick Clicks," short little stories from clicker trainers who have used the technique with all manner of animals, from wallabies to walruses, and have some interesting tales to tell, and "Click Tricks," tips for getting the most out of clicker training.

CHAPTER 2
Click and Easy

In this chapter, we'll get you off to a fast start with some easy basics that can be taught using a clicker and treats. Even dogs without a lot of skills in their repertoires – puppies – should learn these with ease. You can work in two-minute training sessions and be amazed at how much you can accomplish so quickly.

If you have any doubts about what you're doing, go back and consult the "Rules to Remember When Shaping" in Chapter 1. Keep the clicks and treats flowing, make your steps small, and you'll do fine.

These lessons will have you well on your way to good behavior from your dog. Many of these behaviors will be used as the foundation for more advanced work in later chapters. In this chapter we will cover:

Take a treat gently
Sit
Down
Come
Walk on Leash
Wait
Don't touch

With each exercise, we'll mention just a few of the many uses that can be made of it, and how we'll be building on it. You'll appreciate having these behaviors named and on cue. So get your equipment together and set a few minutes aside. Ready? Begin!

TAKE A TREAT GENTLY

The Final Picture: The dog uses his tongue, not his teeth, to take a treat from an outstretched hand. Stops those painful lunges at training treats. Keep this in mind as you practice – it's messy but effective!

Uses: Necessary if you're going to be hand feeding dogs (useful in behavior modification work, which we'll be doing in Chapter 6), for using treats in training, and for life in general.

Preparation and Props: Soft, sticky treats such as peanut butter, spray cheese in a can, cream cheese, liverwurst; chewy treats; dog biscuits; a clicker; a hungry dog.

The Steps Along the Way:
Session One –
1. Mash a small amount of the sticky treat into the palm of your hand and close your fist around it, leaving an opening at the thumb side big

enough for the dog to get his tongue into. (Yes, we know it's disgusting. But you'll thank us in the end, when you don't have to worry about a canine version of a piranha.) Hold your hand out to the dog and let him try to get at the treat. The dog might nibble, chew, or lick to try to get the food. When he licks, click and open your hand. Repeat 10 times. Reload your hand with more mushy food as needed.
2. Require that the dog lick several times before you click and open your hand. Reload and repeat 10 times. If the dog chomps, yelp loudly ("Aip!") and turn your back on him, ending that repetition.

3.   Change to a different treat and repeat steps 1 and 2, gradually making the dog lick longer before being clicked and allowed a big taste of the gooey food. Okay, you get to wash your hands and quit for a while.

CLICK TRICKS

Yelping and ending play is an effective way to inhibit biting of all types – especially with a young puppy. Don't forget to <u>reward</u> playing nicely!

Session Two –
4.   Change locations and repeat steps 1 through 3.
5.   Continue to change locations and repeat steps 1 through 3 until the dog gets clicked for using his tongue rather than his teeth for at least 8 out of 10 repetitions, no matter what gooey food you are using. Now you're ready to add the verbal command.
6.   Add your verbal command just before presenting your food-laden fist. If the dog bites or chomps at it, yelp (make it loud, like you've been mortally wounded – dogs appreciate drama!) and turn your back on him. Let him wait a few seconds before trying again. If he uses his tongue, click and open your hand and let him lick the treat off. Repeat 10 times.
7.   Continue to change locations while you work on adding the verbal command. Remember to also change treats occasionally.

CLICK TRICKS

When teaching a new behavior, you'll need to pair a verbal cue or hand signal with the behavior at least 50 to 60 times (spread over several sessions) before the dog begins to make the connection between what you say or signal and what he should do.

Session Three –
8.   Now use an interesting chewy treat such as steak, chicken, or hot dog slices. Hold it between the tips of your thumb and fingers, covering the treat. Offer it to the dog as you give your command. If he forgets himself and bites, yelp and turn your back, ending that particular repetition. Do not, under these circumstances, let him get the treat, even if it's painful. If he licks once or twice, click and give him the treat. Reload and repeat up to 10 times.

9. Continue to build on the number of licks before you click and release the treat, varying the number of licks each time. Change treats and repeat steps 8 and 9 at least 4 times.

Session Four –
10. Take a hard treat – a biscuit – and hold it with the tips of your fingers as before. Proceed through steps 8 and 9. Change treats several times and repeat these steps.

Remaining sessions, work on variability –
11. Change locations frequently. Dogs feeling some stress (changing locations is stressful) or excitement tend to take treats more quickly and harder. If stress induces your dog to chomp rather than lick, you'll have to gradually work in more stressful environments.
12. Get the dog revved up and excited, then offer a tasty treat.
13. Repeat step 12, but with a toy.
14. Have different people, including children, work on having the dog take treats nicely. Wait until the dog is fairly reliable. If you're still worried about small fingers being chomped, you can cover the child's hand with your own at first.
15. Vary the number of licks required to get the treat – how many licks does it take to get to the center of a gooey treat?

Early Steps: Some dogs give up very easily early in the process and may just sit back and wait for you to give them the treat. You could click and treat this – the dog is learning not to grab at treats, and that can be useful, especially if you have young children in the house. But the dog is not learning to take treats gently. Try using a different type of food if he won't go after it eagerly, or have someone watch you to make sure you aren't accidentally using some verbal correction to stop the dog. Or, if he is very sensitive to your yelp, just turn your back if he bites.

Problem-Solving Tips:
The dog paws at the treat hand rather than biting or licking at it.
▪ Hold your hand still and work on clicking and treating for not pawing the hand as your first step. Once the dog learns pawing is not allowed, he'll try other things, and you can start working on licking.

It hurts too much to work on this. The chomping is getting worse!
- Never jerk your hand away if the dog chomps. It gives the dog the idea he wasn't quick enough or forceful enough, and he'll try harder next time.
- Wear gloves. It will hurt even more as the dog gets better at lunging for treats, so you'd better start working on it now.
- Work in a very low-stress environment, with no other dogs or people around. Dogs will sometimes be less grabby in more secure surroundings.

The dog licks until the click, then grabs the treat forcefully when offered.
- Open your hand just slightly, and yelp when the dog makes a grab for the treat. (It's best not to use the clicker to practice this, because you are really correcting the dog, not rewarding him.
- After you click, place the treat as far into the dog's mouth as you can manage (see the section in Chapter 4 on handling your dog's mouth if you need work on this).
- Put a treat between your forefinger and thumb, hold it in the dog's mouth far back on the tongue. Click when you feel the tongue moving instead of the teeth. This exercise can be tough on your fingers, but the payoff in better food-taking behavior is worth it!

Note that Labrador retrievers, Doberman pinschers, and German shepherds are often particularly difficult to train to take treats gently, so these and similar breeds may take longer to teach this behavior. Your persistence will be rewarded!

Suggested Commands: Gentle, Nice, Easy

Variations: Could you teach your dog to leap up and grab a treat without touching your fingers? Or do a variation on the killer whale leap to take a fish from the trainer's mouth? Don't try this if you don't like jumping dogs!

SIT

The Final Picture: The dog plants his butt on the ground in response to a verbal cue or hand signal, in any environment, on any surface.

Uses: You name it, Sit probably figures into it! Good for preventing jumping on people, working at doorways (as we'll be doing later in the chapter with Wait). The starting position for teaching Down. Sits are used in many types of canine competition events.

Preparation and Props: Treats, a clicker, and a hungry dog. These directions are for a lured sit rather than a purely shaped one because it accommodates a nice hand signal from the start.

The Steps Along the Way:
Session One –
1. Start with the dog in front of you, facing you. Hold a food treat directly over the dog's nose and move it up slightly. Click and treat when the dog tilts his head back. Repeat 3 times.
2. Start at the dog's nose again, but move the treat up and back over the dog's head, keeping it low so the dog doesn't jump up. Click and treat when the dog looks up and begins to bend his back legs. Repeat 3 times.

CLICK TRICKS

If you have trouble seeing when the dog's back legs bend, have someone else watch and click, while you treat, or work from a sitting position for a better view.

3. Start at the dog's nose again, and move the treat farther back over the dog's head toward his rear, until he sits. Jackpot! Repeat until the dog puts his butt on the ground 3 times in a row.
4. Change locations and repeat step 3. Click and treat only when the dog puts his butt on the floor. Repeat 3 times.
5. Change locations and repeat 3 times.

Session Two –
6. Starting in a new location, repeat step 4 3 times.
7. Now, do not hold a treat in your hand, but use the same hand motion up and over the dog's head. Click and treat when the dog touches his bottom to the ground. Don't forget to deliver your treat. Repeat 10 times.

CLICK TRICKS

Have treats in a bowl nearby, but out of the dog's reach. You won't have to have them in your hand but they are readily available. Try to deliver the treat quickly enough that the dog's still sitting when he gets it.

8. Change locations and repeat step 7. Remember to bring your bowl of treats!

9. Gradually modify your hand motion until you are moving your hand up but not forward over the dog. To do this, shorten the distance you move your hand by an inch or so, repeat 3 times, then decrease the distance again, until it looks the way you want.

Session Three –
10. Work in a new location until the dog responds reliably (80 percent of the time) to your hand signal. This means he should get clicked 8 out of 10 times.

11. Change locations and work until the dog responds 80 percent of the time.

12. Change locations and repeat.

Session Four –
13. In a new location, again work until you have a reliable response (correct 80 percent of the time) to your hand signal. Time to add a verbal signal (also called a command or cue word) if you wish.

14. In the same location, add your verbal cue just before you give your hand signal. Remember, it's new cue ("Sit"), old cue (hand signal), action (dog sits), click and treat. Review Chapter 1 if you don't remember why this order is important and why you don't give the verbal cue at the same time as the hand signal. Also see Chapter 7 for when you might use a signal, when you might want to use a command, and why you might not want to use both at once.

15. Change locations and repeat the previous step.

Following sessions, work on variability –
16. Continue to change locations and surfaces, gradually adding more distractions.

17. When the dog sits, wait a few seconds before clicking and treating, building up to a sit stay.

18. Practice a sit beside you rather than in front. Be sure to have the dog on both your right and your left sides.
19. Practice sits when you are facing the dog, standing behind him, or standing with your back to him.
20. Improve the speed of response to your command. To do this, click and treat AS the dog bends his back legs rather than when he completes the sit, release, take a step away from the dog, and repeat. The dog may abort the sit when he hears the click, but don't stress about it. We're clicking for a fast response (one criteria) so the completion of the sit (another criteria) has to be dropped to a lower level. As the dog starts to anticipate, his response will speed up, then you can add back in completion of the sit.
21. Click and treat only the best sits – fastest, prettiest, whatever you like. Gradually wean yourself off the clicks and substitute praise, petting, playing with a toy for food rewards. Remember to release the dog from the sit!

CLICK TRICKS

A release word tells the dog he is done for the moment, the command is no longer in force. Some suggestions for your release word are Release, Break, Free, or Go. If a release is new to your dog, you'll have to teach him what it means. Say the word then make him move – tickle him, pat your thigh, make a sound, jump around. Do something different to make the dog move each time so the word is the cue, not what you are doing. If you use your release word consistently, the dog will begin to wait for it – you're on your way to teaching a stay!

Early Steps: Some dogs may back away from the handler rather than sit. Sometimes just holding your hand a little higher will work. Have someone observe you and tell you if you need to hold the hand higher or lower. Or you can practice in a corner so that the dog can't move backward.

Other dogs may jump up at the treat. This is handler error – you're holding the treat too high. Move it just over his head, close but not touching.

Problem-Solving Tips:
The dog paws at or jumps at you.
- Work in a doorway with a baby gate between you and the dog. Click and treat for calm behavior first, then work on shaping the sit.

- Don't use a food lure. Pure shape the sit instead. It requires more planning, but you won't get frustrated with the dog jumping on you.
- Work on the attention exercise in Chapter 1 ("Another Shaped Behavior" section) so the dog learns that not lunging for the treat gets him the treat.

The dog is biting at your hand as he follows the food.
- Go back and work on Take a Treat Gently earlier in this chapter.
- Offer treats on a spoon or resting on a fork.
- Switch to less exciting treats.

The dog won't sit if I don't have a treat.
- Stop luring with treats and free shape the sit.
- Make sure your hand signal looks identical when you don't have the treat.
- Start from Step 1 using a hand signal and no treat.

Suggested Commands: Sit, Park it

Suggested Signal: Hold your flattened hand out with palm facing the ceiling, and move it upward from approximately your knees to your hip

Variations: Pure shape the sit instead of using a lure. Work on having the dog sit at a distance from you. Once the dog also knows Down, teach a sit from the down position.

DOWN

The Final Picture: The dog puts his body flat on the ground in response to a verbal cue or hand signal, in any environment, on any surface. Some dogs lie on one hip or the other while some lie centered between the hips, sphinx-style. Either way is okay at this stage.

Uses: Down stays, useful for keeping the dog out from underfoot while you are performing some task; part of "Go to Your Spot" (Chapter 4); many varieties of canine competition; the basis for some popular tricks and other behaviors.

Preparation and Props: Treats, a clicker, and a hungry dog. We are again using a lure to facilitate adding a hand signal. It's helpful if the dog knows the Sit command, but not necessary.

The Steps Along the Way:
Session One –
1. Start in a familiar environment with few distractions. You may find it helpful to be on a slick floor surface – the kitchen often fits the bill. Put the dog in a sit, if you've already taught it. If your dog doesn't sit on command, either train that first or see "Early Steps" below for tips on how to start. Draw a treat down from the dog's nose to between his front paws. Move slowly and click and treat if he drops his head to follow the treat. Repeat 3 times.
2. Draw the treat down between the dog's two front paws and slightly behind them. Click and treat for the dog moving his head lower toward the ground. Stay at each head level for no longer than 3 repetitions. Jackpot at any point if the dog lies down.
3. Draw the treat down between his front feet and hold it on the ground. Click and give the treat when the dog lies all the way down to get it. Repeat 3 times.

Session Two –
4. Starting in a new location, click and treat the dog for lying down. Repeat 3 times.
5. Now eliminate the food from your hand. Use the same hand motion, keeping your fingers together as if you had a treat, from the dog's nose to the ground. Click and treat when the dog lies down. Remember to have your treats handy. Repeat 10 times.
6. Change locations and repeat step 5.
7. Gradually modify your hand signal until you are only moving your hand partway toward the floor (see Step 9 for Sit for information on how to do this.). Click and treat the best responses only – such as when the dog is already lying down before you've finished your hand signal. Repeat until you have delivered 10 treats.

Session Three –
8. Working in a different location, work until your dog is responding reliably to your hand signal (lying down 80 percent of the time). In

other words, he lies down 8 out of 10 times as soon as you start the hand signal.

9. Change locations and work again until the dog responds 80 percent of the time.

10. Change locations and repeat again.

Session Four –

11. In another new location, work until your dog is lying down reliably – 80 percent of the time – with your hand signal. Now you can add a verbal signal, if desired.

12. In the same location, add your verbal cue just before you present your hand signal – so it's verbal cue, hand signal, dog downs, click and treat. Review Chapter 1 if you don't remember why this order is important and the verbal cue isn't given at the same time as the hand signal.

13. Change locations and repeat the previous step.

Following sessions, work on variability –

14. Continue to change locations and surfaces (carpet, linoleum, grass, dirt, cement), gradually adding more distractions.

15. Work on getting the dog to lie down whether you are sitting on the floor or a chair, or standing up. You will need to change positions gradually so the dog doesn't get confused. If he does, back up to a previous step and move more slowly.

16. Delay your click and treat until the dog has been down for a few seconds. You can build up to a down stay this way. Remember to use your release word.

17. Practice downs beside you rather than in front. Be sure to work to both the right and left sides.

18. Improve the speed of response to your command. To do this, click as the dog starts to lie down, rather than waiting for the dog to complete the down, release, take a step to get the dog up, and repeat. When he hears the click, the dog may abort the down – that's okay. Remember that when you're changing one criteria (asking for speed), you have to relax other criteria (actual completion of the position). As the dog begins to react more quickly, you can add back in the completion of the down.

19. Click and treat only the best downs – the fastest, straightest, best rolled hip, or whatever you're looking for. Gradually wean off of the

clicks and use praise, petting, your release word, playing with a toy as alternates to treats. Don't reward every response.

CLICK TRICKS

Play the "position game" to see if the dog really understands your commands. Give your dog a cue for sit or a cue for down or say a nonsense word. Only reward what you've asked for. If you delay the reward does the dog change position, hoping to get a click? That's your sign he really doesn't understand your commands.

Early Steps: If your dog doesn't sit on command yet, start with him standing on all fours. Hold a treat in front of his nose and move it down between his front feet. Click and treat when he ducks his head a little. Gradually ask for more head movement, until the dog is putting his head on the ground. Eventually, the rear end should follow. Whenever it does, even if it's while you're still shaping getting the head on the ground, jackpot!

As an alternate method, you can use the additional prop of a chair or coffee table or even your own bent leg (with you sitting on the floor). Lure the dog under with your treat, clicking and treating as he puts his body on the ground. Once the dog starts to get the idea, you will need to wean him off the additional prop as a separate step in your training.

Problem-Solving Tips:
The dog's butt stays up even when his head is on the ground.
- Try moving the treat down more slowly, and drawing it slightly away from the dog's nose once it's on the ground.
- Use the alternate method described in "Early Steps."

The dog is biting at your hand as he follows the treat.
- Teach "Take a Treat Gently" first.
- Offer treats on a spoon or on a fork.
- Switch to less exciting treats.

The dog works fine at home, but won't lie down in public or in more distracting environments or out in public.
- This is usually due to stress. The down is a vulnerable position for a dog,

so if he's unsure of himself in public, you'll have difficulty convincing him to lie down. Work on the confidence building exercises in Chapter 6 to help him be more sure of himself.

- Stay in a safe environment and slowly add more distractions such as other people, other dogs, moving objects. Work until the dog is comfortable with all of this before moving to a new environment.
- Use really exciting treats when out in public.

Suggested Commands: Down, Plotz, Crash, Drop

Suggested Signal: Hold your flattened hand out with the palm facing the floor, and move it from approximately chest height to hip height.

CLICK TRICKS – Command Words

Put some thought into the words you choose as commands, or cues. "Down" can often become a problem because people use it when dogs jump up and they want the dog to stay off of them, or when they want dogs to get off of furniture. To keep English effective in communicating with dogs, words should have one meaning and one meaning only. If you think "down" is likely to be misused to indicate things other than "put your body on the ground," choose another word.

Variations: After you have the basic down reliably on cue, work on having the dog down at a distance. (See Working at a distance in Chapter 7 if you need help with this.) Down is a powerful command, and being able to drop your dog at a distance may save the situation in an emergency someday. Teach the dog to down from either a sit or a stand. Work the down in a play group while other dogs are moving.

COME

The Final Picture: The dog comes directly to you from wherever he is and sits (or remains) near enough to you for you to touch him (and snap a leash to his collar if need be), regardless of what he was doing at the time or what is going on around him. The sit here is optional – the important detail is that the dog come to you and remain near you until given further instructions.

Having a dog run to you but then immediately run away in a sort of "catch me if you can" is not a useful exercise. For obedience competition, the dog has to come and sit in front, facing you.

Uses: In real life, this is one of your essential commands if you ever want the dog off-leash, even in your own yard. It also figures into many dog sports.

Preparation and Props: Treats, a clicker, a hungry dog, a closed container to hold kibble, a boring toy. A safe environment where the dog cannot run off, and where he has few options other than to come to you. It's helpful if the dog will already sit on command.

The Steps Along the Way:
Session One –
1. In a boring environment with your hungry dog, show the dog you have a treat, then back one step away from him. Click and treat when he takes a step toward you. Repeat 3 times.
2. Move to a new place in the room and repeat step 1.

CLICK TRICKS

When working on recalls, the dog should come to you to collect his treat after being clicked. Unless otherwise indicated, don't be "Domino's" – don't deliver.

3. Move to a new place in the room and repeat step 1.
4. Move to a new place in the room. Put a treat on the floor and while the dog is eating it, take 3 steps away from him. When he turns his head toward you to see where you've gone, click, drop a treat on the floor in front of you, and move 3 steps away. Repeat 10 times. (You are clicking the head turn.)

Session Two –
5. Change locations. Repeat step 4.
6. Throw a treat a short distance away from you. While the dog is eating it, move a few steps away and turn your back on the dog. When he comes around in front of you, click, drop a treat, step away and turn your back on him again. Repeat 5 times, then change locations and repeat the entire sequence. (You are now clicking the dog for being in front of you.)
7. Change locations and repeat step 6.

Session Three –
8. Starting in your last location, repeat step 6.
9. Toss a treat away from you and wait for the dog to eat it. Click when the dog turns toward you. Repeat 5 times.
10. Toss a treat away from you and wait for the dog to eat it. Click when the dog is taking 1 step toward you. Repeat 5 times.
11. Change locations and repeat step 10.
12. Now toss a treat away from you and wait for the dog to eat it. Click when he has taken 3 steps back toward you. Repeat 5 times. If he doesn't go for the tossed treat but instead moves toward you, click and Jackpot!!
13. Change locations and repeat step 12.

47

Session Four –

14. In a new location, put your boring toy on the floor and step away from it. When the dog turns toward you, click and treat. Don't worry if the dog picks up the toy and brings it with him. Our only criteria at this point is that the dog turn toward you. Repeat 10 times.

15. Change locations and repeat step 14, clicking and treating for 2 steps toward you.

16. Change locations. Put the same toy on the floor, but now turn your back to the dog. Click and treat when he comes around in front of you. Repeat 10 times.

17. Change locations. Toss the toy and turn your back on the dog. When he comes around in front of you, tell him what a good boy he is, reach down and touch his collar, and click and treat. DO NOT use the hand touching his collar to hold the clicker – the noise of the clicker right next to his ear might be unpleasant or startling to the dog. Repeat 10 times.

18. Change locations. Toss the toy, turn your back to the dog. When he comes around in front of you, praise, reach down and grab and hold his collar for one second. Click and treat and release the collar. Repeat 10 times.

Session Five –

19. Change locations. Put your closed container, with some treats inside, down on the floor, step away from it, and turn your back. The dog should have the hang of this game by now, and come running around in front of you. Grab his collar, hold for one second, then click and treat and release. Note that the treats you are giving the dog MUST be more interesting than the treats in the closed container. Repeat 10 times.

20. If your dog is responding reliably – at least 8 out of 10 times – it's time to add your verbal command. Put the container on the ground and step away from it, turning your back to the dog. Immediately say "come," and when the dog turns toward you, click and treat. If the dog doesn't go for the container at all, click and jackpot, then fill the container with tastier treats for the next repetition. Repeat 10 times. Change locations and continue pairing the command with the behavior for at least 50 repetitions over the next day or two.

Additional sessions, work on variability –

21. Continue to work at short distances with gradually more interesting doggie distractions. The ultimate success of your recall will depend on many many repetitions with a huge variety of distractions in lots of different environments.

22. Continue to work at short distances in gradually more distracting environments. Don't forget to practice in places where an emergency recall may really be necessary some day, like at your front door.

23. Gradually add more distance to your recall – no more than 5 feet at a time. Do at least 10 repetitions at each distance before moving on.

24. Build variability into your rewards. Some options are running away from the dog when he turns toward you (most dogs love chase games), throwing a toy after clicking, releasing him to investigate that smell he was so interested in, or doing a fun activity when he comes to you. Be sure NEVER to punish the dog for coming to you, even if he has your favorite pair of socks in his mouth when he arrives!

Early Steps: Take a look at why the dog isn't coming – does he not know the command (has never been taught it) or know it but not do it reliably (has never been taught in gradually more challenging environments)? If he's never been taught the command, start out right, follow the steps, and you'll do fine. If he's been exposed to a command but it's never been reliable, start fresh with a different command. Make sure that you never do anything unpleasant if the dog comes to you. Go back and work on GRADUALLY adding more and more distractions until the dog ignores everything to come to you.

If the dog won't even take a step toward you, work in a bathroom or other restricted area, use more enticing treats, or take a look at your body language (leaning over is threatening, squatting down is inviting).

Problem-Solving Tips:

The dog comes but he always brings the toy or treat container with him.

- Secure the toy or container so it can't be moved from its spot. Be sure to start practicing with the dog close to you and reward heavily for turning away from the item. Don't forget to change locations of the toy or treats, as well.

The dog does okay in some environments, but loses it when outside or in an area with more distractions.

- Break your distractions into even smaller pieces as you build up through them. For example, if other dogs are a distraction, work with dogs your dog already knows (and who are not exciting playmates), starting with them a great distance away and behind a fence (so that he can't get to the other dogs if he's not working with you). Work gradually closer, then add other dogs your dog knows, then add dogs he doesn't know (again at a great distance), and so on.
- Change your rewards. The same old treats you train with every day may not be enticing enough to compete with really interesting smells, the chance to get petted by a stranger or play with a dog. You (and your rewards) need to be more interesting than any other thing your dog may encounter.
- Some dogs will never be truly reliable off leash. Yours may be one of them. If he is, it's a valuable piece of information to have – you will know that you will have to avoid putting the dog in situations where lack of a reliable recall could have terrible consequences.
- If your dog has had a problem with recalls in the past, it may take a LONG time to retrain. Don't give up, even if you only seem to be making a smidgeon of progress with each work session.

The dog comes, but seems stressed, is crawling, comes very slowly, or urinates.

- Pay attention to your body language. If you are leaning forward and frowning with concentration, you might be freaking the dog out. Stand up straight, breathe deeply, and smile at the dog. Try your initial repetitions while you are sitting on the floor. Don't fawn over a nervous dog – you may actually make the problem worse.

- Have the dog come to your side rather than in front – it may be less stressful for the dog.
- Click for faster approaches. You may have accidentally taught the dog to come slowly.
- Have you called the dog to you and then done something unpleasant, like clipping his nails and giving him a bath? Even one or two repetitions of that can quickly teach the dog that bad things can happen when he comes. Pay attention to what happens to the dog when he is called and make sure that it is ALWAYS a positive experience.

Suggested Commands: Come, Here, Dog's name

Suggested Signal: Hold your arm straight out from your side, parallel to the ground, flattened palm facing forward, then bend at the elbow and bring your palm in to your chest

Variations: Teach the dog to check in with you periodically, even if you haven't formally called him. This is a particularly good idea if you are working with a deaf or hard-of-hearing dog you want to be able to have off-leash. Teach the dog to drop into a down in the middle of a recall (an advanced exercise in obedience competition).

WALK ON LEASH

The Final Picture: The dog walks nicely on leash regardless of distractions. The dog should not pull no matter how long the leash is.

Uses: One of the all-time most-requested behaviors is walking on a leash without pulling so that owners and dogs can enjoy walks together. Once walking is more enjoyable, you may tend to get your dog out there more for more exercise for you both and more socialization for the dog. Also a great start for walking OFF leash.

Preparation and Props: A regular buckle collar and 4- to 6-foot leash, treats, and your clicker. It will be helpful if you have already worked on the attention exercise in Chapter 1 with your dog.

The Steps Along the Way:

Session One –

1. Start in the house, with your dog on leash. Stand still and keep the leash short enough that you can reach the dog, no more than 3 feet. Click and treat each time the leash goes slack. Repeat 3 times. You don't need to worry about where the dog is at this point, only whether or not the leash is slack.

2. Change locations and repeat 3 times.

3. Continue changing locations in your house until the dog is keeping the leash loose no matter where you are.

4. Put a toy on the ground out of the dog's reach. Click when the leash is slack and RELEASE the dog to get the toy. Repeat 10 times, sometimes delivering a treat from your hand and sometimes releasing the dog to play with the toy. Change toys and treats as necessary to keep the dog from getting bored with them.

5. Have a friend or family member sit nearby holding a boring cookie. They should not look at or say anything to the dog (choose a helper who can manage this!). Click when the leash is slack and RELEASE the dog to get the treat from your helper. Repeat 10 times, sometimes delivering a treat from your hand and sometimes releasing the dog to get the treat from the other person.

Session Two –

6. Repeat steps 1 through 5 from Session One with the increased criteria that the dog must now put slack in the leash AND look at you.

7. Continue until the dog won't look away from you, then move to another area in the house and repeat steps 1 through 5 until he won't look away. At this point you can begin working outside, in your back yard.

8. Continue to change locations, gradually adding more distracting environments, until you are able to work in your front yard at the foot of your driveway, with the dog not looking away from you no matter what goes by on your street. Up to this point, you have been standing still with the leash kept about three feet long. From this point on, whenever you have the leash on your dog, you will "become a tree" (stop moving) any time he pulls for any reason. You move forward ONLY when the leash is slack.

CLICK TRICKS

Find some other way to exercise your dog (instead of walking) during the week while you are working on the loose leash exercises! Don't allow him to build pent-up energy.

Session Three –

9. Decide which side you want your dog to walk on. Begin in your front yard at the foot of your driveway. Drop a treat on the ground, and while the dog is eating it, turn and take a giant step away from your dog. Your back is now to the dog. Click and treat when he takes a step toward you on the side you have chosen. Deliver the treat from your hand on the side you want the dog to walk on, held alongside your leg. As soon as you treat, turn your back to the dog and take a giant step away again. Repeat 10 times.

CLICK TRICKS

If you want the dog to walk on your left, have the leash in your right hand and pivot to your right each time you step away from the dog. This will keep the leash manageable and encourage the dog to come up on the correct side.

10. Now click and treat when the dog gets to "heel" position, right next to your leg. Don't click if he runs past, just turn away from him again. Here is where delivering the treats in the correct place can really speed up your training! Repeat 10 times.
11. Change locations and repeat step 10. Change locations and repeat a third time.

12.   Can you predict that the dog will come to your side for a click and treat when you step away? Then it's time to add a name to this behavior. Starting in a new location, step away from the dog, say your command, click and treat when he comes to your side, then step away again. Repeat this pairing of "command, behavior, click, treat" at least 50 times over the next couple of days, changing locations frequently.

Session Four –

13.   Begin in a new location. Give your dog a treat, then step away. As he runs to your side, take a step or two so he must move with you while you are moving. Click and treat when he takes two steps next to you, then turn away again. Repeat 10 times.

14.   Continue in a new location, increasing the distance you walk together before clicking and treating. Repeat 10 times at each new distance – so it's 10 repetitions taking 2 steps, 10 repetitions taking 3 steps, and so on – until you can take at least 5 steps with the dog trotting beside you before you click and treat.

15.   Vary the number of steps the dog is required to take before getting a click and treat. The number should "bounce around" an average count during each series of 10 repetitions. Start with a lower number than you built up to in step 14. For example, if you can take 5 steps with the dog, then bounce around 3 as your average. So the first repetition might be 2 steps, then 4 steps, then 1 step, then 5 steps, then 3 steps, then 2 steps, and so on. Decide before each repetition how many steps the dog will need to take with you in order to get a click and treat. (See Chapter 7 for more information on varying or "bouncing" around an average.)

Additional sessions, working on variability –

16.   Continue to increase your average number of steps taken before clicking and treating, by using the bouncing technique described in step 15. If you find you are often losing the dog at this stage, you are taking too many steps for him.

17.   Continue to add more and more distractions in your environment. Don't forget to jackpot if the dog ignores something particularly interesting to stay with you!

18.   Add changes of pace such as walking faster or more slowly.

19.   Vary your rewards. Sometimes throw a ball or toy for the dog to chase, sometimes pet him, sometimes give him a treat, sometimes release him to sniff an interesting scent or greet a person or dog.

Early Steps: Walking on leash without pulling is one of the most difficult things to teach a dog, mostly because humans don't pay attention to the dog on the end of the leash unless he is causing problems. If you want to be successful, from now on, any time your dog is on leash you MUST work on keeping it loose. If he gets even an occasional reward for pulling, such as getting to touch noses with another dog or greet a person, or get to his favorite park more quickly, he will continue to pull. Remember, variable rewards – sometimes the dog gets something he wants as a reward for pulling – make a behavior STRONGER!

The longer the dog has been pulling on leash, the longer it will take you to teach him that it doesn't work any more. And, if you walk your dog on a retractable leash (Flexi™ or other brand name) and want him not to pull, stop using the Flexi right now. He is learning to pull every time you walk with it because the dog has to put pressure against the collar in order to draw the retractable leash out.

If you really need to get your dog walked, you can introduce a Halti™ or Gentle Leader™ to prevent him from practicing pulling. Keep in mind these devices will have to be weaned off of if you want a loose leash without them.

Problem-Solving Tips:
The dog works okay until you move outside with him, then is uninterested in you and your treats.
- Stress can cause a dog to stop working in a new environment, and stress often appears as "disinterest" in a dog. If you know your dog is on the shy side, build up very slowly through new distractions, changing the environment as minimally as possible each time.
- Work before meals and use the most exciting treats you can find, delivered in his food bowl. Something about having a bowl plopped down in front of him is simply irresistible to most dogs!

The dog isn't trying to pull me forward on walks – I'm usually pulling him along.
- This can be due to fear or shyness. The good news is that this exercise works the same even if the dog isn't pulling. You are still clicking and

treating for coming to your side. Move more slowly through each new environment if you suspect that this fits your dog.

- Stop pulling. If you stand still and only move forward when the leash is slack, neither you nor the dog have any reason to be pulling on the leash. If you are trying to drag the dog along, he may just be putting on the brakes as an automatic reaction to the tension YOU are putting on the leash.

The dog works all right until another dog (or person, child on a bike, etc.) goes by.

- Work separately on getting attention around the particular distraction that is a problem for your dog. See Chapter 3 for Check In and Chapter 6 on confidence building for more information. Wait until you have good attention to begin your work on walking on leash.

Suggested Commands: Let's go, Walkies, Let's walk, Easy

Variations: Teach your dog to touch your hand while you are moving, then use your hand as a target or lure as you walk with the dog on leash (this will result in something a little closer to formal heeling, and the dog will need to stay closer to you – not as much fun for the dog on walks). Teach the dog to do the same "close" walking (no more that a 6-foot leash away) without a leash.

WAIT AT THE DOOR

The Final Picture: The dog waits at any doorway, without moving forward, until released. He does not have to remain in a particular position such as a sit or down, but he must not cross the threshold you have specified. This can (and should!) be used at doorways, in the car, at street crossings, or when opening your dog's crate.

Uses: This is a must-have for all dogs for safety reasons. Remember to practice in the car, too – hatchbacks or the large rear doors of SUVs or sliding van doors give the dog plenty of space to bolt before you can get a hand on him. A building block for sitting at the door to greet friends.

Preparation and Props: Treats, a hungry dog, a leash, and a clicker. An obvious threshold such as a doorway.

The Steps Along the Way:
Session One —
1. Start at a doorway, with the dog on leash. Keep the leash short enough so that the dog is right next to you and can't step through the door. Open the door. Click and treat when the dog stops pulling forward to get through the doorway. Repeat 10 times.
2. Move to another doorway in your house and repeat step 1.
3. Move to another doorway and repeat step 1.

Session Two —
4. Start at your original doorway with the dog on leash. Click and treat when the dog looks at you, then release the dog to go through the doorway with you. Repeat 10 times, working both directions through the doorway.
5. Change locations and repeat step 4.
6. Change locations and repeat step 4.

Session Three —
7. Starting with a new doorway, lengthen your leash so that the dog could step through the doorway if he chose to. (Don't choose a doorway the dog is likely to want to charge out, such as the front door or the door to the back yard – use an interior door, to the basement or a bedroom maybe.) Open the door. If the dog hesitates or looks at you, click and treat, then release and walk through the doorway with the dog. Repeat 10 times.
8. Change locations to a more enticing doorway (but still not the front or back door) and repeat step 7.
9. Change locations and repeat step 7.
10. Is the dog getting predictable yet (does he pause and wait for more information at the doorway)? If so, time to add your command. (If not, continue to work at gradually more enticing doorways until he is pausing at least 8 out of 10 tries.) Say your command, open the door, dog pauses, you click and treat, release to go through the doorway. Continue changing doorways and pairing your command with the behavior for at least 50 additional repetitions.

Session Four —
11.   Start at a doorway with the door already open. Approach the doorway with the dog on a loose leash. Just before the dog reaches the threshold, say your command and stop moving. Click and treat if the dog pauses before he hits the end of the leash. If he doesn't pause, or hits the end of the leash first, do not click. Instead, repeat the process, shortening the leash so he isn't as far ahead of you. Repeat 10 times.
12.   Change to a more enticing doorway and repeat step 11.
13.   Go to your back door and repeat step 11.
14.   Go to your front door and repeat step 11.

Additional sessions, work on variability —
15.   Practice leaving your dog behind while you go through the doorway, then returning to the dog — start with just a step in front of the dog, and gradually get farther and farther away.
16.   Work on the wait at safe doors without the leash.
17.   Work on the wait at enticing doors such as your front door, without the leash. Have a back-up plan ready in case the dog leaps through unexpectedly – can you set up an exercise pen around the front steps or block the driveway?
18.   Have someone standing on the other side of the door waiting to come in. Vary whether people come inside or not.
19.   Have someone with a dog walk by your front door. Have a friend bring a dog your dog likes and stand on your porch. Sometimes they come in, sometimes they don't. Use a brief play session with the second dog as a reward for a good wait.
20.   Practice wait while you open and close the door but the dog does not go through the doorway.
21.   Have your dog do a wait while kids are playing in your front yard.
22.   Don't forget to practice wait when you open the car door, at curbs before you step into the street, and when you open the dog's crate door.

Early Steps: If the dog doesn't seem to get it, use a less distracting doorway, such the door to your bedroom rather than your kitchen. It can be helpful to have a second person holding the leash. This allows you to work in different places in relation to the doorway yet still prevents the dog from crossing the threshold without a release.

Problem-Solving Tips:
The dog does okay while on leash, but bursts through the opening when the leash is off.

- Start with VERY boring doorways. Work slowly up through the progressively more interesting doorways in your house.
- Use your body to block the dog's exit - step in front of and move toward the dog to make him back away from the doorway. (Use your foot for a small dog.)
- Work on the Watch Me exercise in Chapter 3 first so that the dog is more likely to check with you instead of trying to run through the door.

Suggested Commands: Wait, Hold up, Pause.

Suggested Signal: Hold your flattened hand out with the palm facing the dog, and either hold it still or move it slightly toward the dog.

Variations: Have a conversation with a friend or delivery person on the front porch while your dog does a wait with the door open. See if you can teach your dog to wait behind a less obvious threshold such as the change from linoleum to carpet, or with no threshold at all.

SLICK CLICKS

CHICKEN TRAINING

Mandy Book

"Why are you going to Arkansas to train chickens?" my husband asks. "To learn to be a better dog trainer!" And off I fly to Little Rock to train with Bob and Marian Bailey, experts in the art of animal training for many years.

"You are bigger, stronger, and smarter than the chicken," Bob repeats for the 20th time during our training session. I can almost believe him. Then I realize I have taught one of my chickens to peck aggressively at me while I open her cage. I am just a bit intimidated by this chicken, and she has already learned that I move faster, and she gets out faster, if she pecks. So much for the smarter part!

I experiment with ways to prevent getting pecked. I try fooling her by putting one hand close to the cage and opening the door with the other hand, while she is busy pecking toward the decoy hand. That works for one session, but five minutes later she has figured out the hand is a decoy and ignores it completely while pecking at the cage-opening hand. I try to be faster than the chicken and get the door open before she can peck. Not a chance! (I note that Bob did <u>not</u> say we were faster than the chicken.) Finally, I stop and approach the problem from a dog training perspective. What is it that the chicken wants? To get out of the cage and be trained (and therefore fed). So I will wait for the behavior I want – <u>no</u> pecking – before I will open the cage for the chicken.

I sit in front of the cage, waiting for my opportunity to be smarter than the chicken. Her pecking slows, then stops momentarily. I instantly put my hand up to the cage. She pecks. I wait. When the pecking stops again, I move closer to the door. Eventually, I am able to open the door without having to dodge a beak. At each session, I wait patiently for no pecking before I open the door. The chicken quickly learns the game and cooperates – no more pecking. No one is the wiser about my inadvertent chicken aggression training – except my chicken and me. And I <u>am</u> smarter!

DON'T TOUCH

The Final Picture: The dog removes his nose/ teeth/paws from whatever they were touching, or stops short of touching some object.

Uses: A building block for an even stronger command, Leave it, where the dog turns away from something and returns to you to check in. A good basic for teaching paws off the counter.

Preparation and Props: Dog, kibbled dog food, a variety of good treats, and a clicker. Teach Take a Treat Gently before working on this.

The Steps Along the Way:
Session One —
1. Hold a piece of kibble in your closed fist. The dog may lick or paw at your hand. Click and treat (using the kibble in your hand) as soon as the dog stops touching your hand. Repeat 10 times.
2. Change to a more interesting treat and repeat step 1.
3. Change to an even more interesting treat and repeat step 1.
4. Using the same treat, count to 2 with the dog not touching before clicking and treating the dog. If the dog touches your hand before you get to 2, restart the count. Repeat 5 times.
5. Count to 3, then click and treat. Repeat 5 times.

Session Two —
6. Start in a new location. Count to 3, then click and treat. Repeat 5 times.
7. Count to 4, then click and treat. Repeat 5 times.
8. Count to 5, then click and treat. Repeat 5 times.
9. Using the "bounce around" technique described in the section on Walk on Leash, gradually build up to 10 seconds where the dog is not touching your hand. Start with an average of 3 seconds. For example, count to 2 and click and treat, then 4, click and treat, 1, click and treat, 3, click and treat. Repeat 5 times at each new average count.

Session Three —
10. Starting in a new location, bounce under the maximum count of 10 for 5 repetitions. Will the dog stay off of your hand during the entire count? Good - it's time to add your command!
11. Hold a treat in your fist, say your command, wait till the dog doesn't touch for the count you have decided in advance, click and treat. Continue to pair your cue with the behavior for at least 50 more repetitions. Change treats, locations, or the hand you are using after every 5 to 10 repetitions.

Session Four —
12. Put the treat on the flat of your hand and hold your hand in front of the dog. Say your command, click and treat if the dog doesn't touch it. Repeat 10 times, bouncing around an average 10 count. Close your hand if the dog tries to grab the treat and repeat step 11 again.
13. Change treats and repeat step 12.
14. Change locations and repeat step 12.

Additional sessions, work on variability —
15. Place a treat on the floor. Keep your foot poised over it in case the dog tries to snag it. Click and treat if he doesn't touch it. If he tries to grab it, cover it with your foot and wait until he backs away, then click and treat. (You can pick up the treat from the floor and give it to him or give him one from your hand.) We recommend that you hand the treat to the dog, rather than letting him grab it off the ground, just as a good habit-builder.
16. Put a treat on the floor and click and treat if the dog looks at you.
17. Drop a treat on the floor unexpectedly. Click and treat when the dog looks at you.
18. Spill the dog's bowl of food on the floor (start with just a few kibbles in it so he doesn't get a huge reward if he's not ready for this step!)
19. Work the same exercise with a toy and different objects.
20. Have different people holding food or a toy.
21. Work this behavior using other dogs or other animals as the "don't touch" object.

Early Steps: Some dogs (especially puppies) will paw for a long time before giving up. Be prepared for that so you don't accidentally drop a treat and reward that behavior. Be ready to click the instant they stop, even if it seems like a miniscule amount of time. Build up the time from this starting point.

Problem-solving tips:
The dog never paws at the hand or tries to touch it.
- Consider yourself lucky, introduce your command earlier and proceed with the lesson!
- Gentle or shy dogs may be hesitant to grab something from your hand. You can work on the same behavior by dropping a treat on the floor, or offering it in your open hand.

You aren't making progress – say, not getting past a count of 2.
- You have to outwait the dog – patience is required! If you keep giving up and letting the dog have the treat after 2 counts, you're teaching the dog this is as long as he has to wait. . .ever.
- You may have stayed too long at that count before varying it by using the bouncing around. Start your bouncing at a low count. If a count to 2 is as far as you can get, give a few clicks at 1, a click at 2, then a click at 3, then back to 1 again for a few more clicks. Have fewer of the higher counts in the initial stages. Don't shoot for a count to 5 or 6 right off the bat.
- You may be trying to increase your bounce average in too large a step. Start with a lower average count and gradually build up again.

Suggested Commands: Don't Touch, Off.

Variations: Can you tell the dog Don't Touch and leave the room without having him grab the food? (Hint: Put the food in a container initially, so that if he does go for it, he can't get rewarded). Jackpot if your dog shows restraint when you're out of the room or otherwise occupied - this isn't a "normal" doggy response!

CHAPTER 3
Easy Clicker

If you've completed the training exercises in Chapter 2, you've already trained most of the basic commands you'll need to help your dog behave in the home and out on walks. Congratulations! You're already well on your way to having a better canine companion and an enhanced relationship with your dog.

We used food treats as lures for some of those exercises. Not that there's anything wrong with that, mind you. But we'd like to practice a little pure shaping here. We'll let the dog take more of the initiative. In this chapter we will cover:

Watch me
Touch (nose)
Back up
Paw (touch)
Look (and go) there
Off leash walking
Check in

With each exercise, we'll mention a few of the many uses that can be made of it, and how we'll be building on it. You can do a lot with these behaviors – we'll even provide you with plans for a fun at-home flyball game. So get your equipment together, and set a few minutes aside. Ready? Begin!

WATCH ME

The Final Picture: The dog looks at you for ten to fifteen seconds, keeping his attention focused on you no matter what is going on in the environment.

Uses: Prevent barking and growling by helping your dog avoid eye contact with other dogs, precision heeling for competition or just more attentive walking on leash, solid stays, signal exercises (in higher level obedience).

Preparation and Props: Your relationship with your dog must be solid to accomplish this behavior. Is the dog bonded to you? Does he see you as a leader? If you can answer yes to both questions, you're ready to begin. If you can't answer yes, you need to work first on your relationship with your dog. Work on teaching other behaviors – training new things will both bring you closer together and establish you as leader.

The Steps Along the Way: We will offer two complete series of sessions for this behavior, one using luring and one relying on pure shaping. Try whichever you prefer. But after this, you'll be doing some training without lures.

Luring the Behavior –
Session One –
1. Touch the dog's nose with your finger, then move the finger two to four inches from his nose toward your face. Click when the dog looks at your finger. Repeat 3 times.
2. Gradually shape the dog to follow your finger for a longer distance, till you can bring your finger all the way to your face. Repeat each distance no more than 3 times.

Session Two –
3. In the same location, click the dog for following your finger all the way from his nose to your face. Repeat 3 times. Now shape for a longer

look, up to fifteen seconds, at your finger held to your face. (See the "Click Tricks" on page 69 if you need help with how to do this.)

Session Three –
4. Starting in the same location as your last session, begin fading your lure (getting rid of it) by starting with your finger a few inches away from the dog's nose and drawing it to your face. Repeat 3 times.
5. Start farther away from the dog's nose each time, till you are not moving your finger at all, but just placing it on your face and getting the behavior. Stay at each step for at least 3 repetitions.
6. Introduce your command. Say it just before you point at your face. When the dog looks at your face, click and treat. Pair the command with the behavior for at least 50 additional repetitions, changing now and then to a different location, and varying how long the dog has to look up at you before getting a click and treat.

Following sessions, work on variability –
See the section in Pure Shaping, below.

Pure Shaping the Behavior —
Session One –
1. Put the dog on leash and sit in a chair with the dog's food bowl filled with kibble in your lap. Click if the dog looks away from the bowl. Repeat 3 times.
2. Gradually shape the dog to look up at your face (see Chapter 1 if you need help.) Stay at each step for a minimum of 3 and a maximum of 5 repetitions.

Session Two –
3. Sit in a chair, holding a smelly treat. (If you can smell it, your dog certainly can.) Click if the dog looks away from your hand, and give him a treat with the hand he looked away from. Repeat 3 times. Jackpot if he looks at your face!
4. Gradually shape the dog to look up at your face if he isn't already doing it. Stay at each step for a minimum of 3 and a maximum of 5 repetitions.
5. Stand up and repeat step 4.

Session Three –
6.   Sit in a chair. Put some smelly treats in a container on the floor. Click if the dog looks away from the container. Reward him with a treat from another source, such as your hand or pocket, or the counter. Repeat 3 times. Jackpot if he looks at your face!
7.   Gradually shape the dog to look up at your face if he isn't already doing it. Stay at each step for a minimum of 3 and a maximum of 5 repetitions.
8.   Stand up and repeat step 7.
9.   Gradually build up the amount of time the dog has to look at you, to at least 15 seconds. See the "Click Tricks" on page 69 if you need help with this.
10.   Can you predict that the dog will look up at you if you put a treat on the floor? Then it's time to name the behavior. Say your command, when the dog looks up at your face, click and treat. Pair the command with the behavior for at least 50 additional repetitions, changing now and then to a different location, and varying how long the dog has to look up at you before getting a click and treat.

Following sessions, work on variability –
11.   Gradually add more distractions to the working environment by changing locations, adding toys on the floor, or working around other people or even other dogs. You may have to decrease the amount of time the dog must look at you when you introduce a new distraction. Build up to 15 seconds of attention in the presence of each new distraction before moving to a more difficult one.
12.   Vary the amount of time the dog has to focus on you before being clicked.
13.   Vary how many times the dog has to focus on you before being clicked.

Early Steps: Luring is probably easier for a young puppy, especially an active one, but it sometimes encourages jumping. If you're having a hard time getting the dog to follow your finger, hold a treat in your fingertips. Or try pure shaping. If you're getting a lot of jumping, decrease the distance the dog has to follow your finger from his nose before getting clicked. ONLY click when all four feet are on the floor.

CLICK TRICKS

To build up to a longer behavior, you need to bounce around an average count, which gradually increases. Let's say you set your initial "bounce" at 3 seconds (knowing that the dog will maintain the behavior for at least 5 seconds). Your first repetition would be 2 seconds, click and treat, then 1 second, click and treat, 4 seconds, click and treat, 2 seconds, click and treat, 3 seconds, click and treat, and so on. Do about 10 repetitions, then increase your average count a second or two. Gradually build up to the maximum time you want for the behavior – or a little past it, for good measure.

Problem-Solving Tips:
The dog won't look up at you.
- There are too many distractions in your environment. Work in a more isolated spot, with the dog on leash. Use really super yummy treats.
- The dog is very submissive and/or your body language is too threatening, so the dog doesn't want to look at you. Smile while you work. Sit in a chair to be less threatening. Use frequent jackpots and very short training sessions.

The dog won't maintain eye contact for any amount of time.
- There are too many distractions in your environment. Work in a more isolated spot, with the dog on leash, using super yummy treats.
- You are trying to build up too much time too quickly. Review your shaping. Increase your bounce average more slowly, adding only one second at a time.
- You may have accidentally shaped the dog to look at you for a specific amount of time before looking away. You need to vary the length of time the dog has to look at you before being clicked. See "Click Tricks" on bouncing around, above. Or have someone else watch and click at intervals you have randomly written down on a piece of paper, varying the time around your average count. Gradually build up one or two additional seconds at a time.

The dog is jumping up as he follows your finger.
- Click only when the dog's butt is on the ground. Add distance to your shaping more slowly.

Suggested Commands: Watch, Ready, Look

Suggested Signal: Point to your face or eyes

Variations: See "Check In" later in this chapter.

TOUCH (with nose)

The Final Picture: The dog touches his nose, on command, to something attached to you, such as a touch stick or your hand. Both variations are taught the same way and use the same command. The dog can easily determine if you have a touch stick or only your hand. We will refer to both as the target.

Uses: One of the best building block behaviors. Can be used to work on fear problems, for better heeling, to teach dance steps, to focus the dog, for obedience competition exercises, to teach a conformation stack, to direct movement (such as a spin, bow, crawl, or jump on or over something), and to direct the dog to objects. An excellent behavior for helping a traditionally trained dog to get excited about clicker training. The hand touch can even be used as a signal for an off-leash recall.

Preparation and Props: ¼" dowel approximately 3 feet in length (the "touch stick"). Paint the end (the last couple of inches) a different color to provide a better target and help the dog, or wrap a rubber band around the end. Or you can buy a foldable touch stick (see Resources in Appendix), designed just for clicker training. If you don't have a touch stick or a dowel, use your hand to start. Eventually, teach both variations. You may also want a shorter version of your dowel touch stick for particular exercises, for instance, if you have a fair-sized dog and you want to work on targeting for heel position – a long stick would be in the way, but a short (12 – 18 inches) stick would be just right.

The Steps Along the Way:
Session One –
   1.   Present the target just in front of the dog's nose at his level. Click and treat when the dog looks at the target. Remove the target between repetitions. Repeat 3 times.

2. Present the target. Click and treat when the dog touches the target with his nose or paw or body, even if it's accidental. Repeat 3 times.
3. Present your target. Click and treat if the dog touches anywhere on the target with his nose. Repeat 5 times, removing the target after each click and treat.
4. Present the target, and click and treat touches closer to the end of the stick or the palm of your hand. Gradually shape the dog to touch only the end of the touch stick, or the palm of your hand. See Chapter 1 if you need help with this shaping. Repeat until the dog touches the appropriate spot on the target at least 8 out of 10 times.

CLICK TRICKS

If you're using a touch stick, it's helpful to use a rubber band to section off the stick and shape the touch to the end. Start with the rubber band wound around the stick about halfway down it. Move the rubber band down a few inches after every 3 repetitions. That way, you'll be clear on if the dog is meeting your criteria and should be clicked and treated.

Session Two –
5. Change locations and repeat step 4, clicking only for touches in the appropriate spot.
6. Change locations and repeat step 5.
7. Working in the same environment, present your target, but place the target in a different location relative to the dog, so that he has to either reach up, reach down, or move right or left to touch the target. Repeat 10 times, changing the location of the target each time.

Session Three –
8. In a new location, work until the dog will touch the end of the touch stick at least 8 out of 10 tries no matter where you are holding the stick (its location or where your hand is on the stick), or until he will touch your palm no matter where you hold it or if it is your right or left hand.
9. Are you starting to be able to predict that the dog will touch the target correctly? Time to name the behavior. Say your command, dog touches, click and treat. Pair the command with the behavior at least

50 more times, changing one detail – where the target is held, how it is held, where you are working – every time you click and treat.

Following sessions, work on variability –
10. Dog touches end of stick resting against the wall, floor, or some other object (or your hand held on the floor, resting on a table).
11. Dog touches the target multiple times before getting a click.
12. Dog follows the target while it's moving, trying to touch the end of the stick or your palm.

Early Steps: With most dogs, you can start at Step 1. But if the dog doesn't appear to notice the stick, put the stick on the ground and click three to five times for looking in the general direction of the stick. Then click a few times for looking AT the stick. Then click a few times for touching the stick with his nose or foot. Click a few times for nose touches only. Now pick the stick up and proceed from Step 3.

Be careful not to shape a BITE at the stick by being late with your click. This will be difficult to get rid of (see Problem-Solving Tips below).

Do not wave the stick in front of the dog to get his attention. Keep it still. Let him figure out that he needs to approach it and make contact.

By the end of the first training session, the dog should be touching the stick readily, with some of his touches at the end of the stick.

Problem-Solving Tips:
How do I hold the clicker, touch stick, and treats (assuming you only have two hands)?
- Hold the clicker and stick in the same hand with your palm up and the clicker resting on top of the stick (see diagram). Deliver treats with the other hand.

- Tape the clicker to your end of the stick. Be sure that the clicker mechanism is accessible.
- Put the treats in a bowl out of the dog's reach and hold the clicker in one hand and the stick in the other. Reach for a treat as you need it.
- Get a third hand. Have someone help you by dropping a treat on the floor or handing it to the dog each time you click. (Children LOVE to help this way.)

The dog is biting the stick instead of touching it with his nose.
- Click JUST BEFORE the dog touches the stick. Because the dog is getting the click before he actually makes contact, you will short circuit the biting behavior. If you are slow with your clicker and find it hard to get the click in before the dog makes contact, try moving the stick away while the dog tries to bite it – this will give you added time for getting the click in. (Get that click in, so it doesn't become a game of "chase and bite the stick"!)
- Restart the training with the stick lying on the floor. Carefully reshape a touch only.
- Click the dog for doing anything BUT biting the stick, such as touching it with his foot or not touching it at all.
- Change to a metal stick. You might be able to find a telescoping pointer with an alligator clip on the end (makes a good target). Dogs are less likely to bite metal.
- Teach the touch to your hand rather than the touch stick.

The dog appears to be afraid of the stick, or reacts as if IT bit HIM.
- Click JUST BEFORE the dog touches the stick.
- Modify the click sound so it's not so loud – hold the clicker in your pocket or put heavy tape on the metal part of the clicker. Or use a retractable ballpoint pen as a clicker, or click with your tongue.
- Start with the touch stick on the ground and stay at this level for several sessions. Leave the stick out where the dog can investigate it at his leisure.
- Desensitize the dog to the stick. Start with a pencil and gently stroke him across the back with it while you give yummy treats. Do this for brief periods for several days. Gradually use longer and longer straight objects, such as an emery board, ruler, etc. Or use dowels in progressively longer lengths if you have them available.
- Teach to touch your hand first instead of touch the stick.

Suggested Commands: Touch, Nose

Variations: Teach touch your hand. This useful target is always available to you. Use it to refocus a distracted dog, teach a flip finish, train the dog to leap in the air, work on fear of being petted, and fine-tune obedience competition heeling. Teach the dog to touch a Post-It™ note with his nose – you can stick a note anywhere to direct the dog at a distance.

SLICK CLICKS

WOLVES CAN TOUCH, TOO!
Cheryl S. Smith

At Wolf Park in Indiana, I had the opportunity to clicker train a wolf to a touch stick. There were 3 wolves in the enclosure we were standing outside of. One was not interested in us, but the other two were right at the fence, eager to interact. We clicked and gave our chosen wolf, Apollo, a treat for about a dozen repetitions, then stuck the end of a touch stick through the fence. Wolves are curious animals, so Apollo immediately touched and got a click and a treat. We did a half dozen or so repetitions with the stick right in front of him, then started presenting the stick so that he had to move to touch it. If Apollo wasn't quick enough, Karin, the other wolf paying close attention to what we were doing, beat him to the stick, even though she had not received any treats up to that point. Wolves are very good observational learners, and we got two wolves performing the touch from working with only one! They are also quite forceful with biting the stick if you are a hair late with your click, and they hang on!

BACK UP

The Final Picture: The dog will back away from you in a straight line, facing you.

Uses: Helpful for getting the dog to move out of your way. You will need this behavior to work on any distance commands with your dog, so that you can send him back if he comes forward. Used extensively in professional photography, tv, and film work with animals – you'll find it great for taking your own photos of your dog! Used in Freestyle competitions (dancing with your dog).

Preparation and Props: Your dog, a clicker, and treats. Start your behavior in a "chute," such as the area between your coffee table and couch, or between two lines of chairs, to pattern the dog to back up in a straight line. Take the dog forward through your chute area several times until he seems comfortable with it. If he seems really nervous about it, work through that first – see "Confidence-Building Exercises" in Chapter 6.

The Steps Along the Way:

Session One –

1. Back into your chute, encouraging the dog to follow you (you are facing each other). Wait quietly for the dog to do something. Click and treat when the dog stands up while in the chute. Repeat 3 times.

CLICK TRICKS

"Clicker-savvy" dogs will get active right away, and you'll have to be quick to catch a stand instead of some other behavior. A confused or novice dog may just lie down and stop responding at all. Adjust your steps to suit your dog – break them down as much as possible for the confused dog, make them bigger and go through them faster for the confident dog.

---

2. Now click and treat the dog for moving any foot (front or back). Repeat 3 times.
3. Click and treat the dog for moving either back foot. Repeat 5 times.
4. Click and treat the dog for moving a back foot and shifting weight off his front. (Some dogs will move their front feet then their back feet, while others will move their back feet then shift weight off the front – observe your dog so you know what to expect and click.) Repeat 5 times.

Session Two –

5. Click and treat the dog for moving a back foot and shifting weight off his front. Repeat 5 times.
6. Click and treat the dog for moving first one back foot, then the other. Repeat 5 times.

CLICK TRICKS

What the dog is doing with his front feet is not important here, except as it may provide a clue to what is going to happen next, allowing you to time your click expertly for the movement of the dog's back feet.

---

7. Click and treat the dog for taking a step backward starting with either back foot. Repeat 5 times.

8. Click and treat the dog for taking a step backward with both back feet and at least one front foot. Repeat 5 times.

Session Three –
9. Click and treat the dog for taking a step backward with both the front and back feet – all four feet have to move backward a step before you click. Repeat 5 times.
10. Continue to add additional backward steps to your shaping, one step at a time. Stay at each new level no more than 3 to 5 repetitions. When the dog will take at least 3 steps backward, go on to step 11.
11. Fade your forward movement, if you have been using this to help the dog back up. . . unless you want to use this as your signal for the behavior (see Early Steps). To fade, instead of taking a step forward for every step the dog takes backward, try taking a step and waiting for the dog to take 2 steps backward. The dog will get frustrated waiting for you to help him, and will move around a bit. Click and treat any movement backward that occurs without movement on your part. Continue to cycle through steps 9 to here, gradually getting the dog to offer more and more movement while you stay still.
12. When you can predict the dog will move backward without any movement from you at least 8 out of 10 times, it's time to add the cue. Say your command, the dog backs up, click and treat.

Session Four –
13. Continue to pair the command with the behavior at least 50 additional times. While you are doing this, you will also be gradually getting rid of the chute. Start by opening the far end of the chute up a little bit (see illustration), so that it's more of a V shape. Continue to open it a small amount every 5 to 10 repetitions, until the dog has at least 3 feet between him and the chute side. Then work the dog along a wall, with nothing on the other side, and then in an open area.

Following sessions, work on variability –
14. Build up the distance the dog will back up.
15. Work in different environments.
16. Work around other people, dogs, food, and toys.
17. Have the dog back up, then ask for some other behavior, such as sit or down, with the dog away from you.

Early Steps: If you're having a tough time with the early shaping outlined above, you can lure the behavior by putting a treat at the dog's nose (level with his shoulder) and stepping into the dog, or by simply moving toward the dog while in your chute. Don't forget to fade out your forward movement (see step 11 above) or the treat.

If you have difficulty seeing which leg the dog is moving while in your chute, try working the first few steps in a more open area for a better view or position a mirror behind the dog, until you can see the indications of the dog shifting his weight and moving backward. Return to the chute once you know what a "weight shift" looks like.

Problem-Solving Tips:
The dog keeps sitting.
▪ Pay attention to where your hands are – dogs will often sit when they look up, so don't inadvertently be cuing your dog to look up. The dog can't back up from a sitting position.
▪ Click and treat for anything BUT a sit for 5 to 10 repetitions.

I can't get the dog to move his back feet.
▪ Work in a more open area so you can see better what his whole body is doing.
▪ You may be clicking too late – try to anticipate what the dog will do next, and click any minor movement of the back feet.

The dog moves all his feet but doesn't actually move backward.
▪ You stayed too long at clicking for foot movement and probably didn't shape it carefully. Decide before each step exactly what you will click for and break your steps into tiny changes which you can click. Don't change criteria in the middle of a step.
▪ Have someone move the dog backward while you watch to see which legs move first – what predicts backward movement for your dog?
▪ Help the dog by stepping into him, then fade your movement.

Suggested Commands: Back, Back up, Get back

Suggested Signals: Make a pushing motion with your hands toward the dog; Alternately lift your knees, as if marching in place, simulating walking toward the dog, without moving forward

Variations: Have the dog back up to a spot on the floor marked with tape. Teach the dog instead to Move out of the way – ths variation, not necessarily backing up, doesn't require such precision clicking, but is still useful for the dog to know.

PAW (touch)

The Final Picture: The dog touches a horizontal, vertical, or angled target with a front paw. Note that most dogs will show a preference for one paw or the other.

Uses: Shake, wave, ring a bell, close a door or drawer, turn off the lights, flyball or dogapolt.

Preparation and Props: A large target that can be oriented at an angle. This can be as simple as a 10" x 10" square of plywood or Plexiglas™ or a piece of carpet that can be taped where you need it. It's best while you're training if your target doesn't move even if pushed hard. Otherwise you risk spooking the dog, or training a lighter touch. Once you have taught this, you can transfer it to other things, such as the home-built flyball box we offer you at the end of the chapter.

CLICK TRICKS

From here on, we'll often indicate when to "click" in our instructions. This actually still means "click and treat." Do not click without treating. It's not fair to your dog – the click promises a reward – and will make your clicker less potent as a training tool.

The Steps Along the Way:

Session One – start physically close to the target

1. Place your target on the floor. Click for approaching the target. Repeat 3 times.
2. Click for looking at the target. Repeat 3 times.
3. Click for touching the target with any part of the body, nose, or foot. Don't stay longer than three to five clicks at this level, or the dog will think it's the final picture.
4. Click for any touch with ANY foot. At this point it doesn't matter if it's intentional or accidental. Repeat 3 times.

Session Two –

5. Place your target in a new location. Click for any touch with any foot, intentional or accidental. Repeat 3 times.
6. Click for any touch with either FRONT foot anywhere on the target. Repeat 5 times.
7. Click for an intentional touch – the dog is looking at the target, not just tripping over it – with a front foot anywhere on the target. Repeat 5 times. You'll probably find that the dog uses one foot exclusively.
8. Shape a touch to the center of the target. Mentally divide the target into a bullseye. Decide before each 10-treat session where the dog needs to touch to get clicked. If the dog is touching that area (or closer to the bullseye) 8 out of 10 times, move in to the next ring of the bullseye for the next 10-treat session. If the dog doesn't get 8 out of 10, make your bullseye rings narrower so your steps are smaller. Don't forget to jackpot any touches to the center!

Session Three –
9.   Place your target in a new location and continue shaping center touches until the dog is accurately hitting the center of the target 8 out of 10 tries.

Session Four –
10.   If your dog has been somewhat tentative, shape for a harder touch. This will not be necessary with all dogs. See "Early Steps" for some suggestions.
11.   When the touch is as hard as you want and you can predict the dog will do it, name the behavior. Say your command, the dog does the behavior, click and treat. Continue pairing the command with the behavior for at least 50 more repetitions, changing the location of your target every 10 repetitions.

Following sessions, work on variability –
12.   Reorient the target to a flat vertical orientation, as well as at an angle.
13.   Put the target higher or lower so the dog has to work to hit it.
14.   Send the dog from a greater distance to the target.
15.   Gradually fade the target by making it smaller and smaller over the course of several sessions until the dog can accurately hit a one-inch target placed anywhere (cut the target gradually smaller, or use gradually smaller pieces of wood or Plexiglas™.)
16.   Introduce MOVEMENT of the target by attaching it to the front of a drawer or door. Open the drawer or door SLIGHTLY, give your command, and click and treat if the dog moves the target. Don't open the drawer or door very far at first – the dog needs to get comfortable with moving the target a small distance. Gradually increase the distance the dog has to push the target.
17.   If you are ultimately training a flyball box or dogapolt (see end of chapter for instructions on building your own just-for-play dogapolt), you need to load and launch the box a few times so the launch doesn't frighten the dog. Load the box with a favorite ball or treats. Hold the

dog back a little, launch the box yourself, and let the dog catch the ball or treats. Repeat this until the dog appears excited when he hears the launch, and looks for the ball or treats. Now let him launch the ball or treats, helping with your own foot if necessary. As your dog's enthusiasm grows, he will hit the box harder and harder, or you can shape a harder push on your original target.

Early Steps: If the dog does not attempt to touch the target at first, it can help for you to walk around it, encouraging the dog to keep moving. When the dog accidentally brushes against the target, click and treat. Don't do this for more than one session, though, or the dog will become dependent on your movement.

To shape a harder touch, don't click the first touch the dog makes. Usually he will look at you, wondering why you didn't click, then hit the target a second time, harder, to be sure you notice. Click and treat! If the second touch isn't harder, wait for a third. If the dog stops responding or seems confused, go back to Step 9 and stay there until the dog is rapidly and accurately hitting the center. Then try withholding the click again. Click the hardest 5 out of 10 pushes at each step until it's at the level you want. You are shaping a harder push, so the accuracy might be impacted. Don't worry, just work accuracy separately.

Problem-Solving Tips:
The dog doesn't seem to notice the target, or realize he should touch it with his foot. Or he only tries to touch it with his nose.
- If your dog already knows how to shake, use this command to help you lure him into this behavior. Offer your hand over the target area, say "shake," but pull your hand away before he makes contact, so that he accidentally touches the target instead. Click and treat!
- Move around the target so that the dog moves and accidentally bumps the target. But don't do this too much, or the dog will think you have to move before anything happens.
- Write down at least 10 steps to shape from "not noticing" to "touching target." For example;
    1) eye flick in direction of target
    2) head motion in direction of target
    and so on. . .

Pick the target up and put it down after each repetition (don't continue doing this once the dog starts touching the target).

The dog touches the target, but lightly.
- Is the dog afraid the target will move? Make sure the target is completely secure and reshape the behavior from the beginning, using really good treats.
- Hide a ball or a piece of food under the couch and click the dog for reaching for it with his paw.
- Find things that your dog paws or scratches on his own – another dog in the house, a certain patch of ground, whatever – and click and treat that. Come back to the target and try again.
- Work on desensitization and confidence-building exercises (Chapter 6).
- Have someone watch and tell you if you're clicking too early and getting a lighter push.

The dog scratches the target rather than pushing it.
- You were probably late with your clicks. Reshape the behavior from Step 5, CAREFULLY clicking just before the dog touches the target. It will help if you sit at a level where you can easily see the dog's paw approaching the target.
- Use what you've got, and teach the dog to turn off a light switch.

Suggested Commands: Punch, Push, Stomp, Launch, Paw

Variations: Teach the dog to touch a touch stick with his paw, giving it a different name from touching it with his nose.
　　　　Teach the dog to touch a target with each of his paws, front and back. You could use this in stacking for conformation.
　　　　Teach the dog to drag his paw across the target, in preparation for turning off a light switch. Aim for just one gentle swipe, or you may have to repair the area around your light switch frequently. Remember to gradually build up to the switch being at the actual height on the wall. You'll need to construct a dummy switch for the dog to use for practice (a piece of plywood and a light switch screwed into place will work).
　　　　If using a dogapolt, teach the dog to pick up the ball and put it back in the launch mechanism
　　　　Use the diagram at the end of the chapter to build yourself a dogapolt. It only takes some half-inch wood, a screw and wing nut, and an empty

Pringles can. The tennis ball sits on the little ledge in the Pringles can, and when the dog steps on the pad at the other end of the lever, the ball shoots out of the can!

SLICK CLICKS

INNOVATIVE ANIMALS

Kathy Sdao, proprietor of Bright Spot Dog Training
and former marine mammal trainer

We used clicker training at the University of Hawaii to teach two bottlenosed dolphins to be creative (based on the pioneering work done by Karen Pryor and chronicled in *Lads Before the Wind*). One of the dolphins, Akeakamai ("lover of wisdom") grasped the concept better than we ever imagined possible. After a few weeks of training, she would respond to the gestural cue for "do a behavior I've never seen you do before" – basically an exaggerated shrug – with amazing feats of acrobatics and sheer silliness. We researchers got to the point where we had to abandon our attempts to record in words these behavioral creations because we couldn't keep up, and some were literally indescribable. I remember sitting beside the tank with my jaw dropped open, watching Ake leap and fling toys and swim backward. She truly understood that we wanted to see novel behaviors, and she seemed thrilled to demonstrate her skill.

LOOK THERE

The Final Picture: The dog looks at an object that you indicate, then runs directly to it. Variations include bringing the object back, or sitting by it.

Uses: Finding objects; retrieving designated objects; two Utility obedience exercises, the Go Out and Directed Retrieve; assistance work; going to a designated person.

Preparation and Props: A couple of favorite toys that don't roll (so, not a ball). It's helpful if the dog knows Wait (Chapter 2) and Release (Chapter 2), but not necessary.

Session One –

1. Start with the dog seated beside you in a Wait or Stay. Toss the toy in front of you a foot or so away. When the dog looks at it, click and treat then release to get the toy. Repeat 3 times.

CLICK TRICKS

If you and your dog have now done a fair amount of clicker training – say, if you've taught everything in the book thus far – you could also click and release the dog to get the toy instead of giving a treat. The release to the toy is an alternate reward for the dog. You could even introduce a new command, perhaps "Get it," to mean that the dog is allowed to run and grab the toy. The "Get it" command would then be a variation of the release. From now on, we'll indicate for this behavior when to click. You decide whether you will use click/treat/release, click/treat/Get it, click/release, or click/Get it.

---

2. Toss the toy a little farther each time, until the dog has to run about twenty feet away from you in a direct line to get the toy. Repeat 3 to 5 times at each new distance, adding only a few feet at a time.

Session Two –

3. Working in a new location, change toys and repeat step 2 until the toy is 20 feet away.
4. Change locations and repeat step 3.
5. Change locations and toys. Toss the toy about twenty feet and wait a 1-second look before clicking. Remember, you are clicking for looking at the toy! Gradually build up the time interval to about thirty seconds between tossing the toy and clicking the dog. Review the bouncing around technique described in "Watch Me" if you need help with this step.
6. Change locations and repeat step 5.

Session Three –

7. Now have the dog wait (or have someone hold him) while you place the toy about six feet away and come back to stand beside the dog. Wait for the dog to look at the toy for 3 seconds, then click.

8. Place the toy farther away each time, gradually building up distance until it is again about twenty feet away. Repeat 3 to 5 times at each new distance. Vary how long you have the dog look at the toy before clicking (3-10 seconds).

Session Four –
9. Are you able to predict that the dog will look at the toy? Time to name the behavior. Say your command, the dog looks at the toy, click and treat or release to get the toy. To introduce a hand signal, use a sweeping motion of your arm, from your hip extending toward the object. Keep your palm flat and perpendicular to the floor. If you plan to use this behavior for competition obedience, the dog should be on your left side and you will give the signal with your left arm.
10. Repeat the pairing of the cue – whether verbal or signal – with the behavior at least 50 additional times, changing locations every 5 to 10 repetitions.

Following sessions, work on variability –
11. Have someone else place the toy a short distance from you, again gradually building up to 20 feet.
12. Gradually add distractions to the environment.
13. Place four identical toys (such as tennis balls) spaced out around a circle about ten feet in diameter. Stand in the center of the circle with the dog. Turn to a toy, give your command and/or hand signal, click when the dog focuses on the toy, and release him to get the toy. Repeat with remaining toys.
14. Vary the amount of time the dog has to focus on the object before being clicked and released.
15. Vary your reward – click and treat or click and release or just release.
16. As the dog begins to look out toward where you signal, anticipating that the toy will be there, make the size of the toy smaller and smaller until it is gone and the dog is looking ahead only because you have cued it.

Early Steps: If the dog doesn't know Wait and Release, he needs to be on leash for the training sessions. Step on the leash or have someone else hold it so that you have both hands free. When you release the dog, step off of the leash.

Problem-Solving Tips:
The dog gets the toy and runs off with it.
- Get another toy identical to the first, show the dog the one you have in your hand, and have an assistant pick up the dropped toy when the dog comes to get the one you have.
- Keep the dog on a long leash (20 to 30 feet) so you can trade the toy for a treat after reeling in the dog.
- Use a large biscuit-type treat instead of a toy so he can eat it.
- Work on your Come command (see Chapter 2).
- Work on the "Check In" exercise later in this chapter.
- Have someone stand next to where the toy is thrown and step on it or pick it up if the dog moves before the click. (You'll need to "fade" your helper eventually.)

The dog doesn't "track" the toy as it falls, or doesn't look at it after it hits the ground.
- Maybe the dog doesn't see it. Use a bigger toy or throw it closer for the first few sessions.
- Use a toy the dog is more interested in, either one he's never seen before or one he hasn't seen in a while. Something he plays with every day won't be as interesting.

The dog isn't interested in toys or treats.
- Use something he IS interested in – another person, another dog, his leash, his food bowl – to start the marking behavior. Have the other person or person and dog start in front of you and run in a direct line away from you, looking to see that your dog is watching them.

Suggested Commands: Look, Mark

Suggested Signal: With your flattened hand, palm perpendicular to the floor, use a sweeping motion from your hip toward the object

Variations: Teach the dog to look at the indicated object, then go get it and bring it back. Name specific objects or people or dogs and teach the dog to go to the named object or person or dog. Wow your friends with your dog's abilities! Teach the dog to look in the direction you indicate with your arm, then run out straight until you tell him to stop and do something else (an exercise in competition obedience).

WALK OFF LEASH

The Final Picture: The dog will follow along beside you, near enough to be touched, until released. Great for trail walking in areas that allow dogs off leash. (These instructions are a modification of Dawn Jecs' "Choose to Heel" program. If you are interested in competition-level heeling, her book of the same name is an excellent resource that is easily adapted to clicker training.)

Uses: Walking the dog across the street or in a crowd, or controlling the dog as you maneuver a trail. Useful for competition heeling or dance steps.

Preparation and Props: Your dog, treats, a clicker, and a large enclosed area (such as a large boring room, your back yard, or the local tennis courts) or a long leash (30 to 50 feet long). The Touch (to your hand) behavior detailed in this chapter will help immensely with this one. Teach it first.

The Steps Along the Way:
Session One –
1. Start in a distraction-free environment such as a large empty room. Begin moving in a big counterclockwise circle with the dog on the inside, and click and treat one step toward you. Drop the treat on the floor beside you so the dog has to come and get it. Meanwhile, you move off, continuing in your counterclockwise circle. Repeat 10 times.
2. In the same location, click and treat for 1 to 3 steps toward you, varying the number of steps the dog has to take to get clicked. Repeat 5 times.
3. Change your criteria to 2 to 4 steps and continue adding steps until the dog is occasionally getting clicked for having come up beside you. Continue at each new level for at least 5 repetitions.

Session Two –
4. Repeat step 3 until the dog runs to your side immediately after eating the dropped treat.
5. Now you are ready to build up the number of steps the dog must walk beside you to get clicked, starting with just one step. Deliver the treat directly to the dog at the spot you want him to be for your walking, then move away as he is eating. If he won't let you get away from him, you're doing really well! Repeat 5 times.

CLICK TRICKS

With any behavior (but especially if you're moving), it's a good idea to practice clicking and delivering the treat WITHOUT the dog first. This will make your training progress more graceful, and prevent you from flinging treats all over the place.

6. Now click and treat for 1 to 3 steps beside you, varying the number of steps the dog has to take beside you to get clicked. Repeat 5 times.

CLICK TRICKS

This is a good place to use your hand touch as a lure. If the dog already knows he should try to touch your hand when it is held beside your leg, you will speed through steps 6 and 7. Deliver the treat on the same side, but don't hold it in your hand so that you aren't using a treat as a lure, but still give it with the dog in position where you want him to be. You can later wean the dog off the hand touch or not – for this behavior, it's not difficult to keep your hand out when you want the dog next to you and relax it when you don't. Note: If your hand touch is brief rather than "touch till told to do otherwise" and is on a verbal cue, try to get rid of the verbal cue as quickly as possible. Otherwise you risk changing your meaning of touch to "follow my hand" rather than "touch my hand."

7. Change your criteria to 2 to 4 steps and continue adding steps until the dog is walking beside you an average of 20 steps before getting clicked. Continue at each new level for at least 5 repetitions.

Session Three —
8. Starting in a new location, with SLIGHTLY more distractions, repeat step 6. Put a long leash on the dog if you are working outside in an area that is not safely enclosed.
9. Change locations, increasing the distraction level again, and repeat step 8.

Session Four –
10.   Go back to your original training location and start walking in a CLOCKWISE circle. Repeat steps 1 through 9.
11.   If you can predict the dog will come to your side as soon as you start moving, it's time to name the behavior. Say the command, dog comes to your side and stays there for varying amounts of time, click and treat. Repeat for at least 50 additional pairings, changing your location, direction (straight forward, counterclockwise circle, clockwise circle), or the number of steps the dog has to take, every 5 repetitions.

Following sessions, work on variability –
12.   Continue to work in gradually more distracting environments.
13.   Add distractions such as a toy on the floor, another dog in the area, or treats in a closed container on the floor.
14.   Call the dog away from play with another person or dog to walk beside you for a few steps, click and release to return to play.
15.   Practice having the dog come to your side while you are standing still, then begin moving with the dog.
16.   Change directions, walk straight, make turns, or stand still, all while clicking and treating the dog for staying next to you.
17.   Vary the type of rewards, using rewards that are of high value for your dog and might be available on a walk, such as the opportunity to sniff, swim, or run after you.

Early Steps: Be creative when looking for a training space if you don't have indoor space. Ask a dog training facility if you can borrow or rent their space. If you must work outside due to space limitations, give the dog 20 minutes or so of play and sniffing in the area so it will become less interesting by the time you start training. In open areas, be sure the dog is on a long leash so you don't have to worry about him running off before he's trained! If attention is an issue for your dog, work on the "Check In" behavior before attempting this one.

Problem-Solving Tips:
The dog only walks a certain number of steps before wandering off.
▪   Build up your bouncing more carefully. Have someone watch you to make sure you aren't going the same number of steps before clicking – humans are real creatures of habit, and this is a likely problem.

- Use really great treats so the dog is motivated to work hard for them. Change treats between steps to keep the dog interested.
- See "Check In" for other problem-solving tips related to distractions.

Suggested Commands: Heel, By me, Close, Let's go, Side, Left, Right

Variations: Teach the dog to come to both sides, using a different command. This is an easy one if you already have a solid hand touch.

SLICK CLICKS

CHICKEN TRAINING

Mandy Book

What did I learn from chicken training camp? First and foremost, chickens don't care if you like them, and they don't particularly like you. They don't care if you tell them what good chickens they are. Yet they still learn things with speed and intensity. They can also learn tasks which are fairly complicated – for a chicken!

I learned to improve my training results by keeping notes on my training sessions, and limiting sessions to just a minute or two in length. My dogs love the fast training – they don't get bored, lose focus, or shut down, even with difficult tasks. The notes allow me to keep track of progress on three different dogs, who may be learning at different rates or even learning different things. The notes also prevent me from working on more than one thing at a session (which is confusing for me and the dog). They also allow me to review our progress, and to change direction if necessary.

I learned to manage my resources. Dogs, unlike chickens, will work for things other than food, but you still have to be aware of how much you are giving out. I learned to be faster with my timing, and to deliver rewards "in position" rather than tossing treats indiscriminately. In other words, if you want a dog to remain in heel position, don't deliver treats in front of you.

And finally, I learned that I am indeed bigger, stronger, and (usually) smarter than a chicken!

CHECK IN

The Final Picture: The dog will come and work with you regardless of what else is in the environment. This is great for inattentive or independent dogs, dogs that pull on the leash, or those that are "toy nuts."

Uses: Basis for walking off leash, "Come" (recall), any type of competition work.

Preparation and Props: Your dog, treats, a clicker, and a distraction-free room. Make a list of all the things that distract your dog, then rank them from low to high. For example:

> Nylabones→rawhide→tennis ball→squeaky toy→rattling treats packaging→people→other dogs→toys

Now make a list of your dog's favorite food treats, also ranking from low to high:

> dog kibble→cat food→hard treats→soft treats→hot dogs→steak→garlic chicken

The Steps Along the Way:

Session One —

1. Start in a room the dog has little interest in exploring. Click and treat when the dog looks at you, dropping the treat on the floor at your feet. Move away and repeat 5 times. The dog should begin moving toward you to collect the treat when he hears the click. Try to vary the direction you head each time.

2. Now only click and treat when the dog takes a step toward you as you move away from the previously dropped treat. Add more steps, staying at each level for 3-5 repetitions, until the dog is following you around the room as you move away, and getting clicked for moving with you a step or two.

Session Two —

3. Working in the same room as before, repeat step 2.

4. Place three or more similar items on the floor, from the lowest level of distraction in your distraction list. Click and treat when the dog takes 1 step toward you, whether or not he brings one of the items from the floor with him, dropping the treat at your feet and moving away. DO

NOT take the item from the dog. Repeat adding more steps toward you until the dog is following you around the room and completely ignoring the items on the floor. Click and treat occasionally when the dog is walking next to you, especially if you walk by an item and he ignores it. If the dog won't drop an item to take the treat, drop the treat on the floor. Immediately increase the value of treats from your treat list by at least 2 levels. This is usually the most difficult step. It can take from 1 to 5 minutes for the dog to leave a distraction to move toward you. After 1 minute, if the dog doesn't appear interested in leaving the distraction, lower your criteria and click and treat if the dog looks at you, and toss the treat on the floor near his head (without approaching the dog). Repeat 5 times. Then click and treat a look at you, dropping the treat next to you so the dog has to move to get it. Now the dog has to stand up to get clicked (drop the treat at your feet and move off). Up the criteria again so the dog first has to take a step to get clicked. If, after 5 minutes, the dog will not even look at you, stop the training and leave the room. Have someone else pick up the distractions and put the dog on leash. Start again at Step 1 the next day. When you reach Step 4 again, DECREASE the level of the distraction (make it even more boring), and INCREASE the level of the treat (make it even more exciting). Repeat the first four steps daily until the dog is responding within a few moments at Step 4. Only then can you move on to the next step.

Session Three –
5. Put your original items from step 4 on the floor – the dog should have little interest in them by now. Add three or more similar items from the next level of distraction. Continue as in step 4 until the dog ignores everything on the floor. Click and treat occasionally while the dog is walking next to you.
6. Work your way up through the distraction list, adding three or more at each new distraction level to the items already on the floor. If your dog is doing well, you might add several levels of distractions at one time. If progress is slower, you might add one new level of distractions per training session or every other training session. Change treats to a higher value reward each time you add new distractions. Click and treat when the dog comes to you (with or without one of the objects from the floor). Repeat until the dog is following you around the room

without a toy, getting periodically clicked and treated for staying with you and ignoring toys.

Session Four —
7.   Continue as in Step 6, varying when you click and treat the dog for leaving a distraction (sometimes as soon as he turns toward you, sometimes walking toward you, sometimes when he is close to you, sometimes after taking 1, 2, 3, 4, or 5 steps next to you). Jackpot if the dog leaves the distraction quickly when you turn away. If your dog enjoys praise and petting, use them instead of your click and treat about every fifth time. Praise ANIMATEDLY, in addition to the click and treat, if the dog ignores the distractions to walk beside you. Continue at this level until the dog shows no further interest in the distractions.

Following sessions, work on variability —
8.   Put the dog on leash and repeat steps 5, 6, and 7, varying the rewards used (praise, petting, or food). The behavior may change when the leash is on.
9.   Change locations and repeat Steps 2 through 7. Repeat this whole procedure in at least seven different locations, both indoors and outdoors, of varying sizes. (If you are unable to work outdoors in a secure area, the dog can drag a 30-50 foot line for safety.) Dogs do not generalize well, and need to be shown that the same rules apply to different locations.
10.   Gradually introduce other people, dogs, and other real-world distractions.
11.   The "hot toy" variation — Return to your original training location. Put out a variety of distractions and toys. Start walking around the room. When the dog comes to you, click and pick up the nearest toy. Hold on to the toy and encourage the dog to play with you for about a minute, then let go of the toy and move away. DO NOT throw the toy for the dog to play with. We are trying to teach the dog to work WITH you, not AWAY from you. When the dog drops that toy, click and pick up the toy nearest you and have a rousing game with it for one minute. Then let go of the toy and move away. The dog will begin to spit out toys and run toward you each time you move away. DO NOT click and pick up a new toy until the dog has made some effort to seek you out (whether or not he is carrying the old toy). The dog is learning that the

only toys that are fun are the ones you have in your hand. Everything else is boring! Note: This is going to be a difficult step if your dog has regular access to free play with toys without you. His desire to work with you will be low, as he has been entertaining himself.

12.　Use a favorite toy on your walks as a reward for ignoring distractions. While on your walk, if the dog sees a distraction and turns to you, his favorite toy flies out of your pocket and you play together for two or three minutes. Let the dog carry the toy for a minute, then exchange it for a treat and continue on your walk. (If the dog drops the toy when you stop playing, pick it up and put it back in your pocket.) Eventually, the dog will see all distractions as a signal that he will get an opportunity to play with a toy with you. Do not leave the toy accessible during the day, to keep its value high.

13.　If your dog regularly plays with other dogs or has "off-leash" time, be sure to reward him for checking in with you while playing with other dogs, by himself, or with other people.

Early Steps: Work in a confined area where it's safe for your dog to be off leash. At each step, you will continuously wander around the room, always moving away from the dog and changing directions. Don't stop moving!

Do not deliver treats to the dog – the dog must always move toward you to collect the treat, even if it's only a few inches. Change the type of treats you use frequently, and give jackpots as necessary.

Don't give up. This exercise has been successful even with the most confirmed "toy hounds." Start with the most boring distraction you can think of, something you KNOW the dog won't want to pick up (like three spoons or forks) and highly desirable treats, to build up your early success. Make sure your treats are always better than whatever is available on the floor for the dog to pick up. Change treats frequently and throw in an occasional jackpot (see Chapter 1) to keep the dog's interest high. Work in an environment that is familiar and boring to the dog to begin the exercise, one where there are no outside distractions over which you have no control. YOU must be the most interesting thing in the room.

Problem-Solving Tips:
The dog will not look at me if there are any distractions.
- Choose distractions that are in the dog's environment all the time (tennis balls, if you leave them scattered around), and use a really good treat.

- Use your treat to lure the dog away from the distracting item the first few times you work with him.
- Change treats frequently and throw in an occasional jackpot to keep the dog's interest high.
- Work on Watch me first.

The dog is aggressive or possessive around toys or treats.
- Don't move toward him whenever he has an item.
- Start with something the dog won't want to pick up (such as metal items).
- Don't remove items from the dog's mouth – drop the treat on the floor and move away. Let him figure out he can go back to the item; it won't disappear because he lets go of it.

Suggested Commands: Train this as an automatic response, without any specific command, or introduce the command "leave it" or "drop it" in step 7. (For attention on command, see "Watch Me" earlier in this chapter.

Variations: Get together with some friends and have each person work on attention with his or her own dog at the same time.

Train all of your dogs to go only for the toy you indicate. This variation is great for shy dogs in your household, who are nervous about playing with toys when other dogs are around, for possessive dogs (they have their own toy that no one else will get), and at competitive events (someone is always squeaking inside or outside the ring).

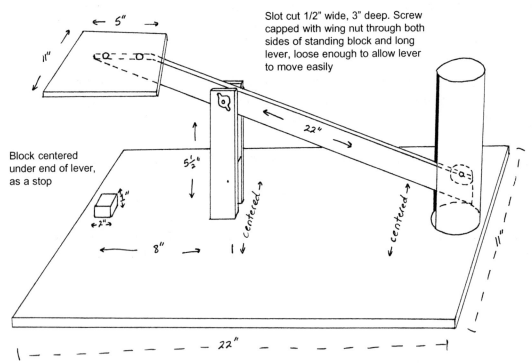

← 5″ →

11″

Slot cut 1/2" wide, 3" deep. Screw capped with wing nut through both sides of standing block and long lever, loose enough to allow lever to move easily

Block centered under end of lever, as a stop

1″

2″

5½″

← 8″ →

centered →

centered →

22″ →

11″

← 22″ →

Pringles can with slot cut, leaving top and bottom rims intact. End of lever is inside can, with small piece of wood as platform for a tennis ball

CHAPTER 4
A Click a Day

You've done some basic useful things, and you've practiced a bit of "purer" clicker training. Now it's time to really apply what you've learned to building a better dog. Teach the behaviors in this chapter, and you'll be the envy of your friends.

If you're like most people, you're going to look at this list and think it's impossible, you'll never be able to do that! Relax. You've already seen the power of the clicker. You've gotten in some practice to get better at using it. You can do this. You know we're going to tell you how, step by step. Your dog will really be a model citizen by the end of this chapter. Who wouldn't want a dog that will:

Go to his place and settle down
Sit-stay while greeting
Relax for veterinary exams
Take medication (Say ahhh!)
Turn around
Stand still for bathing and grooming
Be calm about toenail clipping

Don't doubt it — you can do it (and your dog certainly can). Pick out one of these behaviors you'd like to accomplish and follow the instructions. When you prove to yourself that you can do it, you'll be ready for the next.

GO TO YOUR PLACE AND SETTLE DOWN

The Final Picture: Dog goes to a place indicated (a mat, dog bed, even a sofa if you so choose), lies down and remains there. The dog can sleep or chew a bone or whatever, but must not leave the place until released.

Uses: Traveling with your dog, appropriate greeting behaviors, teaching him to be quiet in the house or in a particular room.

Preparation and Props: Dog, treats, clicker, and a mat, blanket, towel, or whatever you choose. It's helpful if the dog already knows Down.

The Steps Along the Way.
Session One —
1. Starting in a low distraction environment, put your mat on the floor directly in front of you. Click and treat when the dog looks at it. Repeat 3 times. (Pick up the mat and put it down for each repetition.)
2. Click and treat when the dog moves toward the mat. Repeat 3 times.
3. Click and treat when the dog puts one foot on the mat. Repeat 3 times.
4. Click and treat when the dog puts two feet on the mat. Repeat 3 times.
5. Click and treat when the dog puts all four feet on the mat. Repeat 3 times.

Session Two —
6. Click and treat when the dog puts all four feet on the mat. Repeat 3 times.
7. Now when the dog gets on the mat, don't click. If he lowers his body at all (elbow bend, play bow, head drop or full down), click and treat. Release and take the dog off the mat completely. Shape a down on the mat if needed, staying at each step for only 3 repetitions. (Note: If the dog already knows Down well, say Down as soon as he steps on the mat, then click and treat the Down. Stop saying "down" as the dog begins to anticipate it when he gets on the mat)

8. Take one step farther away from the mat, and repeat step 7, clicking the complete down. Repeat 3 times.

9. Continue to work farther and farther away from the mat, until you are at least 20 feet away. When you get too far away to deliver your treat easily, you can click and toss it to the dog OR walk closer and hand it to him. Repeat 3 times at each distance.

CLICK TRICKS

Don't forget to use your release and make the dog get off the mat. It needs to be clear to him that he should wait on the mat for the release command. So when we say "Repeat 3 times," remember to release and move off the mat after each click and treat repetition.

Session Three —

10. Change locations and repeat steps 8-9.

11. Change locations and repeat steps 8-9.

12. Is the dog heading for the mat and lying down predictably? Time to add your command. Start about 5 feet away from the mat, say your command, wait for the dog to go to the mat and lie down, click and treat, then release him from the mat. Repeat 10 times, taking one step farther away from the mat each time.

13. Change locations and repeat step 12. Pair your command with the behavior at least 50 more times, changing locations, and varying your distance from the mat about every 10 times.

Session Four —

14. Send the dog to the mat, count to 1 after he lies down, click and treat, then release. Repeat 3 times. Continue to add time (1 second at a time) to the behavior until he will remain on the mat for a count of 5.

15. Now you will "bounce" around to build additional time on the mat. Vary the amount of time, staying around an average of 3 counts, until you click and treat. For example, 3/click/treat, 1/click/treat, 4/click/treat, 2/ click/treat, release, 5/click/treat, 2/click/treat, 3/click/treat, release, 5/ click/treat, etc. Repeat 10 times, then up your average count to 5, releasing the dog from the mat at least once during your 10 repetitions

and making him move off the mat. Continue adding time in small increments. As you build up past a minute toward 10-15 minutes, give the dog something fun to do (like chew on a bone he doesn't normally get) while he is on the mat. So the sequence becomes send the dog to the mat, give him a chewy, count your time, click and treat, remove the chewy, release the dog. Repeat the entire process, counting up a different amount of time on each repetition and varying how long the dog is on the mat before you let him move off it.

Additional sessions, work on variability —
16. Work in different rooms, including in someone else's house.
17. Gradually increase the number of things going on while the dog is on the mat - bouncing a ball, putting food on a coffee table, bringing more people in.
18. Remember to reward him when he is lying quietly on his mat. To encourage him to spend more time on the mat, you can give him rawhide or other messy goodies when he is on the mat, then take them up if he gets off of it.
19. Put the mat next to you while you are watching television or on the phone. Click and treat when the dog lies down on the mat for a short time without being cued.
20. During meals, put the mat about 10 feet away from the table and cue the dog to lie down on it. Sit at the table and begin to eat while keeping an eye on him. After you take a couple of bites, go to the mat, click and treat the dog, then release him. Continue to build a longer duration of time on the mat.
21. Send the dog to the mat and greet someone at the front door.
22. Practice getting the dog excited and out of control, then sending him to the mat for a brief settle. The reward for settling down is the opportunity to play again.

Early Steps: You will be training Down as part of the Place/Settle behavior. If the dog already knows the Down, you can cue it once he is going to the mat. When he begins to go to the mat readily and lie down on his own, don't bother to give your cue for Down any longer, just click and treat after he lies down. If the dog doesn't yet know Down, and you are shaping it with this behavior, remember to reward small steps toward that behavior (review the section on teaching the Down if you need help with this).

Problem-Solving Tips:
The dog goes to the mat but won't lie down.
- Lure or cue the down after he goes to the mat. Try 5–10 repetitions with help, then see if the dog will do it on his own if you don't help. Click and treat any movement into a down without help. Shape the down separately, then work on this behavior.

The dog gets off the mat without being released.
- Be sure you are releasing him from the mat consistently. If you sometimes let him get off without saying your release word, he won't know he is supposed to wait for it. Click, treat, then release.
- Build time on the mat slowly, a few seconds at a time. If you find the dog is getting up before you click, you may be advancing too fast for the dog to handle.

The dog chews on the mat
- Give him something else to chew on while he is on the mat.
- As a separate exercise, click and treat NOT chewing on the mat. Build up time on the mat not chewing. (Be careful not to click immediately after chewing has stopped, or the dog may chew, then stop, to get the click.)
- Wash the mat thoroughly. Treat remains may be encouraging the chewing.
- Don't leave the mat down if you're not supervising the dog on it.
- Use a sturdier mat, such as heavy-duty carpet remnants or various sorts of doormats.
- Make sure the mat doesn't resemble any chew toys the dog may have!

Suggested Commands: On your Mat, Place, Park it, Settle, Chill out, Relax

Variations: Teach the dog that when you give him a bone or toy to chew, he should take it to the mat and settle down with it. Teach the dog to target an area (such as a corner) in addition to a mat.

SIT-STAY (WHILE GREETING)

The Final Picture: The dog will sit while you let someone into your house, while being petted, or while you are talking to someone on the street.

Uses: Any behavior that requires you to leave the dog behind while you do something else. Used in the Canine Good Citizen Test, but also very handy for a well-behaved pet. Your friends will thank you.

Preparation and Props: Your dog, leash, treats, your distraction list from "Check in" in Chapter 3 and a clicker. Teach the dog to Sit separately. You should have Sit on cue in many environments before attempting to build on it here. The dog should also have a firm understanding of Release (meaning he doesn't move until told to do so).

The Steps Along the Way:
If you haven't worked on stretching the amount of time the dog remains in the Sit, do this first (while you're at it, practice it for the Down too, since you'll need it with that behavior also). Details are in the "Pre-session" below. If the dog holds the Sit until you release him, start at Session One Step 1.

Pre-session —
A. Working in a low distraction environment to start, signal the dog to Sit, then rapid-fire click and treat at least 3 times in a row, pause briefly, click and treat, Release the dog. So a sequence might look like this: click/treat; click/treat; click/treat; click/treat; pause; click/treat; click/treat; click/treat; release
   Repeat 10 times, each time changing the number of times you click and treat before AND after pausing (to a maximum of 5 clicks/treats before or after the pause). With young, active puppies, do a maximum of 3 clicks/treats before or after the pause.
B. Add 2 additional click/treat combos to a maximum of 7 click/treats (5 for pups) before or after your pause. Repeat 5 times. Up the maximum to 10 (7 for pups) and repeat 5 times.
C. Now put another pause in your sequence of clicks and treats. Remember to vary the number of clicks/treats before and after the pauses (have someone check you to make sure you aren't developing a pattern!) Continue to add more pauses until the dog is remaining in a sit in front of you for 2 minutes with only a total of 10 click/treats. Don't forget to say your Release at the end of each sequence!
D. You can also build up time using the bounce around described in Chapter 2.

CLICK TRICKS

If you want to introduce the command Stay, you can do it at this time, although it's not necessary for the dog. (Humans sure like to use it, though!) Say Sit, then Stay, do your sequence of clicks/treats/pauses, then say your Release. No more clicks after the dog is released - all the treats come while the dog remains in the Sit. Lesson for the dog is that getting up doesn't pay well!

Session One —
1. Working in a low distraction environment, do sequence A-C with the dog sitting beside you in "heel position." (Heel position is next to your left leg, with the dog's front feet facing the same direction as yours.)
2. Do sequence A-C with the dog on your right side facing forward in the same direction as you are.

CLICK TRICKS

Practice clicking and delivering treats on your off side (the one that's more difficult for you) WITHOUT the dog first! You don't want to be twisting around like a crazy person to try and deliver treats with your favored hand, or you may encourage your dog to get up.

Session Two —
3. Starting in a new location, repeat steps 1 and 2 with minor distractions. A minor distraction for most dogs would be stationary objects such as old toys and bones laying around, a container with boring treats, or a person they know well sitting and ignoring them. (This is where your distraction list comes in handy!)
4. Change locations and repeat steps 1 and 2 with a few more interesting distractions thrown in, such as a favorite toy laying on the floor.

Session Three —
5. Change locations and repeat steps 1 and 2 with a major distraction in the environment. For most dogs, major distractions come in the form of moving objects, such as a thrown toy, or someone moving around and making noise.

6. Move outside in your front yard and repeat steps 1 and 2.
7. Move to a new outside location with more distractions, such as a park. Repeat steps 1 and 2.

Session Four
8. Go back indoors, into a calm environment. Have a friend (someone the dog knows well and is not overly excited to see) come up and start talking to you, while you click and treat the dog for sitting beside you. Vary how many clicks/treats and pauses you do before releasing the dog, aiming for keeping the dog seated beside you for at least 1 minute, and no longer than 3 minutes. When you release, let the dog greet and get petted by your friend. If the dog jumps up at any time, both you and your friend will stand motionless, until the dog has all four feet back on the ground. Even better, you can have the friend quickly exit the front door if the dog jumps. Lesson for the dog is that jumping ends fun interaction.
9. Continue to work with other friends on step 8, until your dog has successfully remained sitting while you have talked to at least 5 different people.
10. Now have one of your friends reach over and pat the dog on the head, after your friend has greeted you first. Rapid-fire click and treat the dog while he is being petted, then Release after the petting. Ignore the dog when he is released. Repeat with each of your other friends.

CLICK TRICKS

Ignore means don't look at, talk to, touch the dog, or let him touch you! For this behavior, you want all good things for dogs to happen only when dogs are sitting in one place.

Additional sessions, work on variability —
11. Work outside, having people the dog knows greet you and pet the dog.
12. Practice having strangers come up and talk to you, while you work on the dog maintaining a sit. You can do this easily by standing in front of a neighborhood store. Strangers will want to come and see your well-behaved pet! But before you do this, assess your dog's reaction to

strangers and to being touched. If your dog is nervous about it, go to Chapter 6 and work on "People and Physical Contact Fears". Then reassess. Some dogs just need some work and experience, and others may never be relaxed around strangers. Don't jeopardize your dog, and the public, by putting him in situations he can't handle.

If your dog is okay with being touched by strangers, we recommend two strategies as extra insurance that all will remain well. First, teach your dog a hand touch and click/treat him for touching many different hands held above his head. This will make a hand coming over his head a good thing. Second, protect your dog from being frightened by well-meaning strangers by using the rule that the person must always ask first. This also lets you educate people (nicely) who don't ask that they should always ask first. This is especially important for children, who can suffer a face bite if they run up to pet the wrong dog.

13. Have friends with dogs walk by your dog while he is sitting next to you.
14. Have friends with dogs walk up to you, sit their dog, and have a conversation with you.
15. Have friends greet your dog while squealing or come up to you walking weirdly, or with a cane, crutches, or in a wheelchair.
16. Practice all of the above without a leash on the dog.

Early Steps: If you have already taught the Sit with a Release, and worked on it in a variety of locations, this behavior will start very quickly. If you haven't already worked on it, allow yourself several extra weeks to get a solid Sit in different environments and build the amount of time the dog holds the Sit waiting for a Release.

Problem-Solving Tips:
The dog works okay until the distractions are too high.
- See problem-solving tips for Come, Chapter 2
- Fine tune your distraction list and add a few more levels in between, then build up more slowly.
- Use a variety of super yummy treats.
- Work before meals.

The dog works okay until the distraction is a person.
- As a separate exercise, teach the dog to keep "four on the floor" for greeting by clicking and treating that and departing or ignoring him if he

doesn't keep all feet on the floor. Add more people as he gets the idea, then teach the sit for greeting.

I'm having difficulty building up time in the Sit.
- Review the Click Trick on bouncing in Chapter 2.
- Make sure you are working in a low distraction/high reward environment (like your kitchen).
- Reduce the number of click/treat/pause combos until the dog is successful remaining in a sit, then build up SLOWLY.
- Have someone watch you - are you delivering treats quickly enough, before the dog gets up? Practice without the dog if you need to.

Suggested Commands: Sit,Sit/Stay

Suggested Signal: For stay, you hold the flat of your palm toward the dog's nose.

Variations: Work on a Sit for greeting while you are a distance from the dog and pretending to be busy doing something else while someone comes and pets him.
	Have him Sit, then step away and have him do another behavior while still in the same spot.

RELAX FOR VETERINARY EXAMS

The Final Picture: The dog lies quietly on his side or back, without struggling, while you check his feet, tail, ears, teeth, eyes, etc. He will allow another person (such as your veterinarian) to examine him with equal ease.

Uses: This is great for general care of your dog, as well as a great building block for Taking Medications (Say Ahhh), bathing and grooming, and toenail clipping. It will also prove useful for other socialization exercises in Chapter 6. You'll find that each time you break through a problem area, the next one moves much more quickly.

Preparation and Props: A clicker, treats and a sleepy, relaxed dog.
It's also helpful if the dog already knows how to Play Dead (see Chapter 5 for more information) or Down (Chapter 1).

The Steps Along the Way:

Session One —

1.   Play some calm, relaxing music (this is for you, not really for the dog!) Sit in a chair if you have a large dog, and on the floor if you have a small dog. Put the clicker in your non-dominant hand, and a bowl of treats out of reach of the dog but where you can get them easily. Allow the dog to be in whatever position he's comfortable with - sitting, standing or lying down. Using your dominant hand, touch the dog's side for one second, click (with your non-dominant hand) and treat (using the dominant hand). (So the only job of your non-dominant hand is to click – it's good practice for you to be ambi-clicks-trous!) Touch the dog's chest, click and treat, touch a front leg, click and treat. Continue until you have touched the dog on every part of his body for one count, working to the back legs, tail (base and out to the end), up along his back, the ears and teeth, in that order. Pay attention if the dog seems stressed (changes position, pulls away, moves the limb or turns abruptly toward you) about any part of his body so that you can work on this separately. (See Early Steps below for help on this.) Do not move on to step 2 until you can touch every part of the dog's body, even if only for a second.

2.   Touch each part of the dog's body again, putting more pressure on your touch, and holding it for about two seconds before clicking and treating. You want to click while your hand is still in physical contact with the dog. Once you click, you can remove your hand and grab a treat for the dog.

CLICK TRICKS

For the dog who dislikes physical contact, this is doubly rewarding because the touching stops as long as he is still and allows it. Keep the sessions brief, progress slowly (work at the same step for several sessions), and spread them out throughout the day to help a dog like this.

---

3.   Change treats, and touch each part of the dog's body again, going from least to more stressful as described in step 1. Vary each touch from 1-5 seconds, clicking and treating the dog for quiet, relaxed behavior - i.e., not struggling, wiggling, or moving away from your touch, relaxed body, lying down, yawning, stretching.

CLICK TRICKS

We're changing treats here because after 20 to 30 repetitions, the dog may be getting bored with the same treat, and because we are upping the stress level in this step.

Session Two —
4.   Change locations and repeat step 3.
5.   Change locations and treats, and repeat step 3. Try to work in a location with a different floor surface from where you started originally.
6.   Change locations. Now rather than just resting your hand on the dog, you are going to encircle the smaller parts like legs and ears, and grasp a little skin over the back and sides. Don't grab or pinch, be gentle about it, but do be a little more assertive. Vary the amount of time you maintain each hold from 1-5 counts, but always click and treat when the dog is relaxed, not pulling away or resisting.

CLICK TRICKS

If at any point the dog seems stressed (panting, resisting, moving away or stiffening, etc.) you should end the session. Start the next session at a previous step (where the dog wasn't stressed) and build up more slowly from that point, breaking your steps even smaller than indicated here. Remember to breathe deeply yourself! Your own relaxation will definitely help.

7.   Continue to change locations and repeat step 6 until the dog seems totally bored with the whole process.
8.   At this point you can add the cue, remembering to click and treat for calm, relaxed behavior only: command name, hold dog, dog is relaxed, click and treat.

Session Three —
9.   In a new location, begin by touching the dog firmly all over, then hold and move at least two parts of the dog's body (legs, tail, ears, lips, eyelids, etc.), clicking for calm behavior.
10.   Repeat step 9 over the course of several days, changing locations each time, and adding one or two new body parts at each step.

11. Now gently massage each body part as you move around the dog's body, clicking for relaxed behavior. If the dog seems to be enjoying it at this point, you can dispense with the clicker, and talk calmly to the dog while you massage/examine him. That may be in a matter of weeks for puppies or dogs that resist physical contact, or a matter of days for a quiet older dog. Remember to reward RELAXED AND QUIET behavior with treats and/or release from restraint. Use low, drawn out praise while you are touching the dog. Breathe!

12. As you move around the dog's body, check each part to make sure it's healthy - spread toes, look in the ears, check teeth, touch toenails, check the belly, look at the skin, etc. Remember, you're rewarding with treats for being still while you examine each part of the dog.

Session Four —

13. If your dog already knows how to Play Dead, have him do it, then massage his hips and shoulders and briefly down the legs and back to hips and shoulders. Keep this step SHORT - the whole process should take less than 10 seconds. Click and treat when you get back to the hip/shoulder area. Repeat 10 times, having the dog Play Dead, Hold Still, massage, click and treat. If you haven't already taught Play Dead, have the dog lie down, then massage the hips and shoulders on one side. Most dogs like it enough that they will roll onto their side to get more, but if your dog doesn't, don't force him. You'll undo all your hard work up to this point! Instead, teach the Play Dead and reinforce often and well for that behavior, then come back to this step.

14. Change locations (to a new floor surface) and repeat step 13.

15. Continue changing locations and floor surfaces and repeating steps 12 and 13. Don't forget to practice outside – you never know when you will need to check an injury at a park or some other outdoor venue.

Additional sessions, work on variability —

16. Handle the dog's feet, squeezing out each toenail, tapping toenails and holding the leg firmly, in preparation for toenail clipping or foot bandaging. Press on the end of the toenail (you might have to put styptic powder on to stop a bleeding toenail.)

17. Handle the dog's mouth, opening it and looking at all the teeth, in preparation for teeth brushing and the Take Medication command we'll work on next. Practice wrapping your leash around the dog's mouth in case you have to do a makeshift muzzle some day. Hold the dog's

mouth firmly but gently and take a good look at his eyes, lifting each lid, and nose.

18.   Lift the dog, clicking and treating him if he's not wiggling. Start with just a second or two of lifting and build up to carrying the dog for some distance. An injured dog may have to be carried, or lifted into a car or onto a table. Be careful of your back with a large dog! (This will also tax your dexterity with your clicker!)

19.   Practice having the dog stand, sit, turn around (see that behavior later in this chapter), lie down and roll over on an elevated surface. A picnic table works well for a starting point. Your goal is to be able to do this on the vet's exam table.

20.   Have several people the dog knows well and is comfortable with do steps 8 to 19 while you click and treat calm behavior.

21.   Have someone the dog doesn't know well do steps 8 to 19 while you click and treat calm behavior.

22.   Take the dog to your veterinarian's office to get treats from the people in the waiting area, and your veterinarian, get clicked and treated for being on the scale, and get clicked and treated going into an exam room. Repeat many times before the dog actually needs to have a procedure done so the dog thinks your veterinarian's office is cookie heaven instead of doggy hell.

23.   Have your vet practice steps 12-19 while you click and treat. You may have to pay for an extra office visit to practice this but it will be WELL worth the money in the long run. If your veterinarian understands what you are doing, he or she should be all in favor of it. This training may make your dog the darling of the practice.

CLICK TRICKS

Remember, it's your dog, and you have the right to direct how things are done with him. Discuss things with your veterinarian in advance if you have concerns. Mandy had a vet (not her regular one) that pooh-poohed the need for treats with a 14 week old lab puppy she was training. Mandy was vindicated 10 minutes later when the vet complimented her while the dog held absolutely still on the table for a painful catheter procedure because she was clicked and fed the entire time. More on social and fear stuff in Chapter 6.

Early Steps:
For a dog who can't be touched, just hold your hand over the area (as close as you can get without stressing the dog), keep it there until the dog is still, then click, treat and STOP. The dog's reward for not pulling away or reacting is that you LEAVE HIM ALONE. Come back ten minutes later and repeat, trying to get an inch closer to the dog each time, until you are able to touch him in one place. Continue as indicated in the instructions, taking extra time at each step.

Alternatively, teach the dog to touch your hand (see Chapter 2) or shake (see variations on Wave in Chapter 5) to give the dog the opportunity to control the initial touch. Proceed as the dog gets more comfortable with physical contact.

If your dog is nervous about being handled and will only let you touch one or two parts of his body (generally the shoulder, side or under the chin), start there. Touch it until you can get a 10 second touch without the dog pulling away. Then move to the next least stressful area for your dog (see diagram below for suggestions) and repeat. Add a third touch area, then a fourth. Keep adding and repeat until the dog allows touching on any body part, then proceed with step 1 in the instructions.

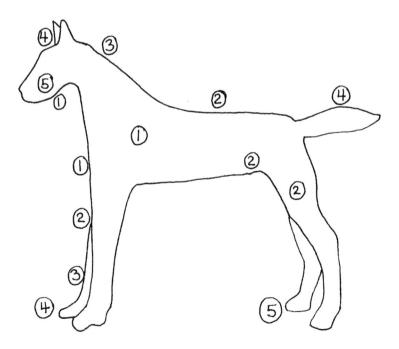

Each time you work with the dog, try to get further along the dog's body, but without making the dog stressed. Short, frequent sessions are the way to go with this! It is critical with this behavior that you not move on to the next step until the dog is comfortable with the one prior. Your eventual goal with a touch sensitive dog, though, is not to get him to merely tolerate it, but to actually LIKE it. You'll know you're there when the dog turns a formerly untouchable part to you to touch first!

Problem-Solving Tips:
Dog won't take the treat
- If the dog isn't eating, you are moving too fast for him
- Use better treats and work before meals
- Sit on the floor instead of in a chair.

The dog goes along well and then seems to regress quickly
- You moved too fast and spooked the dog. Start all over from step 1, and move slowly when you get to the point where the dog was spooked before.
- Something else spooked the dog - maybe something in the environment that you weren't even aware of. Move back to a few steps prior, and move more slowly through the steps.

Suggested Commands: Hold Still, Settle, Relax (has a nice drawn-out sound).

Variations: Think about the other grooming tasks you will need to accomplish with your dog beyond brushing and bathing. Does he need to be professionally groomed, get up on a surface, be restrained for regular medical procedures or testing? All of these things can be taught using treats, a clicker and a little creativity. You'll make your life (and your dog's) a lot easier if you spend the time to introduce these basic handling exercises BEFORE you need them!
Teach the dog to wear costumes, backpacks and hats.

SLICK CLICKS

THE SPEED OF TRAINING
Mandy Book

I took my boxer, Twister, to the veterinarian because she seemed to be having some kind of urinary problem. A standard procedure is to get a urine sample, which they can do with a syringe or by a direct void. They needed a direct void to check for problems in the lower part of the urinary tract. The vet tech who followed me outside had a little contraption to collect the urine - a long metal pole with a plastic cup on the end. I told Twister to "Hurry Up" and waited for her to comply. The tech stood ready, following her as she moved around. Twist was a little unsure about this stranger following her with a stick, but she finally squatted and peed. The tech quickly stuck the cup between Twist's legs, banging it against one of them in the process. She unfortunately missed the catch, and that was quite enough for Twist, who wouldn't let the lady get near her again, with or without the stick. I told her I would try it at home and bring back a sample. How hard could it be? After all, they teach whales to pee in a cup using clicker training, so I ought to be able to do it relatively quickly with a dog. Once I got home, I made a device similar to the urine-catcher with a hanger and a plastic cup. During the course of the next 2 hours I shaped Twister to allow me to put the "catcher" between her back legs and hold it there, without her moving away from it. This took about 10 sessions, lasting about one minute each. I even added a step where I banged the cup against her legs, just in case. And I gave her water. When I felt like she was comfortable with the process, I took her outside and told her to "Hurry Up." When she squatted, I angled the cup between her legs. She filled it, not minding it in the slightest, and got a cookie to boot! The morals of the story? 1) You never know what you'll need to teach or how fast you'll need to teach it! It was possible because of the power of the clicker. 2) If I had thought to spend ten minutes using the clicker at the vet's office before they tried to get the sample, I wouldn't have had to devote 10 sessions to it at home and then drive all the way back to the vet!

TAKE MEDICATION (SAY AHHH!)

The Final Picture: The dog allows you to open his mouth to give medication, pull something out, or check his teeth.

Uses: You'll be able to take something from the dog's mouth or even just have him Open and drop it himself. Or you can put something – such as a pill from your veterinarian – in without having to count your fingers afterward. You'll need this behavior before you know it!

Preparation and Props: Dog, dog kibble or really tiny treats, clicker, an assistant or a Bridge word (see Click Tricks below). Introduce Relax for Veterinary Exams above first.

CLICK TRICKS

A bridge word fulfills a similar function to the clicker. Both are called "behavior markers" because they provide a time connection between the behavior and the reward received. The advantage of a bridge word is that it doesn't require your hands. But the disadvantage is that it isn't very precise or distinct, and it's more difficult to use it to shape a behavior. Still, it has its uses and we recommend you condition a bridge word so that you have the flexibility to be able to use it. Pair it with food the same way you did the clicker - Bridge, treat; bridge, treat; etc. The word itself should be one syllable, quick and upbeat to say, like Yes, Wow, Right, Yep, Bink, Treat, Yeah. Don't use Good, because we all say it too much and it won't have the strong association to food you will need for the word to be effective as a bridge word.

The Steps Along the Way:
Session One –
1.   Hold the bottom of the dog's muzzle firmly but gently, supporting his chin with one hand, for one count, click and treat or bridge and treat if the dog remains still. (From here on, we'll indicate click/treat but use either option for this exercise.) Repeat 5 times.

2. Hold the bottom of the dog's muzzle firmly for a count ranging from 1 to 5, click and treat for remaining still. Repeat 10 times, varying the count each time.

3. From this point on, you'll either need an assistant to click (you treat), or you'll have to use your bridge word and treat, because both your hands will be occupied. Grasp the bottom of the dog's muzzle with one hand as you have been doing, but then use your other hand to grasp the top of the muzzle. Hold firmly for one count, click and treat the dog remaining still and not resisting. Repeat 5 times, varying your count between 1 and 3.

4. Open the dog's mouth a small amount for one count, click and treat for remaining relaxed. Repeat 10 times. If your dog resists, go back to step 1 and start all over.

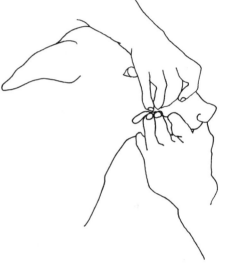

5. Continue to open the dog's mouth a little bit further each time, until it is open wide enough that you could get a hand in there. Repeat at each degree of opening at least 5 times. Keep the time the mouth is open short, no more than a second – it's not comfortable for the dog, and you need to let him get used to it.

Session Two –

6. Repeat Step 5 until the mouth is wide open.

7. Open the dog's mouth wide, hold for a count of 2, then click and treat for not resisting. Repeat 5 times, then add one additional count. Build up to a count of 5, repeating at each new count 5 times.

8. Bounce around (see Chapter 2) an average of 5. Repeat 10 times.

9. Is the dog relaxed while you hold his mouth open, regardless of how long? Time to add your command. Command, hold dog's mouth open, click and treat. Continue to pair the command and the behavior for at least 50 additional repetitions, changing treats and locations every 10 times.

Session Three –
10. Open the dog's mouth and run your finger along his tongue, click and treat for being still. Repeat 10 times, bouncing around an average of 5 counts.
11. Open the dog's mouth and hold his tongue down with one hand, click and treat being still. Repeat 10 times, bouncing around an average of 3 counts.
12. Open the dog's mouth, then tuck a treat in the back of his mouth. Click and give another treat if he doesn't resist. Repeat 10 times.

Additional steps work on variability –
13. Work in different environments.
14. Work with different size treats.
15. Give the dog an item, then remove it from his mouth. Be sure to click and treat for letting go of the item!
16. Have someone else tuck a treat in the back of the dog's mouth while you hold it open.

Early Steps: Teach the Relax for Veterinary Exam before trying to mess around in the dog's mouth! Don't clamp your hands onto the dog's muzzle - it will make him resist and pull away from you. Hold the muzzle gently but firmly from underneath and over the top of his nose.

If you've ever done something nasty to the dog around his mouth (like pinch his lip or grab and squeeze his muzzle to "correct" biting, or a lip pinch for a forced retrieve), expect it to take a very long time for your dog to be comfortable with mouth handling. You've already taught him that fussing around his mouth is unpleasant. Practice often in very short sessions. Instead of correcting him physically, teach the dog to be gentle with his mouth by using the instructions in Chapter 2 on Take a Treat Gently.

Problem-Solving Tips: See Relax for Veterinary Exam.

Suggested Commands: Say AHHH, Open

Variations: Teach the dog to open his mouth as soon as you touch it, in addition to being calm while YOU open it. Then give it a good trick name like "Baby Bird." Teach the dog to catch and swallow pills tossed to him (talk about being easy to medicate!)

SLICK CLICKS

TAKE YOUR MEDICINE
Kathy Sdao, proprietor of Bright Spot Dog Training
and former marine mammal trainer

Our female walrus, Georgie Girl, at Point Defiance Zoo & Aquarium had major abdominal surgery to remove a plastic toy she'd ingested. Her recovery was long and agonizing, involving lots of medications, as many as 150 pills three times a day. The standard way to give pills to marine mammals is to stuff each one into the gill slit of a herring or mackerel, then feed the fish to the sick animal. But with so many pills for Georgie, that process took forever! So we decided to clicker train her to swallow pills. After very few sessions, we got to the point where we could dump dozens of pills, all in a pile, into the back of her throat as she leaned her head back, and she'd swallow them down. Her reward was a squid when she was feeling well, or a Tums if she was off her food.

TURN AROUND

The Final Picture: The dog turns 180 degrees from left to right, right to left, front to back, or back to front.

Uses: Bathing and grooming, direction work in agility competition, fancy footwork for freestyle (dancing with dogs) competition, spin in a circle.

Preparation and Props: Dog, treats, clicker, touch stick. If the dog already knows a hand touch and/or touch stick, this variation will be a piece of cake! If not, teach the hand touch first.

The Steps Along the Way:
Session One - Left to right and right to left
1. Start by sitting or standing in front of the dog. You want to be at a level where you can hold either hand comfortably out from your body, parallel to the ground, and have the dog be able to touch it while he is standing (on all four feet). With a very small dog, you might want to sit

on the floor. Put your right hand out, say Touch (or whatever your cue is for this behavior), then click and treat when the dog touches. Drop your right hand, and put your left hand up, say touch, then click and treat when the dog touches. You can hold the clicker in either hand, but keep the treats in a bowl or pocket until you click. Deliver the treat from the hand the dog touches each time. Repeat 5 times, alternating hands (the dog touches each hand 5 times).

CLICK TRICKS

People (including your authors) tend to be sloppy about exactly what the cue is for "Touch." Do you expect the dog to make contact when you simply hold your hand out, or do you say "touch" (or whatever your command word is) every time? Most people use both techniques indiscriminately. Fortunately, our dogs are pretty forgiving about our less-than-perfect procedures, and usually get it right. But you'll make it easier for your canine student if you're more consistent about your cue. If you always want to use a verbal cue, don't click and treat the dog for touching your hand when you hold it out without saying anything. If you want presentation of your hand to be the cue, be aware that if you use your hands a lot when you talk, you may have a dog doing touches you didn't really want. Choose the method you're going to use, and do your best to stick with it.

---

2. With your left hand out, say Touch and immediately drop your left hand and hold up the right, so that the dog will at first face the left hand, but then turn to touch the right hand because it's the only option you're giving him. Click and treat as soon as the dog <u>begins the turn</u> to your right hand (before you get a touch). Repeat 10 times, alternating between the two hands. (Try this without the dog first if you have any uncertainty about when you will be clicking.)

Session Two —
3. Put both hands by your side, then lift your left hand, click the dog for beginning to turn to the left hand. Put both hands by your side, then lift your right hand. Click the dog for beginning the turn to the right.

Repeat 10 times (you no longer should be saying touch, since we are not clicking the dog for touching, but for turning).

4. If the dog is reliably (80 percent of the time) beginning to turn to the opposite hand when it appears, add your new command if desired (or you can use the touch command or hand signal, allowing the dog to touch the hand, and skip this step). Tell the dog "turn," put the hand up you want him to turn toward, dog turns, click and treat.

5. You will now build time with the dog standing facing the direction he has turned to, without the hand in front of the dog's nose. Start with the dog facing right. Hold up your left hand. Cue the dog to turn to the left hand, drop the left hand briefly, click and treat, return the left hand to the front of the dog's nose. Drop the left hand again, click and treat, return the left hand. Repeat 5 times. Continue adding more time with the left hand lowered, using the bouncing around method described in Chapter 2. Repeat until the dog will remain standing for up to 5 seconds, facing left, even when your hand is not there.

6. Repeat step 5, turning the dog to face right and building time remaining there.

7. If you want to get rid of the visual signal for turn, you can begin to fade it at this point. To do that, give the cue for turn, then lift your left hand up but not all the way to the dog's nose (about 3 to 5 inches lower than you were holding it previously). Repeat 3 times, alternating hands. Lift the hand, again lower than the previous time by 3-5 inches. Continue to alternate hands. After every 3-4 repetitions, you will gradually lift the hand less, until the dog is turning without any hand movement at all. Remember, you are clicking each time as the dog begins the turn.

8. Change locations. Put the dog in front of you, facing either LEFT or RIGHT. Put both hands by your side, say your turn command, and click and treat the dog for turning. Repeat 10 times.

Session Three - front to back and back to front

9. Get your touch stick out, and start with the dog standing in front of you, facing you. Put the touch stick behind your dog, say Touch (or whatever your command is to touch the stick), then click and treat when the dog touches the stick. Put the stick in front of you at the dog's nose level. Say Touch, then click and treat when the dog turns and touches the stick (he should now be facing you). Hold the clicker in the same hand as the touch stick and feed from the other hand.

Alternate holding the touch stick behind the dog and in front of you until the dog has touched in each direction 5 times. (Note: For a small dog, you may be able to comfortably reach behind him. If so, alternate with your hands instead of using the touch stick.)

10. Hold the stick behind your dog, say Touch, click and treat as soon as the dog begins the turn to the touch stick (before you get a touch). While he is facing away from you, say Touch and offer the touch stick in front of you, click and treat for turning toward you, before he touches the stick. Repeat 10 times, alternating between turning away from you and turning toward you.

Session Four —

11. Start with the dog facing you. Put your touch stick behind the dog, and click the dog for <u>beginning to turn</u> to the touch stick. Put the touch stick in front of you (so the dog turns to face you again), and click the dog for beginning to turn to the stick. Repeat 10 times. (You are no longer saying Touch, since we are clicking the dog for turning, not touching.)

12. If the dog is reliably (80 percent of the time) beginning to turn to the correct direction when you move the stick, add your new command. (You can continue to use the stick, and skip this step, if desired.) Command, place the stick behind the dog, dog turns, click and treat.

13. Build time with the dog facing the correct direction (toward or away from you) without relying on the touch stick, following the instructions in steps 5 and 6.

14. Continue as in steps 7 and 8 for the left to right turn, fading the touch stick prompt, if desired.

Additional sessions, work on variability —

15. Work the dog on a bench, grooming table, bleachers or other raised surface.

16. Practice in the bathtub or shower, with no water on.

17. Practice in the bathtub or shower, with the water running.

18. Teach the dog to turn and stand still while you run your hands or a brush all over his body, using the bounce around an average.

19. Turn the dog and send him over a jump or through a tunnel.

Early Steps: The variations (left to right/right to left and front to back/back to front) stand alone, so you don't need to teach both if you don't want to. If you only teach one, right to left/left to right is probably what you'll use most often.

It may be helpful to have someone else click the turn, or practice a few times without the dog to get your timing right as you work on steps 2 and 10.

Think carefully about your command selection - you could give a different name to each direction, which would be very impressive! But then you have to remember which is which, and you don't have those extra commands available for some other behavior. The dog can learn that one word means "turn 180 degrees from where you are facing" but will need extra repetitions and some well-timed clicking from you early on. You could just use the hand held up as your turn signal, eliminating steps 4, 7, 12, 14. But then you have to have one hand free to give the signal. Put some thought into how you will be using this behavior (see Stand Still for Bathing and Grooming below) before you make your decision!

Practice some of the repetitions in steps 8 and 12 in your bathtub, or on a low table, in anticipation of steps 16 and 17.

Problem-Solving Tips:
The dog anticipates the hand moving and turns before you say the command
- Say your command BEFORE you move your hand
- Use a hand signal instead of a verbal signal for the turn

Suggested Commands: Left, Right, Front, Back, Turn, Touch, Compass

Suggested Signal: Your hand held up where you want the dog's nose to be

Variations: Teach the dog to do all four directional changes at a distance from you.

Teach the dog to turn 180 degrees regardless of where he is facing, not just left to right or front to back.

STAND STILL FOR BATHING AND GROOMING

The Final Picture: The dog stands while you bathe or groom him, without fussing or struggling.

Uses: Obedience stand for exam, pet therapy work, any procedures where the dog needs to be standing, such as brushing, bathing, veterinary exams, toenail clipping. (Some people may choose to do some of these things with the dog lying down – that's okay too. You can teach the dog to stay lying flat the same way.)

Preparation and Props: Clicker, treats, dog, bathtub, grooming tools (brush, clippers). Teach Relax for Veterinary Exam and Touch first. A Turn Around (see above) is also handy but not required.

The Steps Along the Way:
Session One —
1. Start with the dog sitting in front of you, facing your left or right side. Hold your hand out far enough that he has to stand up on all fours to touch it but not so far away that he will have to take a step beyond that, tell him Touch (or whatever your command is for that behavior), then click and treat when he stands up and touches your hand. Put him back into a sit. Repeat 10 times.
2. Put the dog into a down in front of you. Hold your hand out far enough that he has to stand up on all fours to touch it, tell him Touch, then click and treat when he stands up and touches your hand. Put him back into a down. Repeat 10 times.
3. Put the dog into a sit. Put your hand in front of him and tell him to Touch. DO NOT click the first time he touches. The dog will probably look at you, wondering why you didn't click him. Wait for him to touch your hand a second time, then click and treat. Repeat 10 times, starting from a sit every time, varying whether the dog has to touch your hand 1, 2 or 3 times before clicking and treating each time.
4. Put the dog into a down and repeat step 3.

Session Two —
5. Now stand the dog using your hand touch signal, then drop your hand and quickly bring it back, click and treat if the dog hasn't moved, Release the dog. Repeat 10 times, varying how long your hand disappears from sight, and clicking and treating the dog for remaining in a stand, then releasing the dog.
6. Can you predict that the dog will wait patiently, with your hand dropped, until you click? Then it's time to add your command. Say your command, use your touch hand signal, drop your hand, and when

the dog is still for the amount of time you decide, click, treat, and release the dog. Repeat the pairing of your command with the behavior at least 50 times, changing locations every 10 times.

7. Slowly build up the amount of time the dog remains standing still while your hand is gone, until the dog will remain still for up to five minutes. Use the bounce around technique described earlier.

Session Four —

8. Repeat step 11 in a new location.
9. Stand the dog, then pick up a front foot, click and treat if the dog doesn't move, and release the dog. Be aware of how you hold the foot – don't clamp down on it like a vise. Simply lift it and support it. Repeat 10 times, alternating front feet and varying how long you hold the foot up.
10. Stand the dog, then pick up a back foot, click and treat if the dog doesn't move, and release the dog. Repeat 10 times, alternating between the back feet and varying how long you hold the foot up.
11. Stand the dog, lift his tail, lift an ear, click and treat when the dog doesn't move, release the dog. Repeat 10 times, touching one, two or three different body parts each time, and holding for varying amounts of time.

Additional sessions, work on variability —

12. Work the stand in a bathtub, shower, or on a raised surface. Make sure the surface the dog is on is very secure so the dog doesn't slip or fall. Start with the water off, then turn it on as the dog gets good at standing still in the bath.
13. Practice toweling the dog dry while he stands still. Dry for a short amount of time (a few seconds) initially, gradually building up to more time while the dog stands still.
14. Practice brushing the dog while he stands still. Introduce the dog to the brush first, then incorporate the stand, brushing one part and clicking, treating and releasing the dog, then building up to more and more complete brushing.
15. If your dog is clipped, introduce the dog to the noise of clippers, holding them in your hand and picking up body parts while he is standing still, then gradually touching the dog with the clippers, then using them on the dog.

Early Steps: Experiment with where your hand is to get the dog into a stand rather than a sit (too high) or a down (too low). If your dog will be professionally groomed, bring him to the groomers and click and treat for getting on the table and into the tub. Do this several times BEFORE the dog has to be groomed, and things will go much more smoothly for the dog when he actually has to be groomed. You should also socialize the dog to your local pet wash if you won't be bathing him at home.

Problem-Solving Tips:
The dog moves when I take my hand away.
- You were too slow bringing the hand back. At first, keep it away for the briefest of moments.

The dog moves when I start touching him
- The dog may dislike having you touch him. Review the Relax for Veterinary Exam until the dog is 100% comfortable with being touched all over.

Suggested Commands: Stand, Stay, Freeze

Variations: Teach the dog to stand still while you briefly move away to do something else (such as get towels or shampoo).

TOENAIL CLIPPING

The Final Picture: The dog will allow you to clip his toenails without fighting, biting or unpleasantness. If zookeepers can do this with elephants, you can certainly do it with your dog! Teach being calm for clipping even if you never plan to do it yourself, as it will make the dog's trip to the vet or groomer smoother and less stressful for both of you.

Uses: Not just toenail clipping, for clipping the fur around the feet as well. Checking for thorns or burrs, or foot bandaging and general foot care.

Preparation and Props: Toenail clippers, dog, super yummy treats, clicker. Teach Relax for Veterinary Exams first. Stand Still is also a helpful behavior to have.

The Steps Along the Way:

Session One –

1. Start with the dog standing. If you haven't taught the Stand Still exercise above, you might want to do that first. It will make the rest of the process more rewarding for the dog. Otherwise, just stand the dog physically. Touch the front leg, click and treat. Repeat 5 times.

2. With the dog standing, touch the other front leg, click and treat. Repeat 5 times.

3. Now grab and hold one front leg firmly (high up on the leg) for 1 second, click and treat if the dog does not resist. Make sure the timing of your click is at a relaxation point for dog. The dog then gets doubly rewarded — he gets a food treat and he gets relief from physical restraint. (If you encounter resistance, go back and review the Relax for Veterinary Exams earlier in the chapter until the dog really likes having you touch him.) Alternate between front legs, grasping and holding the upper part of the leg for 1 to 3 counts each time. Repeat 10 times.

4. Grasp the front leg at the elbow for a count varying between 1 and 5, click and treat when the dog is relaxed. Alternate with the other leg, repeating 10 times.

5. Continue working down the front legs, grasping successively closer to the foot, and holding firmly for 1 to 5 counts, until you have reached the foot and can hold it firmly without the dog struggling or trying to pull away. Stay at each place on the leg for a minimum of 5 repetitions.

CLICK TRICKS

Hold the leg close to the dog's body rather than pulling it away from the body. It's more comfortable and allows the dog to balance. He'll be less likely to resist.

Session Two —

6. Repeat steps 1 through 5 with the back legs.

7. Change locations and repeat steps 1 through 5. (We recommend that you include outdoor locations and consider doing actual toenail clipping outside. That way, if you accidentally cut the quick and make him bleed, you don't have to chase the dog all over the house with a cleanup rag!)

Session Three —
8.   Change locations and repeat steps 1 through 5.
9.   Stand the dog, and lean over him to grab his front foot, bending his leg at the elbow, and squeezing one toe gently. Breathe deeply while you do this (humans have a tendency to hold their breath during toenail clipping, signalling to the dog they should be stressed!) Hold for a count of 1-8, click and treat. Repeat, alternating feet, up to 20 times.

Session Four —
10.   Change locations and repeat step 9. Add a command if you like, by saying the command, holding the dog's foot and gently squeezing, then clicking and treating relaxed behavior.
11.   Bring out the nail clippers and repeat step 9, holding the clippers in the hand you would use to clip with, but not actually cutting a toenail. Either have someone help you by clicking at the right time, use your bridge word instead of the clicker, or hold the clippers in one hand and the dog's foot and the clicker in the other.
12.   The big moment! Lift the front foot, BREATHE, clip one nail, click, treat. Repeat 5 times with the front foot, clipping a different nail each time (4 times if your dog's dewclaws have been removed). It's not important if you actually get a lot of clipping done, just take the tip of the nail off for now. You'll get better as you get more practice. The goal at this point is to get the DOG comfortable with the whole process.
13.   Repeat step 12 with each foot.

Additional sessions, work on variability —
14.   Lift each foot, and press against the cut edge of the nail for 1-5 seconds, click and treat relaxed behavior (you don't need to be holding the clippers for this). This is what the dog will need to tolerate if you have to put styptic powder on because you cut a nail too close. Repeat 10 times, varying which nail you choose.
15.   At the end of a clipping session, do something really fun with the dog. For our dogs, they get to run around the yard chasing a ball, or play a rousing game of tug. This makes the whole process of toenail clipping something to look forward to. (The formal term for it is the Premack Principle – read about it in Chapter 7.)
16.   Have someone else the dog knows clip his nails.

17. Have someone the dog doesn't know hold his feet and work up to step 10. If someone else will be clipping your dog's nails, make sure he gets practice having lots of strangers touch his feet. They don't have to clip, and they probably shouldn't if they don't really know what they're doing, but they should handle his feet.
18. Practice up to step 10 regularly with the dog, without clipping a single nail. This makes the actual clipping less stressful.
19. Practice on a raised surface such as a grooming table.
20. Clip nails while the dog is standing, sitting, and lying down.

Early Steps: Teaching the dog to shake (offer his foot so you can grasp it) is a good way to introduce this to a nervous dog. Start by clicking and treating ANY movement of the front foot, gradually building up to the dog lifting his foot high enough for you to grasp it. At that point, you will click and treat after you physically touch the dog. (See Wave in Chapter 5 for more help on how to teach this). Teach him to shake with both front feet, then introduce toenail clipping as indicated above.

Stay at each step until the dog is very relaxed, spreading the process out over several weeks if you need to. The better the foundation you lay for being relaxed, the easier the next ten years of toenail clipping will be.

Problem-Solving Tips:
The dog pulls away when I touch his elbow
▪ Make sure you are clicking for relaxed behavior. Have someone spot check you. Stay at that step for an additional 50 repetitions, then move more slowly on the remaining steps.

The dog is fine until I get the clippers out (he had a bad experience already!)
▪ Make the clippers fun by clicking and treating the dog for touching them, pawing them, picking them up or chasing them. Remember the warmup exercise you did with a canvas bag from Chapter 1? You're doing the same thing with the clippers here. Work on steps 1-10 while you're doing this. When the dog gets excited about the clippers and is thrilled to see them come out, start from step 1, using playing with the clippers as part of his reward.
▪ Have someone feed continuously while you do all the steps up to and including clipping a nail, using super treats, spread out over several days

of practice. Pay attention if the dog starts getting forceful with the treat – it means his stress level is increasing.

Suggested Commands: Hold Still, Toesies

Variations: Try introducing the dog to a nail grinder. If he will be a show dog you'll need this more professional looking toenail grooming.

CHAPTER 5
Clicks are for Kids

Okay, we'll admit it right at the beginning – this chapter isn't just for kids, it's for grown-ups who like to have fun, too. Training should be fun, and if teaching tricks helps you make it that way, then go to it!

If you've skipped straight ahead to this chapter, we don't mind. Looking to have fun is a good thing. But to be ready to train these behaviors, you'll need to understand the information in Chapter 1 and have done the training in Chapter 2 (we'll be using those position commands here). So go back and do that now if you need to. . . it won't take long, and you and your dog will both be more ready to tackle the exercises in this chapter.

You and your dog will be able to show off some cool behaviors and play a nifty game when you've done the lessons here. You may want to build on these or teach other fun things you think of – you should be ready by now if you've worked through the book up to this point. In this chapter we will cover:

Head down
Find me

Wave/high five
Play dead
Speak
Put 'em up/dance
Skateboarding

A lot of these have variations. . . like having the dog go belly up when playing dead rather than just lying on one side. They can be changed and enhanced and combined in all sorts of wacky ways. Think up fun and creative names for the behaviors – the best tricks have clever commands – and you'll wow your friends. We know you'll have a good time with this chapter and these behaviors.

HEAD DOWN

The Final Picture: The dog lies down with his head resting on the floor between his paws.

Uses: As the suggested command indicates, this is a perfect behavior for having the dog do a little acting, portraying shame or guilt. Combine Head down with Attention (see Chapter 1) to have the dog also roll his eyes up and look even more pathetic.

Preparation and Props: A clicker, treats, and your dog. We will be starting from a down, so it will be helpful if you've already put that command on cue. (If you haven't, see Chapter 2 for instructions.)

The Steps Along the Way:
Session One –
1.   Start sitting on the floor or in a chair with the dog lying down in front of you. We're going to use the hand touch to begin the behavior. Hold your hand out in front of the dog, slightly below his nose. Give your touch command and click and treat just before the dog touches your hand. Repeat 3 to 5 times.
2.   Pay careful attention to how the dog is moving in response to where you're holding your hand. You want the dog's chin parallel to the floor, not nose pointing to the floor. Adjust your hand position as necessary.

Hold your hand out, say your touch command, and click and treat before the dog touches your hand. Repeat 3 times.

3. Hold your hand a couple of inches lower than in the previous step. You may need to also hold it a little farther away from the dog's nose horizontally to encourage him to keep his head flat. Give your touch command and click and treat before the dog touches your hand. Repeat 3 times. (If the dog is starting to stretch toward your hand, stop using the verbal command for Touch. We don't want the dog to think "touch" means "not quite all the way.")

CLICK TRICKS

With this behavior, the click is likely to end the behavior because the dog wants to pick his head up to get his treat. That's okay – we'll work on holding the position in later steps.

4. If you're having trouble keeping the dog's head aligned with the floor, hold your hand horizontally farther away from the dog's nose and click and treat for the dog stretching to reach your hand, without getting up from his down. Stretching will automatically flatten out the head position. Repeat 5 times.

Session Two –

5. Starting in a new location, with the dog in a down, repeat step 4, keeping your hand as far from the dog as needed to keep the head flat. Repeat 3 times.

6. Gradually lower your target hand, an inch or two at a time. Repeat 3 to 5 times at each level. Keep working gradually lower until the dog's chin is resting on the floor.

7. In a new location, with the dog in a down, position your hand so the dog's chin will be on the floor, click and treat when he assumes the position. Repeat 3 times.

Session Three —

8. Now repeat step 7, but withhold the click and treat for a count of 1. Only click and treat if the dog keeps his head on the floor for your count. Repeat 5 times.

9. Build up the duration of the head down gradually, to a count of 5, rewarding each new level 3 to 5 times.
10. Now bounce around an average of 3 as your hold. So it might be head on the ground, count 4, click, treat, release; 2, click, treat, release; 5, click, treat, release; 4, click, treat, release; 2, click, treat, release; 3, click, treat, release.
11. Increase your average count to 5 and bounce around that.

Session Four –
12. In a new location, bounce around an average of 5.
13. You can modify the hand touch you have been using toward what will be your hand signal. An often-used signal for Head down is pointing at the floor with your index finger, the rest of the hand closed into a loose fist. You have been using a flat hand for a palm touch, so start by curling in your pinky. Present this slightly modified hand cue, and when the dog puts his head down, click, treat, and release. Repeat 3 to 5 times. Fold two fingers in and repeat 3 times. Continue folding in fingers until you are holding your hand in a fist, except for your index finger, which points at the floor. Repeat 3 times at each new hand position. Remember to continue bouncing around your average count as you modify this hand signal, so that the dog keeps his head on the floor for varying amounts of time before getting clicked, treated, and released from the Head down.

CLICK TRICKS

Many behaviors involve some sort of body cue, often a hand movement, while you are training them. This body cue can become your signal as is, or you can slowly modify it to whatever signal you desire if it's reasonably close, the same as changing your sitting position to standing. Or you can introduce a completely new signal the same as you add a verbal command – new cue (signal), old cue, behavior, click and treat.

---

14. Now you will begin putting a little distance between your target and the dog. This will allow you to start changing to a more upright position with your body. First, merely raise your target hand a little, pointing at

the floor. Click and treat when the dog settles his head on the floor. Repeat 3 to 5 times.

15. Raise your hand a little more, and repeat step 14.

Session Five —
16. Begin gradually modifying your body position. So if you were sitting on the floor, sit on a low stool or hassock instead, or crouch. If you were sitting in a chair, start straightening up. Eventually, you want to be able to stand straight up or only bend slightly at the waist to signal the dog. At your first change, try to keep your hand at the same level as in the previous session. Click and treat once the dog rests his head on the floor. Repeat 3 to 5 times.

CLICK TRICKS

Your body position can be very important to your dog. Some dogs will not recognize a command or signal if you suddenly give it sitting down when you've always previously been standing up. So change your position gradually. If your dog stops responding correctly, you probably made too big a change. Go back to your previous position and make smaller changes.

---

17. Change locations and continue working toward your final posture. Repeat 3 to 5 times at each new position.
18. When you are satisfied with your body position, check the reliability of response. Does your dog respond correctly at least 8 out of 10 times? Time to name the behavior. Add your verbal cue just before you give your hand signal. So it's "Head down" (or "Look ashamed" or "Splat" or whatever you like), hand signal, dog puts head on floor, click, treat, and release. Continue to vary how long the dog stays in the position as you pair the command with the action at least 50 times, changing locations every 10 repetitions. (You don't have to add a verbal cue if you don't want or need one.)

Following sessions, work on variability —
19. Continue to change locations and surfaces, gradually adding more distractions to the environment.

20. Practice with the dog in different placements in relation to you – in front of, on either side. Think you could do it with the dog behind you? With the dog five feet away from you?
21. Practice on top of or under things such as couches, boxes, tables.
22. Also put "Head up" on cue, so you could have the dog bob his head up and down on command. Use the same hand touch lure. It should go more quickly. Be careful to do more Head down than Head up so you don't lose the harder behavior (Head Down).

CLICK TRICKS

One of the trickier bits of training is keeping one behavior in place while you train a related one. People tend to concentrate so much on the new behavior that they forget to reinforce the old one. So even in the process of working on "head up," be sure to intersperse practice with "head down" or you risk misinforming the dog that the head down position was not actually the finished position, and you are now asking for something else in its place. So a training session might go, head down, head down, hand target for head up, head down, repeat for head up, head down, head down. Because the dog has learned that putting his head in different positions can pay off, he'll be more eager to try different things, and you shouldn't need as many repetitions for head up as you did for head down. Training will progress quickly, and you'll soon have both positions on cue.

Early Steps: It will help when you are starting this behavior if you deliver the treat with the dog in position. Most dogs will pick their heads up to eat, but getting the reward to them while they are still performing the lowered head behavior will help them understand.

The dog is likely to want to put his nose rather than his chin on the ground. You want to shape for a full head down, lower jaw on the ground posture as soon as possible so the dog doesn't get "stuck" in the nose-down position. Work first on positioning your hand cue so that the dog stretches forward and flattens his head position (or take the nose down position and go with it, if you like that!).

The dog doesn't follow your hand touch cue, or doesn't extend his head enough to be flat.

- Is there a physical problem? Any soreness in the neck may make the dog reluctant to extend the head this way. If you think there may be something physical going on, check with your veterinarian.
- This may just be the dog's preferred method of moving. Help get the idea across by changing hand positions. Maybe offering the back of your hand rather than the palm, or knuckles on top and thumb down will cause the dog to have to think about how to make the touch on your palm, and change how he presents his head.
- Try holding a treat in your hand, either directly offered to the dog, or with the back of your hand toward the dog.
- Shape more slowly, looking for only minute changes in head position at each step.

As soon as you get up from sitting on the floor, kneeling, or crouching, the dog no longer does the behavior.

- Your steps were probably too big when you changed position. Go back to your original training posture and modify it more slowly. (Yes, we know this can be a real challenge to your flexibility and balance – bet you didn't realize dog training can be great exercise!) You can use a chair and gradually bend over less and less.
- Practice other behaviors you already have on cue, and change your position often – stand up, bend over, turn sideways, sit in a chair, sit on the floor, stand with your back to the dog, so the dog starts to realize your body position isn't important to the behavior.

You are a tall person with a small dog, and your back is killing you!

- Train the dog on a table. You will first have to accustom the dog to working on a table. Many small dogs are put up there for grooming and nail clipping and are not very happy there. It may take a few sessions of just clicking and treating before the dog starts to think of the table as a fun place to be. (And if you skipped Chapter 4, there's help for you there with nail clipping and grooming.)

Suggested Commands: Head down, Look ashamed, Sad puppy, Tired puppy, Splat, Nighty night

Variations: Teach Head up to go with Head down, so you can have the dog alternate positions. Teach Head down with the dog on his side, so that he places the side of his head flat on the floor (useful for keeping "dead" dogs from picking their heads up to look at you). Practice at a distance with a hand signal only, as you would have to for actual film work. This is a standard behavior for commercial work.

FIND ME

The Final Picture: The dog waits in one place until told to play the game, then locates a hiding person or an item.

Uses: This is a fun and nifty way to start introducing a dog to the more formal world of tracking (a dog sport, where you can earn titles). You can give the dog both mental and physical exercise, especially when you have moved outdoors. You can, literally, ask the dog to find someone for you rather than shouting or searching youself. Attach notes to the dog's collar and have an instant courier! Teach the dog to find an item you commonly lose track of, like your wallet or keys.

Preparation and Props: Your dog and treats or a toy. If you're going to be playing this game alone with your dog, the dog will need to know Wait so that you can leave the dog and hide. If another human is playing, you can take turns and one can hold the dog. (But Wait is a really useful command, so we really hope you'll train it – see Chapter 2 if you haven't already.)

CLICK TRICKS

Wondering what happened to the clicker? Well, you could use it here, but it's not necessary. You're not working on a precise behavior that you need to be able to mark in small increments. And finding you is the dog's initial reward, so if you tried to click that, you would inevitably be late. So concentrate instead on greeting your dog joyously and giving a treat or playing with a toy. We'll get back to the clicker in the finding items variation toward the end of this behavior.

The Steps Along the Way:
Session One –
1. Put the dog in a sit and tell him to wait, or have an assistant hold him. Show him that you have a treat, then duck around a corner or behind a chair with the dog watching. Tell him your release word if you left him in a Wait, or have your assistant release him. As soon as the dog is released, he should zoom straight to you. Praise and treat when he "finds" you. Repeat 5 times. If you're working with an assistant, you can hold the dog once he has found you, and have the assistant hide a similar distance away from you.
2. Repeat, but hide a little farther from the dog, or in a slightly more complex location, such as around 2 corners or in a closet with a partially closed door. Praise and treat each time the dog finds you. Repeat 3 to 5 times. If the dog is rushing to find you each time, and you are working with an assistant, have the assistant say "find (your name)" as she releases the dog. If you are on your own, you can say "find (your name)" or "find me" before you say your release.

CLICK TRICKS

In other behaviors, we have been working through a fair number of repetitions before adding a command to a behavior. So why are we practically starting out with a command here? Because if the dog comes to find you the first few times, the odds are very good that he will continue coming to find you. The 80 percent or better reliability is already there.

---

3. Now don't let the dog watch you hide, so he isn't getting so much visual information. If you're working with another human, she can have the dog face away from you, or actually hide the dog's eyes. If you're working alone with the dog, you'll have to use visual barriers such as sitting the dog behind a couch, so you can move away without being seen. (Be aware that this can cause the dog to break the Wait command. If this becomes a problem for you, end this session. In your next sessions, work on strengthening the Wait command before continuing with this behavior.) Say your "find name" and Release to your dog and wait to be found, or have your assistant say the same

and release the dog. Praise and treat when the dog finds you. Repeat 3 to 5 times.

Session Two –
4.   Start in a different location – have places in mind where you're going to hide. Put the dog in the place where you will leave him, tell him to wait, go out of sight, and, being as quiet as you can, go hide. Try to keep it the same level of difficulty – how long it takes you to hide, distance from the dog, and how distracting the environment is – as in step 3. If working with an assistant, have her cover the dog's eyes before you depart. Say your command and release, or have your assistant do so, and praise and treat when the dog finds you. Repeat 3 to 5 times.
5.   To keep this from being the same static situation all the time – the game only happens if you leave the dog in a wait – find times when you are out of sight of the dog, hide, and simply wait for the dog to find you. This is terrific for improving the dog's attention because he learns that you'll try to run off if he's not watching you carefully. This is especially good practice with puppies. It's a great game to play in the woods, where you can duck behind a tree while the dog is sniffing something (in a safe area, of course). But you can also play it in the house by slipping behind doors or into closets while the dog is around a corner. You will probably only be able to do this one trial at a time, because the dog will stay with you once he's found you, anticipating more fun. Find times to do this whenever you can. Also mix in some practice of the Wait command by telling the dog to Wait, then coming back and releasing him instead of having him find you, so he doesn't get the idea to automatically run to look for you any time you leave him. (In this case, you want to reward the dog with a treat before you release him, so that waiting for you to come back also provides a payoff.)

Session Three –
6.   Keep playing surprise "find me" games when the opportunity arises.
7.   Take the game outdoors. Be sure you're in a safe fenced environment. You're likely to have a lot more distractions in the great outdoors, so you may have to take less time hiding in a place closer to your dog so you don't lose him to distractions. If he doesn't come to

find you when you say your command and release, go back indoors and practice some more. Start back at step 1 when you move back outdoors. Repeat 3 to 5 times.

8. Work your way through the steps back up to the difficulty you achieved indoors.

9. If you have only been having the dog find you, switch to having another person hide. You might want to make the hiding place a little easier. Repeat 3 to 5 times.

10. Work back up to your previous level.

Session Four –

11. Transfer the "find" concept to objects rather than people. Hold your touch stick next to the object – perhaps your car keys – say "keys" as the dog goes to touch, and click and treat when he touches the object. Repeat 5 times.

12. Place the keys slightly farther from the dog, place the touch stick next to the keys, say "keys" as the dog goes to touch, and click and treat. Repeat 5 times.

13. Continue placing the keys in different positions, placing the touch stick next to them, saying "keys," and clicking and treating when the dog goes to touch. Repeat for at least 50 more repetitions, changing locations every 10 repetitions. Fade the touch stick at the same time, by holding it farther away from the keys every 3-5 repetitions.

14. Place the keys down close to the dog. Say "keys" and click and treat when the dog goes to them. Repeat 5 times.

15. Gradually place the keys farther from the dog. Say "find keys." Click and treat when the dog touches the keys. Repeat 3 to 5 times at each distance.

Following sessions, work on variability –

16. Change locations and have the dog find you sometimes, the other person sometimes, and the keys sometimes. Repeat 8 to 10 times.

17. If you have only been using food as a reward, play with a toy when the dog finds you instead. Vary your rewards. Include petting and praise.

18.   Gradually make the game more difficult. Add twists and turns to your path away from the dog. Go to a hiding place you've used before, but then go from there to a different hiding place. Hide the keys in tougher places. Be inventive.

Early Steps: You want the dog to be successful, so don't make things too difficult at the beginning. If the dog doesn't come to find you at all, examine why. Is coming to you a fun experience, or does it mean the end of a romp or the start of a bath? You'll have to work on being a fun person for the dog.

If the dog comes to find you sometimes, but not always, perhaps the distractions in the environment are too high or your reward isn't motivating enough. Switch to a more boring environment or to a better food treat or to a toy the dog really likes. Make a big fuss when the dog does find you. At the beginning, keep it quick and easy so the dog only has to wait a few seconds before coming to find you.

Problem-Solving Tips:
The dog doesn't remain where left when you're working on your own.
- Go back and work on Wait (see Chapter 2) until it is solid.
- Make the time the dog must wait as short as possible – sit the dog only a couple of feet from where you can duck around a corner or behind a door. Release the dog to find you as soon as you're out of sight.
- Practice leaving and coming immediately back and rewarding the dog for being where he was. Vary the amount of time you're gone. Only release the dog every fifth or sixth time so he can't anticipate.
- Enlist the services of another human to help you play the game.

When released, the dog does something else rather than coming to find you.
- Work in a less stimulating environment, where the dog really doesn't have anything else to do.
- Make yourself more interesting – really get excited when the dog finds you, have a celebration, use really high-level treats or a favorite toy.
- Practice "come," being sure to make it upbeat and pleasurable.

The dog has trouble finding you when you hide in more difficult places.
- You may have made too big a jump in difficulty. Back up a couple of steps and work up more gradually. Plan your sequence of hiding places in advance.

- It's possible some medical problem is impairing the dog's sense of hearing or smell. Have you noticed any other indications? Is the dog eating well? If you think something physical may be going on, consult your veterinarian. Medications may also impact the dog's sense of smell.
- If you have skipped ahead to this chapter, your dog may not be confident enough to think for himself and problem solve. Go back and work on clicker training more behaviors to get the dog used to initiating behavior.

Suggested Commands: Find (fill in the name), Where's (fill in the name), Search and rescue, Seek

Variations: Use individual names (including your own) when you tell the dog to search, and you can soon have the dog looking for specific people. Rather than one person hiding at a time, you can all hide at once, and have the dog find you one after another. (Either all those hiding walk together to the first hiding place, one person stops there while others continue to the second hiding place, where one person stays, etc., or you can teach the dog to lead each found person back to the starting point – great for rounding up kids!)

SLICK CLICKS

FINDING KEYS – A USEFUL TRICK

Turid Rugaas, author of On Talking Terms with Dogs: Calming Signals

Turid has group classes in her native Norway, in a field surrounded by woods. At one class, a woman declined to take part, saying she didn't believe dogs could be trained by positive methods and would just observe for herself. She walked her large dog around the perimeter and into the woods the whole time the class was progressing. When class was over and people were leaving, the woman was still wandering around the woods. Turid finally asked what she was doing, and the woman was forced to admit that she had dropped her keys and couldn't find them. Turid called over one of her positively trained dogs, told the dog to "Find keys," and the dog set off around the woods, tail wagging, and in less than a minute had found the missing keys. The woman, in a less than gracious response, shoved her dog into her car and drove off. But Turid knew she'd demonstrated that dogs could indeed be positively trained to do quite useful things.

WAVE/HIGH FIVE

The Final Picture: The dog, on command or signal, picks one front leg up high into the air, paws at the air, and brings it back down (wave) or brings a front paw up to connect with the person's hand, pads to palm (high five).

Uses: This is a simple little trick that's always well-received – people just seem to love a dog who waves hello or good bye. It also offers some good stretching for the front end assembly of the dog, for some nice low-key exercise.

Preparation and Props: A clicker, treats, and your dog. It's easiest to teach this with the dog in a sit, so having Sit on cue will be helpful.

CLICK TRICKS

Have you ever determined if your dog is right- or left-sided? It will help make it a little easier when teaching some new behaviors if you know. If you've never thought about it, here are some ways to find out — While the dog is moving directly away from you (have someone else crouch down and clap or whistle to get the dog started toward them, if need be), call the dog. Does your dog turn to the left or right to turn around and head toward you? Try it three times – two out of three or better to the left indicate that your dog is left-sided.

When you taught Turn around in Chapter 4, was it easier to get your dog to turn in one direction than in the other? The easier direction of turn indicates the dog's favored side.

Use a treat to lure your dog around in a tight circle in front of you. Most dogs will follow the treat much more readily in one direction than in the other. Going clockwise well indicates a right-sided dog, while good counterclockwise movement means a left-sided dog.

If you don't get clear results, maybe your dog is ambi-paw-trous!

The Steps Along the Way:
Session One –
1. Put your dog in a sit. Stand or sit facing the dog and wait for the dog to move one front foot. Click and treat when he does. If you've been teaching the behaviors in this book, your dog should be offering all sorts of movements, and being in a sit will mean that it's easiest for him to move his front legs (and his head, but you'll ignore head movements). Your dog will favor one foot over the other, so once you start seeing movement, concentrate on that foot. Repeat 3 times.
2. Wait for a slightly higher foot lift, maybe 1-2 inches off the ground. Click and treat. Repeat 3 times.
3. Again, wait for the dog to lift the foot slightly higher. Remember not to change criteria in the middle of a step – so if the dog suddenly gives you one beautiful high foot lift, don't wait for him to do that again before clicking. Click and treat whatever you have decided meets your criteria for this step. Repeat 3 times.
4. Continue to require a slightly higher lift for a click and treat, repeating at each height 3 times. End this session when you have worked for approximately 5 minutes.

Session Two –
5. In a new location, start at the height you reached in step 4. Repeat 3 times.
6. Continue clicking a gradually higher foot lift until you achieve a nice high reach, repeating 3 times at each increment. Most dogs can raise their paw above nose level, and many can reach their elbow to nose level, so see how high you can get.

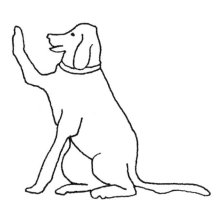

143

7.   When the dog is reaching as high as you want, start to shape the Wave. (You can teach both High five and Wave, but you have to put one on cue before you can work on the other.) When the dog lifts his foot, delay your click. The dog, used to being clicked for the behavior, will try harder to make you click, and may lift the paw even higher, or wave it up and down. Choose what you want your wave to look like – we like a nice up and down motion – and click that. Repeat, selecting the best 5 out of 10 foot lifts to click and treat.

Session Three –

8.   In a new location, continue shaping the Wave until you have it the way you want it.
9.   Can you predict that the dog will offer the Wave and be right at least 80 percent of the time? You're ready to add your cue. Say "Wave bye" or whatever you choose, wait for the dog to offer a good wave, and click and treat. Continue to pair your cue with the behavior for at least 50 additional repetitions, changing locations every 10 repetitions.
10.   When you believe you have Wave on cue, intersperse it with other commands such as Down and Turn around (or others you choose). Only click and reward the dog for offering a requested behavior that matches the cue. If you find that this doesn't work well for Wave, you don't have it firmly on cue yet. Go back and repeat step 9.

Session Four –

11.   When Wave is reliable, you can work on High five. Attach a Paw target to your hand – a plastic coffee can lid or margarine tub lid with a rubber band you can slip over your finger will stay in place while you move your hand around. Present the target and give your Paw command. Click and treat when the dog touches. Repeat 3 times.
12.   Cut your target slightly smaller. In a new location, repeat step 11.
13.   Continue cutting down the target and changing locations until the dog is eagerly reaching to connect with a very small target. This will go very quickly because you have already been working on a behavior involving foot movement, and you are using a cue the dog already knows.

Session Five —
14. When the dog is eagerly connecting with your target, delay the click so that the dog keeps the paw in place. You don't need much duration for a good High five, but a little is good. Wait 1 second before you click, and only click if the dog keeps his paw against your palm target. Repeat 5 times.
15. Change locations and repeat step 14.
16. When the dog is eagerly holding his paw on the target at least 80 percent of the time, add your new cue. Say "High five" or whatever you choose as you present your target. Click and treat when the dog touches. Continue to pair the cue with the behavior for at least 50 additional repetitions, changing locations every 10 repetitions.

CLICK TRICKS

In clicker training, the dog learns the behavior before he knows what it's called. Once the dog is reliably doing a behavior (8 out of 10 tries), it's time to give it a name. This gives you control of the behavior so the dog only does it when he's told and doesn't offer it when he's not told to.

Following sessions, work on variability –
17. Practice interspersing both cues with other behaviors that the dog knows, only rewarding when the dog performs the correct requested behavior.
18. Continue changing locations, working in more challenging surroundings.
19. Practice with the dog in different positions relative to you. Can you twist and have the dog High five you from heel position? Can you have him Wave to the crowd from heel position? Remember to make your position changes gradual.

Early Steps: If your dog doesn't offer a lot of foot movement, try shifting your weight as you stand facing your sitting dog. Sometimes the dog will mirror you, and shift his own weight in response.

You could teach the Wave with a Paw target, clicking before the dog touches. Be careful that you don't untrain Paw in the process. Stop giving the Paw command as soon as possible.

Problem-Solving Tips:
The dog lifts a paw a little bit, but never raises it any higher.
- Is there a physical problem? Dogs need good free-moving shoulders to give a nice wave or high five. Check with your veterinarian if you suspect there may be something wrong.
- Your timing may be off. Are you clicking as the dog's foot is moving up, at its highest point, or on the way back down? Highest point is the best, but better to be early rather than late, or the dog may think all you're after is a foot lift and back down.

The dog sits up (balancing on his haunches) or jumps up (standing on his hind legs).
- You may be trying to do too much too quickly. Be sure you are clicking for one paw moving, and go for a higher lift in very small increments.
- Take what you're getting and call it Sit pretty or Dance! While it's usually important to be precise in your shaping, these are tricks after all, and one is as good as another to your audience.

Suggested Commands: Wave or Say bye; High five or Gimme five

Suggested Signal: Wave at your dog

Variations: Teach the dog to wave or high five with either foot. Signal with the hand closer to the foot. After you have both on cue, add in "shake," working from your High five, but grasping the dog's foot gently. Remember to practice your established behaviors so you don't lose what you've already taught.

Teach the dog to wave from a standing position. If we teach this with both feet, it can become a very pretty dance step for the canine sport of Freestyle (dancing with your dog).

PLAY DEAD

The Final Picture: The dog, from a standing or sitting position, lies down and falls over flat on one side, with his head on the ground.

146

Uses: Always one of the favorites when you're showing off tricks. Useful if you want the dog to assume a totally nonthreatening posture for greeting small people or some other reason (as long as the dog feels secure). Can be helpful if you want to groom the dog while he is lying down. (See Chapter 4, Relax for Veterinary Exams, for more information.)

Preparation and Props: A clicker, treats, and your dog. Being able to have the dog lie down on cue will be helpful.

The Steps Along the Way:
Session One –
1. With the dog in a down, hold a treat in your hand between your thumb and forefinger, the rest of your fingers folded into your palm, and move it from the dog's nose toward the dog's shoulder. When the dog turns his head to follow the treat, his body should start to roll onto one hip. Click and treat. Repeat 3 to 5 times. (If your dog customarily lies on one hip, skip to step 2.)
2. With the dog in a down, lure the dog onto one hip, then keep moving your lure over the dog's shoulder until the dog puts more of his side, at least part of the rib cage, onto the floor. Click and treat. Repeat 3 to 5 times.
3. With the dog in a down, lure the dog further onto one side, so his shoulder facing the floor is starting to touch down. Click and treat. Repeat 3 to 5 times.

4. With the dog in a down, lure the dog completely onto one side. Click and treat. Repeat 5 times.

Session Two –
5. Repeat step 4 in a new location.
6. Now make the same hand motion, but without any treat in your hand. Click and treat when the dog lies flat on his side. Repeat 3 to 5 times.

7. Change locations and repeat step 6.
8. Change locations again and repeat step 6, but when the dog is on his side, use a lure to position his head flat on its side on the floor. Click when the dog lowers his head toward the ground. Repeat 3 to 5 times. Continue working on getting the head to lie flat on the ground, repeating at each step no more than 5 times. (Hint: It should go quickly if you've already taught the Head down behavior.)

Session Three –
9. Repeat step 8 without a treat in your hand, until the dog lies flat out without the additional hand signal. This should not take many repetitions.
10. Give your initial hand signal, but when the dog lies flat, delay the click for a count of 1. Only click and treat if the dog holds the flat out position with his head on the ground. Repeat 3 times, then raise your count to 2 and repeat 3 times. Raise your count to 3 and repeat 3 times. Raise your count to 4 and repeat 3 times.
11. Bounce around an average of 3. Repeat 10 times.
12. Raise your count to 5 for 3 repetitions, then bounce around an average of 5. Repeat 10 times.

Session Four —
13. When the dog starts to anticipate that you will have him do a dead dog (he lies on his side and puts his head down as soon as you give the hand signal), you're ready to add your verbal cue. With the dog in a sit, say "Bang" or whatever you've chosen, give your hand signal, and click and treat when the dog is on his side with his head on the ground. Pair the verbal cue with the behavior for at least 50 repetitions, starting from a down and changing locations every 10 repetitions, and varying how long the dog has to maintain the position.

Following sessions, work on variability –
14. Continue changing locations, gradually making the surroundings more challenging.
15. Start with the dog in a sit.
16. Start with the dog in a stand.
17. Switch among starting with the dog in a sit, a stand, or a down.
18. Try working while sitting in a chair.

Early Steps: If your dog is reluctant to lie flat on one side, try moving to a more secure, entirely boring location. Some dogs view this as a very vulnerable position, and will resist doing it unless they are sure of their security. Get on the floor with the dog and pet or massage him quietly to help him relax. Some scratching in the little "pocket" under the front of the rear leg may help the dog to lie down and relax. Increase the number of sessions working on getting the dog to lie on his side until he will readily move into the position and stay there without popping back up. See Chapter 4, Relax for Veterinary Exams for more information.

Problem-Solving Tips:
The dog doesn't follow the lure.
- Maybe you're moving it too fast, too far, or not in the right place. Try going a bit more slowly, asking for less, moving it in a different arc. Watch where the dog's head goes and how far he will follow the lure.
- Try changing lures. Maybe your treat isn't enticing enough.
- If you had a difficult time teaching the down, this side position will also be difficult.
- Click and treat even a tiny head movement back toward the shoulder. Break your steps down even smaller and build up very gradually. Be sure to click and treat often or the dog may become stressed or discouraged.
- Are you distracting the dog with movements of your body or other hand? Hold everything else as still as possible. Let him concentrate on the lure.
- Make sure the dog is physically able to bend his body that way – there may be a reason he can't do this!

The dog will follow the lure, but pops right back up or gets up from the down.
- Treat the dog in position. He's likely to pop back up to chew the treat, but delivering it while he's in the desired position helps him understand what is being rewarded.
- Use the "hold still" from Chapter 4 once the dog is on his side. Remember to use your release when you want the dog to get up.
- Have someone else try working with a treat to see if your hand position might be the problem.

Suggested Commands: Bang, Sleep (if you'd rather practice hypnosis than a violent act), Play dead, Dead dog

Suggested Signal: Make your hand into a gun and point your index finger at the dog. For the Sleep alternative, make a hand motion as if you were swinging a pendulum.

Variations: Lure the dog past the "on your side" position to a feet in the air posture. (Note that some dogs can balance well on their backs and some can't.) This makes an even more impressive "dead dog" position. "Shoot" the dog behind you while looking in a mirror – you'll have to train the dog to respond even when you're facing away.

SPEAK

The Final Picture: The dog barks on command and keeps barking until told to stop.

Uses: Good to have on command when you want to discourage someone at your front door. Being able to start the dog barking means you can also work on stopping the dog barking (see Variations). Fun for silly games like having the dog bark for how many fingers you're holding up.

Preparation and Props: As usual, your clicker, treats, a hungry dog, a bridge word. It will be helpful if you know some environmental cues that generally cause your dog to vocalize. It doesn't have to be a bark if your dog doesn't offer a lot of barking – a growl or a whine will do at first. If you don't know any environmental cues, here are some triggers that might work:

> waiting while you fill his food bowl
> trying to get a toy that's under the couch
> playing tug with you
> watching you pick up your car keys
> waiting to go out the front door
> seeing a squirrel out the window
> playing with another dog
> chasing a ball
> you barking at the dog

The Steps Along the Way:

Session One –

1. Have your clicker at the ready and treats handy as frequently as possible so that you have maximum chance of catching any vocalizations your dog makes. If your dog is "barky," wait for barking, but if he is not, accept whines or "humphs" or growls. Click and treat whatever vocalization you get. Try to get in 5 or 6 repetitions, but you have to go with what the dog gives you. With quiet dogs, the click may startle the dog into silence and you will have to wait again. Be especially ready to click and treat in any of the circumstances you think might encourage your dog to make a sound.

CLICK TRICKS

You could use your bridge word instead in the early steps to "capture" those initial sounds, if you're too often caught without your clicker. As the dog starts to vocalize more, switch to your clicker so you can better shape exactly the sound you want.

---

2. Try one of the events you think may convince your dog to vocalize, either from your own experience or from our list. Be ready to click and treat any vocalization. Be careful that you don't click the same non-barking sound for too many repetitions or you will convince the dog that whatever sound he is making is the final picture. Choose the best 3 out of 5 or 5 out of 10 noises that are closer to a bark that the dog makes so that you are shaping toward what you want right from the start.

3. Change locations. Click and treat the best 5 out of 10 noises the dog makes.

Session Two –

4. If you are getting mostly whining (possible if your dog is confused about what you're asking of him), try to use an event that might cause him to growl instead. Playing tug will encourage some dogs to growl, especially if you growl first. Click and treat the best 5 out of 10 repetitions.

5. Change locations. If the last trigger you used worked well, use it again. Click and treat the best 5 out of 10 repetitions.

6. In the same location, wait for the dog to offer a vocalization on his own. If the dog doesn't vocalize, work with triggers that have worked before for another 10 repetitions before trying again. If he does vocalize, jackpot! Repeat 5 times.

Session Three –
7. If you were successful in getting the dog to vocalize without any cue other than yourself in the previous session, warm up with one of your successful triggers, clicking and treating the best 5 out of 10 sounds the dog makes. Then wait for a vocalization without any cue. Repeat 5 times.
8. In a new location, continue shaping toward the vocalization that you want. Don't be too picky and lose the dog – remember, you should be clicking and treating every few seconds. If you want loud, protective barking, work toward that. If you'd rather have howling or mumbling or some other variation, work toward that. Know your goal and how you plan to get there, what the steps are in between. So if your dog is barking, but quietly and you want loud, click and treat the loudest 5 barks out of 10. If he's whining and you want barking, click and treat the 5 out of 10 whines that come the closest to a bark or are least like a whine. Remember to decide before you start to train what you'll be clicking.
9. Change locations and continue shaping toward your version of speak for 10 repetitions.
10. Change locations again and repeat step 8 for 10 repetitions.

Session Four –
11. Now can you predict when your dog will vocalize? Will you be correct at least 80 percent of the time? If so, time to add your cue word. Say "speak" or whatever you've chosen just before you predict your dog will bark. Remember to click and treat when he does. Repeat 5 or 6 times.
12. Change locations and repeat step 11 for 5 repetitions.
13. Continue changing locations and pairing your cue word with the action for at least 50 additional repetitions over the next couple of days.

Following sessions, work on variability –
14. Spring surprise requests to speak on your dog when you're not involved in a formal training session.

15. Give your Speak cue, but wait for a second bark before clicking and treating. Repeat 3 times. Cue and wait for a third bark. Repeat 3 times. Reward varying numbers of barks, so that the dog will keep barking until the click tells him to stop.

Early Steps: If your dog is the strong silent type, don't be at all picky about what sort of sounds you'll reward. Give the dog plenty of time to understand that vocalizing of any type is a rewardable behavior before you ever begin to raise the criteria. Use especially good treats to help keep the dog interested and excited.

Problem-Solving Tips:
The dog doesn't make any sound.
- Are you really listening? You have to be quiet yourself to hear any sort of soft whine.
- Work your way through the suggested environmental cues to see what might get you a sound..
- Carry your clicker and treats with you at all times and be ready to click for any vocalization the dog makes any time. This capturing will take longer, but it may be your only choice if you really can't induce your dog to bark.
- Young dogs may not bark very readily. They often get noisier when they reach 8 to 10 months of age. If you're working with a young silent dog, try again when he's older.

The dog makes one sound, but then just stands and stares at me.
- That's the power of the clicker! The dog wants to earn clicks and treats, but doesn't know what the current rules are. Repeat the same trigger and see if it will get the dog to bark again.
- Try outwaiting the dog. Frustration will often cause a dog to vocalize, and not being able to get you to click is frustrating for the dog.
- Work in single repetitions many times a day. Carry your clicker and click and treat any time the dog vocalizes, or use your bridge.

The dog doesn't stop barking when I click.
- Your trigger is too exciting and is overshadowing your click (for more about overshadowing, see Chapter 7). Use something less exciting.
- Your dog is a natural talker and doesn't need any encouragement. Just capture the speak (and shape Quiet, for your own sanity).

Suggested Commands: Speak, Alert, Who's there, Sound off. For quiet, Shush or Quiet

Suggested Signals: For Speak, hold your hand in a loose fist, fingers pointing toward the dog, then open all your fingers so your hand is spread wide. For Quiet, put your index finger to your lips in a "shush" gesture.

Variations: Once bark is on command, work on "Quiet". Cue the dog to bark several times and click and treat each time. Now don't say anything. Click and treat if the dog doesn't bark for one count. If he starts barking immediately, click and treat when he stops barking long enough to breathe. Build up the length of time the dog needs to be quiet to get a click, using the bounce around technique (see Chapter 2). Introduce the command when you can predict the dog will be quiet. Pair the command with the behavior for at least 50 repetitions.

Teach the dog hand signals for both speak and quiet – remember, it's new signal, old signal, so it would be hand signal, command. Being able to cue the dog without being obvious about it will make a more impressive act to show off your trick, and could be really helpful if you ever feel a little uneasy somewhere and would like the dog to make a fuss.

Teach the dog to howl, whine, or mumble, in addition to barking.

PUT 'EM UP/DANCE

The Final Picture: The dog stands up on his hind legs, either stationary (put 'em up) or moving about (dance)

Uses: As already mentioned, this requires strong musculature in the rear end, and can help keep those muscles toned. Obviously, if you want to have a dancing dog, a la circus dog acts, this is the behavior you want. Small dogs are terribly cute at it, but bigger dogs can be impressive too.

Preparation and Props: A clicker, treats, and your dog. Before you begin this, you want to be sure that your dog doesn't have any structural problems that would make it painful or impossible. Ask your veterinarian if you aren't sure. You could use a lure or a touch stick as alternatives. If you are going to lure, having previously taught Take a Treat Gently will help to preserve your fingers.

SLICK CLICKS

BETTER THAN SEX!
Sophia Yin, DVM, MS, UC Davis

I trained a number of yearling horses using a combination of clicker training and natural horsemanship, to prepare them for UC Davis' horse auction. After they were successfully trained and sold, the professor overseeing the project wanted to learn more about clicker training. I suggested working with the stallions, as I'd never worked with stallions before. She immediately told me that stallions are too dangerous and have no attention span, and insisted we work with the mares instead.

But I went ahead and trained the stallions with a friend. We worked with four stallions and found that they learned just as quickly as the mares. They all learned to associate the click with food within three 5-minute sessions in one day. By the third day, they had all learned to be polite about taking treats. And as for attention span, during one session, a mare in a corral eight feet from where we were working was coming into season during our second day of training. She put on her most coy face and displayed by urinating for the breeding stallion I was working with. At first, he started getting excited and fixating on her. He was ready to breed her. Until I walked away. Then he turned around and came over to me to be trained. He chose to be trained for a few bits of grain, over ogling a mare coming into heat.

The Steps Along the Way:
Session One –
1. With the dog in a standing position on all fours, hold your hand target above the dog's nose, raise it high enough that he has to stretch up to touch it, say "touch," and click and treat when the dog extends his neck to touch your palm. Repeat 4 or 5 times.
2. Move the target a little higher so that the dog has to rear up a little higher, so that his front feet come off the ground, say "touch," and click and treat when the dog touches. Repeat 4 or 5 times.
3. Rather than starting at the dog's nose, hold the hand target out at the same height as in step 2 and say "touch." Click and treat the dog while his front feet are off the ground. Repeat 4 or 5 times.

155

4. Change locations and repeat step 3.

Session Two –
5. Start at the same height at which you ended your last session and repeat 3 times.
6. Hold your target slightly higher, so that the dog has to rise higher on his rear legs, say "touch," click and treat when he touches. Repeat 4 or 5 times.
7. Hold your target just slightly higher. Continue as in step 6. Repeat 4 or 5 times.

Session Three –
8. In a new location, hold your target at the height at which you finished the last session and proceed as in step 6. Repeat 4 or 5 times.
9. If your dog hasn't reached a balance point yet, continue gradually raising your target until he can maintain the rearing position. Repeat 3 to 5 times at each level.
10. When your dog is rearing high enough that you think it's possible for him to balance – for most dogs, at something like a 60 degree angle from horizontal – delay your click and treat for a count of 1. Raise the target, say "touch," and click and treat only if the dog remains in the rearing position for the count. Repeat 5 or 6 times.

11. When you have been successful in keeping the dog upright for one second, delay your click and treat for two seconds. Repeat 3 to 5 times. Now raise your count to 3 seconds and repeat 3 to 5 times.
12. Change locations and bounce around an average of 3. Repeat 10 times.

Session Four –
13. In the same location as you ended your last session, delay your click and treat for a count of 4. Repeat 3 to 5 times. Raise your count to 5 seconds. Repeat 3 to 5 times.
14. Bounce around an average of 5. Repeat 10 times.
15. Now convert the touch into a hand signal. Hold your hand higher than the dog can reach it. Say "touch," count anywhere from 1 to 5, and click and treat for remaining balanced on his back legs. Repeat 5 times.
16. When you can predict that your dog will hold the rearing position for any of your counts up to 5 at least 8 out of 10 repetitions, it's time to add your verbal cue. Remember, it's new cue (verbal), old cue (hand signal), action, click and treat. Continue to pair the cue with the action for at least 50 repetitions, changing locations every 10 repetitions and varying how long the dog must hold the position.

Following sessions, work on variability –
17. Work with the dog to your side rather than in front.
18. Work on gaining distance from your dog – it's much more impressive. (See Chapter 7 if you need a hint.)

Early Steps: If your dog has trouble rearing up, first ascertain that there are no physical difficulties. Then try working from a sit. At first, lure the dog into a begging position – this is good for strengthening the hps and lower back muscles needed to stand up. Just hold your target hand lower, so the dog only has to lift his front legs, into a sitting up position. After the dog learns to balance his body, you can use your hand target or a lure to have him rise up out of the sit.

Problem-Solving Tips:
The dog doesn't follow the target.
▪ Has the dog been reprimanded for jumping up? He may be understandably reluctant to offer this behavior. You'll have to really

encourage him and reward any little effort, such as lifting a front foot, at first.
- Have him "Paw" a target held at his chest level in front of him, and gradually raise the height of the target.
- Use better treats.
- Take smaller steps, asking for only tiny changes.

The dog will rear up, but won't hold the position.
- He may not have the necessary muscle tone. See "Early Steps" for a way to develop those muscles.
- He may not have very good balance. Moving the target so that the dog is taking small steps forward rather than standing in one place may help him keep himself centered.
- Ask for less – use a count of 1 for more repetitions and build up very gradually.

The dog tries to leap up rather than rearing up.
- You're probably holding the target too high too quickly. Start with it directly over the dog's head so that the only option for the dog is to put his head back and pick up his front feet.

Suggested Commands: Dance, Put 'em up, High

Suggested Signal: Hold one hand out in front of your body, palm facing the floor, at a height where the dog would have to stand up to touch it

Variations: Have the dog move rather than stand in one place, or turn in circles in the classic doggie dance. Dance together – when you move forward, the dog moves backward, and vice versa. Have him wave with alternating front legs while he's balanced on his rear legs. Have him push a cart or a stroller while walking on his hind legs.

SKATEBOARDING

The Final Picture: The dog puts both front feet and one rear foot on the skateboard (though really large dogs may only be able to fit either both front feet or one front and one rear foot), and pushes with the other rear foot.

Uses: A great behavior for wowing your audiences. Enlist your friends and have a parade group of skateboarding dogs.

Preparation and Props: A clicker, treats, your dog, and you'll need a skateboard. You can find plain, low-class ones for $20, more or less. There are even smaller models good for smaller dogs. You could use a touch stick to teach this, or a paw target, or a food lure, or you could shape it. We'll shape in these directions, but feel free to try other methods if they appeal to you.

The Steps Along the Way:
Session One –
1. Put the skateboard down between you and your dog. Secure it so it doesn't move. When the dog looks at the skateboard, click and treat. Repeat 5 times.

CLICK TRICKS

It will help for you to have the board stabilized, either with blocks under the wheels, or by using your own foot to keep it from rolling, while you work on getting the dog into position. Some dogs aren't affected by the movement at all, while others may be frightened by it, and reluctant to touch the board. You will be removing the blocks and controlling how far the board can move in later steps.

---

2. Wait for the dog to touch the skateboard with any part of his body. Click and treat. Repeat 3 to 5 times.
3. Wait for the dog to touch the skateboard with either front leg or front foot. Click and treat. Repeat 3 to 5 times. If the dog places a foot on the skateboard, jackpot.
4. Wait for the dog to touch the skateboard with either front foot. Click and treat 3 to 5 times.
5. Wait for the dog to put either front foot on the skateboard. Click and treat. Try to deliver your treats to the dog while he is still on the skateboard.
6. If the dog keeps the foot on the skateboard, click and treat for that, up to 5 times. Repeat 3 to 5 times.

Session Two –
7. Now work on getting the second front foot on the skateboard. Wait for the dog to put a front foot on the skateboard and put weight on that foot. Click and treat. Repeat 3 to 5 times.
8. Now wait for the dog to have his weight on the foot on the skateboard and lift the other front foot, even slightly. Click and treat. Repeat 3 to 5 times.

CLICK TRICKS

If you're working with a "clicker-savvy" dog – if you've worked through the book to here rather than skipping to this chapter – shaping can go a lot faster than our step-by-step instructions. If your dog puts both front feet on the skateboard as soon as you put it on the floor, click, treat, and rejoice! If he repeats that behavior several times, that's where you can start. And that's why you need to have the final picture of what you want, and the steps to get there, firmly in mind before you begin. Otherwise, you'd have to stop and figure out where to go from where the dog started.

If the dog puts both front feet on the skateboard initially, but then just stares at it after that, start at step 1, looking at the board – don't stand around waiting to click and treat both feet on the board. In other words, one repetition or two does not make a pattern.

---

9. Wait for the dog to put one front foot on the skateboard and raise the other foot higher than in the previous step. Click and treat. Repeat 3 to 5 times.
10. Wait for the dog to put one front foot on the skateboard and touch the board with the other front foot. Click and treat. Repeat 3 to 5 times.

Session Three —
11. Wait for the dog to put both front feet on the skateboard. Click and treat. Repeat 10 times.
12. If the dog remains with both front feet on the board, continue clicking and treating every 1 second for a total of 10 clicks. Repeat 10 times.
13. Now repeat step 12, but click when the dog moves either rear foot. Repeat 3 to 5 times. Jackpot if the dog puts the rear foot on the

skateboard. Ignore any repetitions where the front feet come off the board (do not click them).

14. Click when the dog has both front feet on the skateboard and the correct rear foot (the one nearer the skateboard) moves. Repeat 5 times.

CLICK TRICKS

If you have trouble seeing what the dog's feet are doing, it may help for you to sit on the floor so you are nearer the action. Or, you could have someone else concentrate on the dog's feet and deliver the click at the appropriate time.

---

15. Repeat step 14, but wait for the rear foot to be lifted higher. Repeat 3 to 5 times, then advance to the next increment (the rear foot touching the skateboard) and repeat 3 to 5 times. Keep advancing until you have one rear foot on the skateboard with the front feet. Repeat 10 times.

Session Four –
16. Wait for the dog to put both front feet and one rear foot on the skateboard. Click and treat. Repeat 3 to 5 times
17. Repeat step 16 but delay your click and treat for a count of 1. Click and treat only if the dog's feet remain on the skateboard. Repeat 3 to 5 times – the dog can either remain with his feet on the board or get off the board between repetitions. Raise your count to 2 and repeat 3 to 5 times.
18. Raise your count to 3 and repeat step 16 for 3 to 5 repetitions. Raise your count to 4 and repeat. Raise your count to 5 and repeat.
19. Bounce around an average of 3. Repeat 10 times

Session Five –
20. In the same location, unblock the skateboard's wheels so that it can roll a couple of inches forward or backward (place the blocks a couple of inches in front of the front wheels and behind the back wheels, so the wheels can make one revolution in either direction). Wait for the

dog to put even one foot on the board and make the board move. We are introducing movement, so we need to relax all other criteria temporarily. Repeat 8 to 10 times.

21.   Wait for the dog to have a foot on the board, make it move, and keep the foot on the board for the duration of this small movement. Click and treat while the dog's foot is on the skateboard. Repeat 3 to 5 times.

22.   Now wait for two feet to be on the skateboard when it moves. Click and treat for keeping the feet on the skateboard through the movement. Repeat 3 to 5 times. If necessary, reshape getting two feet on the board (see steps 7-11).

23.   Now wait for three feet to be on the skateboard when it moves, reshaping if necessary (see steps 13-16).

Session Six –

24.   Move the blocks about six inches from the wheels, so the wheels can roll about two revolutions. Wait until the dog's three feet are on the board, the dog moves the board, and stays on. Repeat 5 times.

25.   Unblock the wheels farther, so the board can roll about a foot. Click and treat for the dog taking a step with the back foot on the ground, keeping the other feet on the skateboard. Repeat 5 times.

26.   Gradually increase how far the board must move before you click and treat (work in increments of 3 to 6 inches, depending somewhat on the size of your dog), rewarding each distance 3 to 5 times.

27.   Work up to being able to move the skateboard across your kitchen.

28.   Can you predict that the dog will place his feet on the skateboard and push it along? Time to name the behavior. Say "Ride" or whatever you have chosen, wait for the dog to move the board, and click and treat. Pair the cue with the behavior for at least 50 repetitions, varying how far the dog must move the board, and changing locations every 10 repetitions. Be aware that different surfaces will affect how the board moves.

Following sessions, work on variability –

29.   Move to different rooms or outdoor spaces with the skateboard. The dog will have to push harder on surfaces where it's harder to move the board.

30.   Vary where you are in relation to the dog and the skateboard.
31.   Borrow a different skateboard to use, or decorate yours differently.

Early Steps: Insecure dogs may be unwilling to approach the skateboard. Leave it out in the room where you and your dog spend most of your time and allow the dog to become used to its presence. Practice some behaviors the dog knows a little distance from the skateboard, gradually moving closer. Keep the skateboard wheels blocked to keep it from moving until you are sure the dog is perfectly happy working with the skateboard.

Play "101 things to do with a canvas bag" game (see Chapter 1) with the dog and the skateboard.

CLICK TRICKS

You can teach the dog, as a separate exercise, to stand on moving surfaces by creating a "Buja" board (named after the person who invented it). It's a 3-foot square plywood board with a hole in the middle large enough to rest on a tennis ball. Sprinkle the top with sand when you paint it, to give it texture so it's not too slick for the dog. Start with the board on a squishy ball on a carpeted surface and gradually use a stiffer ball and a harder surface. Shape the dog for putting first one, then two, then three, then four feet on. Click and treat when the board moves and the dog doesn't shy away. Build up to the dog balancing on the board.

Problem-Solving Tips:
The dog won't keep his feet on the skateboard.
- Make sure the skateboard wheels are blocked so that it can't move. Some boards also move sideways on the wheel axles, so having something beneath the board, almost enough to lift it off the ground, will keep it more still in the beginning.
- Target the dog onto the skateboard and delay the click for 1 second (then 2 seconds, 3 seconds, etc.).
- Deliver the treat in position.
- Work on "feet up" on a variety of other objects as well. Use your hand touch to target the dog's front feet up onto a picnic bench, tree stump,

your leg while you're sitting down – whatever is the right height for the dog and NOT something you definitely don't want dog feet on.

The dog jumps over the skateboard without touching it.
- Spend more time working around the skateboard at the beginning.
- Click and treat for touching any part of his body to the skateboard.
- Work more slowly and quietly, reinforcing calm behavior.
- Have the dog sit close to the skateboard, facing it, and ask him to wave. Click and treat if his foot touches the board.

The dog does okay until you let the skateboard move, then jumps off.
- Are you asking for too much too quickly? Only let the wheels move half a revolution or less at first, and increase very gradually. Use blocks of wood on both sides of the wheels only an inch or two from the wheels, so the skateboard contacts the wood after rolling a very short distance and stops.
- Work with the skateboard on a rug rather than a smooth surface so it will only tend to roll a little.
- Teach the dog to push the skateboard with his nose or foot, rewarding movement. The dog controls the movement, so it isn't so scary.

Suggested Commands: Board, Ride

Variations: You could use the same general training to teach the dog to "roll out the barrel" or roll a ball. Have the dog stand with all four feet on the board while you pull it, or going downhill. Teach the dog to ski or surf.

CHAPTER 6
Clicks of the Trade

If you accomplished the training in Chapter 4 but still have some issues with your dog, we're here to help. We would be remiss if we didn't point out that we can't see your dog and your particular problem, and you may need some one-on-one, face-to-face help from a humane local trainer or behaviorist (see Resources for help in locating a trainer). But the exercises we offer here will certainly do no harm, and may well solve your problem.

In this chapter we'll look at excitable dogs, fearful dogs, noisy dogs, and pushy dogs, and see what we can do about them. Behavior modification is an excellent way to put your clicker to work, and just might be the most valuable training you'll ever do.

The one thing we can guarantee about behavior problems is that they WILL get worse if you ignore them or hope that the dog will "grow out of them." It is also worth reminding you that you should move forward slowly with any fear or aggression-related problem, always working within the dog's comfort zone. Trying to push the dog beyond what he's comfortable with can quickly make your problem MUCH WORSE. And it's also worth reminding you that dogs are carnivores, and therefore capable of inflicting great damage with their teeth -- you want to have respect for that. If you're at all concerned with how to proceed, working with a private trainer will be the best investment for you and your dog. Choose a trainer who uses reward-based training methods (including counter-conditioning and desensitization - see Chapter 7 for more information on these techniques) to help the dog overcome his fears.

The good news is that clicker-training can often have a significant positive impact on problem behaviors, with the most likely side effect being no change at all in the behavior. ALWAYS consult with a trained behaviorist who can work individually with you and your dog if you don't see improvement within two to four weeks of daily work on these problems.

It's best to nip these problems in the bud, so if any of these fit your dog, get out your clicker and turn to the exercise that best fits your needs. Take a deep breath and try to relax. You already know this stuff works, so have faith, take your time, and you may find yourself and your dog a whole lot happier with each other. Remember, if you feel like you're in over your head, consult with someone who can help you and your dog. We'll begin with a little bit of a discussion of how you got to this place. We also need to discuss more technical stuff, so bear with us. We're adding a section to our Road Map for the behaviors in this chapter – "What's in it for the Dog?" These are suggestions for how the behavior might have some built in rewards you'll need to be aware of. Notice that we haven't broken these behaviors into sessions. You should progress at whatever speed is best for your dog, staying at a step for as many sessions as you need to. Review the previous step a bit with a couple of clicks and treats each time you start a new session. Finally, we refer to a bridge word throughout these instructions. Refer to Chapter 7 for more information on what that is and how to use it.

We will cover:

Barking at the window (or door)
Calming excitable dogs (focus, focus, focus)
Possession problems and resource guarding - give me that (bone, toy, ball, remote control, kleenex)!
Confidence-building exercises - getting over fears
Creating an interest in toys – life is fun!
Object fears – approach and touch objects
Noise fears
People and physical contact fears – pet me!
Modifying dog-to-dog interactions

WHY DOES MY DOG DO THAT?

Remember that a main principle of clicker training is that what gets rewarded gets repeated. For your dog, these behaviors that you find obnoxious are somehow being rewarded. The scary person leaves when your dog barks or growls at the door. Or you stroke your dog while he's lunging at the neighborhood child (which may be how the dog perceives things, even though you think you are just "holding him back" and "calming him down"). A key to solving behavior problems is understanding how the behavior is rewarding for the dog. You are going to need to change the reward for the dog, and substitute a behavior you like that will still be rewarding for the dog.

Take a look at what your dog gets out of the behavior. It can even be helpful to have someone else who is not emotionally invested in the problem watch the dog. Ask yourself these questions: When does the behavior start? What is the trigger and how close does it have to be before my dog reacts? How specific is the trigger (i.e., is it all dogs, or just white dogs walking toward me that my dog reacts to?)

What does my dog do in response? Make your answer more specific than "he's aggressive" or "he's afraid" - what form does it take? Is the dog lunging, growling, snapping, barking, hiding behind you? How serious is it? Has the dog bitten someone? How hard was the bite? If your dog has ALREADY tried to make contact with his teeth, whether that was a "snap" (no teeth on the person, but an "air bite") or a "nip" or a puncture, you need to work with someone who is a professional to solve this problem. Remember that practice makes perfect. The more "nips" your dog gets in, the better he will get at it until he ends up being killed.

What happens when my dog reacts? Do I yell at or grab the dog, does the person move away or leave?

What stops the behavior? (This can be a clue to what is rewarding for the dog.)

What do I WANT the dog to do? Phrase it in terms of what you would like the dog to do, not stop doing. For example, "Instead of barking at the window when people walk by, I want my dog to come to me and sit quietly." This is different from "I want the dog to stop barking at the window." The first sentence identifies behavior that can be rewarded, the second does not.

Give the dog an alternative to what he was doing that isn't compatible with the problem behavior. The behavior you want can then be rewarded (and therefore controlled) by you forever after. For example, if lunging at other dogs isn't good, what is? Sitting quietly while they pass by would be one alternative. (You'll have to work up to sitting quietly, of course. See our last behavior in this chapter for more information on how to shape this.) But he can't both be sitting quietly and lunging - they are incompatible.

The more desirable behaviors you reward while clicker training your dog, the more behaviors he has in his repertoire, and the less likely he will be to engage in undesirable behaviors. If the undesirable behaviors no longer have a reward built in (which we'll take care of as part of the training) and the dog has a substitute behavior that WILL be rewarded, the undesirable behaviors start to disappear. This is the principle of extinction - read more about it in Chapter 7. You could also shape the behavior into a more acceptable form. For example, teach the dog to dig in a specific area for toys and treats so that he stops digging haphazardly in your yard. But it's essentially the same thing - you've given the dog something to do that still offers a worthwhile reward for him.

COUNTER CONDITIONING - NOW AVAILABLE FOR ALL HAIR TYPES!

Counter conditioning essentially involves changing the dog's emotional reaction to something. (At least, this is what we think is happening based on observing body language – we can't ask the dog.) This method is very effective with fear-based problems (and really, almost all aggression problems are fear-based). So, for example, if in the past the presence of a child meant something painful was going to happen to the dog (tail-pulling, ear-grabbing, isolation or collar-correcting), the dog understandably would prefer that children not be around. He's learned that barking and lunging makes children go away. Having them go away is rewarding, so he continues to bark and lunge. And children go away. We can change that association. If every time a child is visible the dog's favorite treats magically appear from your pocket, his favorite toy gets thrown or you roll on the ground being silly, then pretty soon a child appearing means that something fun is about to happen -- it predicts it just like a clicker predicts a treat. Now, you can't just start by taking the dog to the school grounds and throwing a toy around. You have to start with the least distressing level and gradually build up the association. So, you might start inside the house at your front window during the time school lets out in your neighborhood. Every time a child appears, you drop a piece of steak on the floor. The dog quickly figures out that child = steak. After a couple of days (or weeks!) of practice, the dog starts to look for children going by the window and comes to you, anticipating a juicy tidbit each time they appear. Now you can put the dog on leash and stand on your porch, building the same association. Then move to the middle of your walkway, and so on. Eventually you just might be able to have the dog around kids and have it be a pleasant experience for everyone.

While we're on the subject of kids, we need to discuss safety issues. The behaviors we chose for this chapter are pretty low risk in terms of creating a potential biting situation. But if you decide to build on them, please exercise caution. Be particularly careful when the object of your dog's concern isn't you. Dogs can do tremendous emotional and physical damage with a bite. We would hate for the recipient to be an unsuspecting child (or adult) who trusted you to keep them safe. Never assume that any dog will be safe - ANY dog under the wrong circumstances will bite. And, we need to mention again, when you're in over your head, seek the help of someone who is knowledgeable about dog behavior to help you work through a tough situation.

Now that you have an idea why you might be having some of these problems, let's get to work on them!

BARKING AT THE WINDOW (OR DOOR)

The Final Picture: The dog comes to check in with you, without barking, when someone walks by the front window. You can train just a come, or come with a sit.

Note that while we don't allow our dogs to bark at passersby, we do allow them to bark when someone rings the doorbell or knocks on the door. Then they have to be quiet when we tell them, or the door doesn't open. (Our friends understand this, and will wait on the porch, but sometimes we miss signing for UPS deliveries! During your training, you can put a sign on the door that says "Hang on, I'm training my dog" if you don't want to risk missing any visitors.) If you need help with teaching the dog to sit when the door opens, check out Sit Stay for Greetings in Chapter 4, and Speak/Quiet in Chapter 5. You could also train the dog to be quiet when someone knocks on the door, although this is a significantly harder variation.

Uses: You already know what you need it for, but we want to point out that allowing your dog to bark uncontrolled at the window at passersby is not just a noise problem, but can actually increase or create aggression toward people and dogs.

Preparation and Props: Dog, SUPER treats (we're talking garlic flavored chicken, steak, cheese tortellini, hot dogs, liverwurst, cheese), and your clicker. Check In from Chapter 3 and Come from Chapter 2 are good foundation behaviors for the dog to have under his belt, but not required. Don't feed the dog at least 8-12 hours prior to a session for the first two weeks of working on this behavior. Keep the dog away from any area where he could bark at people passing by during the weeks you are working on this problem (remember, practice makes perfect!) You want to make sure you limit what he is practicing.

What's in it for the Dog? Barking at the window is fun; you come to check it out and interact with the dog (yelling is interaction, don't forget!); you may have rewarded it earlier by praising the dog (only now it's out of control) or cooing at him ("it's okay, don't be worried"); those scary people run away when the dog barks (especially delivery people -- remember the dog doesn't know they only planned to be there for a short time anyway!); movement-oriented breeds such as herding dogs (Border Collies, Shelties), and protection breeds (Rotties, Boxers, German Shepherds) may react because of a hard-wired genetic component to their behavior.

The Steps Along the Way:
1. Pick a time when you know there will be some activity going by your window. Summer evenings are good, when there are likely to be a lot of people out walking. Early mornings or after work are also good. Or enlist a friend to walk back and forth in front of your window, if you need to. Get comfortable in a chair away from the window - you're going to be there for a while. Each time someone appears at the edge of your property, drop a treat on the floor (no click necessary at this point). What does the dog do? If he notices the treat immediately and goes to eat it while the person is walking by, perfect! Give him a second and even a third treat while he's right there next to you. If he doesn't come to get it until after they've left, that's okay too, but he only gets one treat for that. If he never notices it because he's so agitated, put him on leash, tie the leash to something sturdy close by you, and drop the treat right in front of his nose. Make the treat more enticing if you need to. Your timing of the treat is important, even if the dog doesn't notice at first. You want it to coincide with the appearance of a person at the edge of your property. Don't try to stop the barking or

control the dog (that's why you're not holding on to the leash). Stop the session when the dog has received 30 treats. Remain at this step until the dog looks for a treat while the person is still visible in front of your property — whether or not he barks.

2.   Sit in a different part of the room. Now you are going to give the dog multiple treats from your hand while a person walks by. Make the treats unavailable (keep them in a container) until a person appears, then offer them to the dog during the entire time the person is walking by. As soon as the person disappears, the opportunity to get treats is gone. What we're doing here is making the treats available for a limited time. After that, "the bar is closed," even if the dog does the behavior. This is what will impact the barking later on. If the dog doesn't notice you are offering a treat, don't say anything to the dog, just quietly put the treat back in the container, or eat it yourself. Then go back to step 1 for a while. Feed treats rapidly (1 treat per second) while the person is visible and the dog is near you. The dog will interrupt his barking and start to come for the treats earlier and earlier, or may get his treat, bark at the window, then come and get another treat. Repeat until the dog has received 50 treats, then end the session. At each new session, wait longer between the delivery of treats (i.e., 1 treat every 2 seconds, then 1 treat every 3 seconds, etc.) Remain at this step until the dog comes to you as soon as someone appears and remains with you until they are gone, with at least 3 seconds between each treat delivered. The dog may still be barking while he is eating treats. Don't worry about that at this step as long as he remains close to you.

3.   Time how long it takes someone to walk from one side of your property to the other. We will now shorten the amount of time the treats are available for the dog. This, combined with clicking for quiet, will get rid of the barking, because the treats will only be available for a limited time. The dog won't be able to bark AND get treats.

    If it takes an average of 10 seconds for someone to walk across your property, you are going to offer treats rapid-fire for the first 9 seconds, pause, then click and treat the last second if there is NO barking during that last second. The treats are available rapid-fire for the first 9 seconds only. If he doesn't immediately come to you, he shortens the amount of time he gets continuously fed. (If it takes longer or shorter for someone to cross your property, adjust accordingly.) The dog will learn best if it takes a long time for a person to cross your property, so if you can corral someone into helping you with this step, use them! Repeat 5 times, then continuous feed for one second less, and click and treat one additional second of quiet. In our example of 10 seconds, you would now be feeding for 8 seconds, then waiting two seconds, clicking and treating if there is no barking during the last two seconds. Practice at each level for 5 repetitions, then reduce the amount of continuous feeding by one second and add one second to the clicked and treated quiet time.

When you get to 5 seconds of rapid-fire feeding followed by 5 seconds of quiet, you will click quiet behavior multiple times as you add more seconds to it, varying for a count of 1, 2, or 3 when you click and treat. So it would look like this: rapid-fire feeding (at least 10 treats) for 5 seconds, then 1 second of quiet, click/treat, 3 seconds quiet, click/treat, 1 second quiet, click/treat. Continue to reduce the amount of continuous feeding and add time to the quiet, 1 second at a time. Click and treat every 1, 2, or 3 seconds during the quiet time. Restart your count if the dog barks before he gets clicked. End the session when the dog has received 20 treats. Each time you start a session, review at the previous level for at least 5 click/treats. Continue at this step until the dog is quiet while the person crosses your property, even if he barked upon first sighting the passerby.

4. Now reduce the number of clicks the dog gets for being quiet by gradually upping your count before clicking, using the bouncing method described in earlier chapters and in Chapter 7. So if he was getting an average of 10 clicks initially, gradually reduce it, so that he gets 4 clicks randomly spaced during that 10 seconds, and so on, staying at each new step for at least 5 click/treats. Continue at this step until the dog comes to you in anticipation of getting a treat when someone appears and remains quietly with you, with only two or three clicks and treats.

CLICK TRICKS

Remember to always deliver a reward (a treat in this case) when you click, even if we don't specifically indicate in the instructions. These instructions are lengthy, and we're just trying to shorten them up where we can.

5. The dog might bark initially, then be quiet for the remainder of the time. If so, you'll need another step. For this step, only the quiet time preceded by NO barking is clicked and treated. Immediately click/treat the appearance of a person with no barking, then click at two other points during their passing, varying how long you wait for the second and third click. Your timing must be impeccable for this step. If you waited too long to click and the dog barks, cheerfully say "ooops, too bad!" and leave the room, taking the treats with you. If the dog follows you, great! Just ignore him. Return to the room when the person passing is gone. The dog gets another chance the next time a person walks by. If you continue to have problems, try timing your click just before the person appears (the dog knows they are there anyway!). Repeat until 20 treats are delivered. Continue at this step until you have no barking (not even a peep) at least 80% of the time when someone appears in front of the window.

6. Now we'll teach the dog to come find you to collect his treat. Stand at the far edge of the room you started working in. The dog at this point should assume that the appearance of a person means you'll be delivering treats, and come to you in anticipation (if not, go back to step 4 until he does). As soon as he reaches you, click/treat, then click at least two other times while he's with you (varying how long between each click). After each repetition, go two feet farther away. Repeat until you deliver 20 treats, then end the session. Continue at this step until you are in the room you spend most of your time in (for us, that's the home office down the hall).

7. Add the sit if you want to. When the dog comes to find you, tell him to Sit, then give him a treat and release him. He gets a couple of extra treats if he remains with you after he gets released from the sit. Continue at this step until the sit is automatic. You don't need the clicker any longer at this point, by the way.

8. Pay attention when the dog comes to you and sits so you can be sure and reward the behavior (with treats, petting and games) as often as possible. You won't know that someone has crossed in front of the window since you won't be in a position to see any more. We always assume the dog has made the correct choice if he comes running without being called, and he gets rewarded for it. It's a good idea to occasionally do tune ups where there is a lot of activity in front of the window and you are in the room to click not barking. It's also a good

idea to change rooms periodically so the behavior holds no matter where you happen to be.

Early Steps:
If you can't get the dog to eat a treat no matter what you do because he is so agitated, try working as your first step in a room where he can hear people go by but not see them. If you are still not getting any response, you need to talk to a behaviorist for help with this problem.

Problem-Solving Tips:
Your canine genius figured out running to you in your office is a good way to get treats from you, even though no one is walking by your house!
- Only reward during times of day when you know people are likely to be walking by. Behavior that is randomly rewarded like this – not every repetition gets a reward — will still be maintained.
- Have someone walk back and forth during a time that you specify, so you will know the dog's behavior should be rewarded.
- Periodically sit in the same room and reward quiet attention on you when people walk by, and ignore quiet attention on you when no one is there.

Suggested Commands: None, train as an automatic behavior

Variations: Have the dog be quiet when someone knocks on the door by enlisting a friend to do it over and over, following the steps outlined above. Add different people as the dog begins to get the idea.

CALMING EXCITABLE DOGS (FOCUS, FOCUS, FOCUS)

The Final Picture: Whatever the dog wants, he looks to you first for permission, and does a "default behavior" such as sit, down, touch, paw or an easy trick. The more intense the distraction, the more intense will be his focus on you. Sometimes he gets what he wants, sometimes he doesn't.

Uses: This is great for a dog that likes to chase animals, is highly distracted or distressed by the world.

Preparation and Props: Decide what your default behavior will be and train that first, with NO distractions. The longer he has been doing that behavior, the better your success will be. For our example, we'll use a hand touch. See Chapters 2, 3 and 5 for other behaviors. You can use a clicker, or substitute your bridge word where click is indicated (see Chapter 7), to mark the correct behaviors for this exercise. For this behavior, we'll indicate specifically when you should offer a treat (as opposed to some other reward) after clicking. You'll need treats, toys, and a variety of other rewards for your dog. If you've taught Check in from Chapter 3, it'll make this exercise go quickly, but it's not required. You'll need to create a "table of doggie distractions" – a list of at least 10 items in each of 10 categories that distract your dog, ranked from low distraction to high distraction. To create your table, start with the things that distract your dog the most and work backward Ask other people if you need help. Keep in mind that distance can change where a distraction falls on the table. We've given you a couple of suggestions to get you started. For example, a level one for Mandy's boxer is a small leaf on the ground. She'll sniff it to see if it's a treat she missed, but not hang around to investigate beyond that. A level 10 is a stranger coming toward Mandy with a dog Twister doesn't know. (Level 12 if that dog is off-leash!) You'll also need the Watch from Chapter 1. Don't let your dog have anything for free while you're trying to establish this behavior.

1	2	3	4	5	6	7	8	9	10
leaf on ground	bug crawl- ing	leaf blow- ing	old toy on floor	other dog in sight	hand in open bait bag	horse drop- ping	bicycl- ist	on- leash dog	off- leash dog
plane flying over	flag flap- ping	car door closing	doorbell ringing on tv	closed contain- er of treats	some- one missing fr pack	crowds of spec- tators	cat running past	person playing with cat toy	squirrel chat- tering
clean spoon on floor	waves crash- ing	wind blowing through trees		rustling paper		young girls playing nearby		young boys playing nearby	person sitting eating hot dog

(and so you would continue, until you had 10 full lines of 10 levels of distraction)

What's in it for the Dog? Some dogs are highly prey-driven — you'll know this is your dog because he's been doing since he was a young puppy, chasing everything that moves whether or not it's alive. This exercise will have an impact, although success may be limited. Other dogs may be reacting from fear that something can hurt them. Excitability and hyperactivity can be a sign of a stressed dog (see chapter 1 for a more thorough description). The dog is afraid, he wigs out, and you respond by removing him from the situation – he is rewarded for his fearful behavior. Focusing on something to do and removing ALL correction from the situation is very successful with these dogs. Or the behavior may be a combination of both reasons. Believe it or not, high-activity dogs are the BEST dogs to work with; they quickly learn to focus on the behavior they need to get what they want.

The Steps Along the Way:

1. Start by asking for your default behavior (in our example, a hand touch) before anything the dog wants to do or have. Some examples include: going outside, coming inside, getting his leash put on for a walk, getting the leash taken off, getting into the car, getting out of the car, getting out of a kennel, getting his dish put down, getting his water bowl put down, greeting a person, greeting a dog, or getting a toy thrown. Think of as many examples as you can, and use the hand touch throughout the day as often as possible. Bridge or click when the dog touches, then immediately allow him to do what he wanted or get what he wanted to get. The dog will start to anticipate that you will ask for the hand touch before anything he wants. When the touch is immediate (80% reliable) upon presenting your hand and/or giving the command, regardless of how exciting the opportunity to do something else that's available, go to step 2.

CLICK TRICKS

If you haven't practiced substituting other fun real-life rewards for food, you may initially need to say your release word in addition to your click or bridge word. Your timing for giving the reward to the dog needs to be as immediate as it would with a treat. Also be sure that your DOG thinks what you're offering is a reward! (If your dog doesn't like to leave the house, going for a walk is NOT a reward just because you think it should be). These types of rewards can be even more powerful than food with a dog who is highly distracted. If your dog isn't yet interested in these rewards, see the section on Confidence-building Exercises for help.

2. Now add attention to your "please may I" default behavior. To do this, set up a situation where you have something the dog wants that you can quickly give him. For example, you are standing at the door with the dog ready and eager to go outside (don't do this if your dog isn't yet housetrained - it's not fair to make a puppy wait for that!) Say Watch once (or your command for that behavior). Wait patiently as long as it takes to get the Watch, then immediately offer your hand and/or give the Touch command when the dog glances at you. When the dog touches, click, then open the door. Continue at this step with a variety of real-life rewards until the dog anticipates that he has to look at you to get a chance to touch, which then gets him what he wants. In other words, he looks at you <u>before</u> you give the command to Watch about 80% of the time.

CLICK TRICKS

Offering the opportunity to do another behavior (which is then rewarded) on completion of a first behavior is called the Premack Principle. Read more about it in Chapter 7.

---

3. Now vary how many times the dog has to Touch before you click and let him get the reward. Start with 1 or 2 touches, add another touch after every 5 reps, varying the number required each time, until the dog will reliably touch up to five times before getting clicked and rewarded. For example, "watch," touch, touch, click, reward.
4. Get out your table of doggie distractions. You'll also need portable rewards such as the opportunity to go for a walk, treats or toys that the dog likes. Starting with the lowest level distraction, present the distraction, cue the Watch, cue the Touch when he watches, then click and reward with a low-level reward for touching (ie, not something they would kill for, but something that they're mildly interested in.) Cue another solid behavior, such as sit, praise the dog when he sits. Cue Watch, Touch, click/reward. Sometimes ask for the Sit and sometimes for Watch, Touch in a varying pattern. For example,
    sit/praise,
    watch/touch/touch/click/reward,
    watch/touch/click/reward,
    watch/touch/touch/touch/click/reward,
    sit/praise,

sit/praise,
watch/touch/click/reward,
sit/praise,
watch/touch/touch/click/reward.

Click and reward ONLY the Touch behavior paired with the Watch. The reason for doing this is that you'll need other behaviors out in public with the dog besides Watch and Touch, but we want Touch to be VERY strong for the dog. Repeat until the dog has been clicked and rewarded at least 5 times, then pick some other distraction that's a level one for your dog. Continue with this session until you have worked with every distraction at level one, changing the reward every time but using the lowest level rewards you can. At the next session, review with one or two distractions at the last level you were at, then work through all 10 distractions in the next level. Stay at this step until you have worked through to level 6 or 7 distractions. Change your rewards frequently, using play or privileges in addition to a variety of treats.

CLICK TRICKS

You can create a really strong desire to have a toy by keeping it away from the dog in a drawer, and periodically taking it out, looking at it like it's incredibly interesting, tossing it around a bit, dragging it on the ground with a string attached, and putting it back in the drawer. Occasionally drop it on the floor and quickly grab it before the dog does. Once in a very long while the dog gets to grab it while you're holding it and tug a bit. Pretty soon you'll have the dog's instant attention as soon as you get close to the drawer. (Thanks to John Rogerson for this method of creating "toy envy.")

5.   When you get to level 6 or 7 on your distraction list, you have available to you a whole different level of reward -- yes, reward. Anything that your dog considers to be a distraction, can also be used as a reward for him. Now we're going to give him the opportunity to do whatever is distracting him, as a reward for giving you attention, and touching your hand. You'll need that distraction to be something he could actually have, like a new squeaky toy. So let's use that as our example. Put the distraction on the ground and walk toward it with your dog. At the point your dog notices it, stop moving and wait for the dog to look at you (by

this point, you won't ask for a Watch -- you've done almost 300 repetitions, so the dog should be figuring out he needs to look at you), then cue Touch, click and release to get the toy when he touches. Have a rousing game with the toy, then repeat the whole process 5 times. Out of those 5 repetitions, three will involve interaction in some way with the distraction, and two will involve some other type of reward that's just as interesting for the dog, say another new squeaky pulled out of your pocket that he didn't know you had. Do 5 repetitions with each distraction in level 6, then end the session.

Get creative with how the distractions can be used as a reward for the dog for the behavior you like — play with another dog that you know, the opportunity to sniff or roll in something unmentionable, etc. Don't reward with the distraction every time (every 3rd or 4th time is sufficient) but try to offer a reward that's consistent with ignoring the distraction, for example, you can run and chase ME if you pay attention to me when something you want to chase is around. At the next session, repeat a few level 6, then move on to level 7 distractions and continue at this step until you have worked through all the distractions on your list.

CLICK TRICKS

On our dogs' list of level 7 distractions would be birds. We both have dogs who love to chase them, but the dogs also know they can't really catch them (as do we). The opportunity to chase would be a HUGE reward for these dogs, but the downside to letting a dog chase birds is that you could be creating a stronger desire to chase all animals. In some cities, letting your dog (or encouraging them) to chase wildlife of any kind can be illegal. Finally, you might just encounter a bird who is wounded and can't fly, and what will you do if the dog DOES catch it? These are things you need to be considering as you decide how to reward your dog.

Adding variability:

6. Experiment with changing the speed of the touch (rewarding only the fastest or slowest), getting touch when the dog starts a distance away from you, or having the dog keep his nose on your hand for an extended period, or multiple times. Each time you change one of the variables, work in a distraction-free environment and gradually add in

distractions by level. Changing how the dog performs the touch forces the dog to think about completing the task, which means less focus on the distraction.

7. Add other commands such as Down, Wait or Come as precursors to the Watch/Touch combo. Vary how many behaviors you ask for before giving the dog an opportunity to touch.

8. Vary how long the dog has to look at you before getting the opportunity to touch. Work with low level distractions while you're building up time.

Early Steps: Fearful dogs sometimes don't have a lot of real-life rewards that they're interested in. If that's the case with your dog, you could substitute a super treat (see Barking at the Window for suggestions) as a reward for the default behavior. Use whatever you can and in the meantime build up the idea in your dog's mind that life is exciting, by reviewing Confidence-building Exercises later in this chapter. Or, for a highly stressed dog, use a trick the dog loves to do, one with audience appeal. Both you and the dog will be calmer if you have something to do that has built in rewards for both of you. Reward heavily early on, even if it's not perfect to start with.

Problem-Solving Tips:
I can't get the dog to pay attention no matter how low the distraction is.
- Spend a great amount of time having the dog look at you and perform his default behavior before he can do ANYTHING.
- Have someone else give you a list of things that would be totally boring, level 1 distractions for your dog that you could start with.
- Work with a private trainer to make sure your timing, reward and distractions are appropriate and at a level that will ensure early success.

Suggested Commands: Train as an automatic behavior, or use Watch, Touch

Variations: Experiment with clicking and rewarding "calm behavior" -- what does it look like in your dog? Don't forget you'll need to start at a low level and shape calmer behavior. For example, if your dog is bouncing off the ceiling, the first step might be clicking a less enthusiastic bounce, gradually building up to four feet on the floor, attention on you, then being on his side sleeping.

Teach the dog to give you the default behavior when he's stressed, as an indicator to you that he's stressed. Pay attention if the dog tries to touch in a situation where you haven't asked for it, he may be trying to tell you something.

POSSESSION PROBLEMS AND RESOURCE GUARDING (GIVE ME THAT BONE, TOY, BALL, REMOTE CONTROL, KLEENEX!)

Doggy Laws of Ownership –
> *If it's in my mouth, it's mine.*
> *If I like it, it's mine.*
> *If I had it a little while ago, it's mine.*
> *If I can take it from you, it's mine.*
> *If I'm chewing something to bits, all the pieces are mine.*
> *If I saw it first, it's mine.*
> *If it just looks like mine, it's mine.*
> *If you're playing with something and you put it down, it becomes mine.*
> *If it's broken, it's yours.*

The Final Picture: The dog willingly gives up anything he has, whether that's a bone or your underwear.

Uses: Being able to take ANYTHING away from your dog is a core behavior that all dogs should have. Otherwise, at some point, you may find yourself competing against your dog for something that might be dangerous for him.

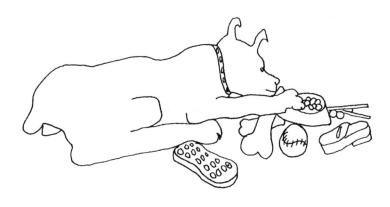

Preparation and Props: Clicker, variety of treats, dog, variety of items the dog might be interested in keeping. Keep items off the floor, trash cans covered, and doors closed while you're working on this behavior. Or, even better, put the dog on a light leash he can drag around the house and bring him with you as you move from room to room. We don't want him to practice stealing while you're trying to solve this problem!

What's in it for the Dog? Possession aggression usually starts as a small puppy. The typical scenario is a puppy who is exploring his environment and checking out everything — with his mouth. Concerned owners take things away, justifiably worried that they might be harmful. Now it becomes a game for the dog, to either hold on to it or eat it as quickly as possible so you can't take it away. A game of chase while you try to capture the puppy adds a huge reward for him. Stop chasing the dog, and don't punish the dog for having forbidden items. This is the worst thing you can teach your dog. It not only creates problems with possession, it also creates problems with recalls. (Having the dog chase you, on the other hand, has some benefits!)

Possession aggression pays off for the dog in terms of attention from you, or because it successfully prevents someone else from getting what he has (either you, or another dog). High possession-instinct dogs (like retrievers) can be particularly bad with this problem, especially if you add punishment to the mix for having something they shouldn't.

A dog who eats non-food items may also be suffering from a physical or food imbalance. Try changing foods or discussing it with your veterinarian.

Special note: Because you are working close to the dog with this behavior, there is the potential for a bite. If you see ANY signs of problems, please consult with a knowledgeable behaviorist. If you are working with an older dog who's been practicing possession for a while, or with a dog whose history you don't know, please proceed carefully. Look for signs of stress — panting, tucked tail, stiffened body, grabbing forcefully at the offered treat — along with more obvious signs of a problem such as growling. Do not punish growling by yelling at or striking the dog. Growling is an indicator that you have pushed the dog too far — you do <u>not</u> want to make it go away. Then the dog no longer growls a warning, but goes directly for a bite.

SLICK CLICKS

Mandy Book

On one occasion, clients dropped their terrier at Mandy's house for boarding during spring time. They said to be careful, because he liked to eat snails. Mandy told them not to worry, she didn't set out bait, so eating snails would at worst lead to a minor parasitic infection.

The first time he went outside, he instantly grabbed a snail, then turned and looked at Mandy. She looked at him but said nothing, and didn't move from the doorway. He held it in his mouth for a moment, then promptly spit it out. He didn't really like snails, he liked the chase game that ensued when he picked them up. Since Mandy wasn't playing, he didn't bother. He didn't eat a single snail while he was at Mandy's house, although he checked a few times to see if she might play his game.

The Steps Along the Way:

1. Offer the dog an item that he would consider low in value - such as a Nylabone™ or toy that he has free and regular access to. You are going to hold onto the item when you offer it to the dog — do NOT let him have it. (Once the dog has possession, the rules change!) Show him a treat (also low in value, but more interesting than what he's giving up.) When he removes his mouth from the object (even if it's just to reposition his bite!) say your bridge word and give him the treat. Offer the object again as soon as he has eaten the treat. It's very important that the dog learn that the item won't disappear if he takes his teeth off of it. Repeat 10 times, then change items and treats. Repeat with two more item changes (you've now traded for four different items.)

2. Hold a treat in one hand and the clicker in the other. Using the same items from step 1, give the dog an item (you no longer hold onto it.) Do not offer a treat, instead click when the dog takes his mouth off the object, even for a second. Do not lean over the dog to give the treat, just open your hand and let him take it once you click. Repeat 10 times for each item. Each time you change to another item, change to a more enticing treat, and wait for a slightly longer pause from the

dog (with his mouth off the item) before clicking and treating. End the session after you have practiced with four different items. Start the next session with one old item (from the previous session) and three new items. Continue at this step until the dog immediately drops what you give him and waits for a treat, for up to 10 seconds, before you click and treat.

CLICK TRICKS

Leaning over a dog (casting your "shadow" on him) is considered very dominant body language for dogs. You want to make your behavior non-threatening at this point to avoid stressing the dog and possibly inviting a bite or encouraging him to swallow the item or run away with it.

---

3.   Put the treats on a counter nearby. Give the dog a slightly more interesting object (like a toy he hasn't seen before) and wait. When the dog drops the object, click and treat. Repeat 10 times, varying how long he has to wait before clicking each time. Repeat the entire process with three other slightly interesting objects. At each new session, pick four objects that are higher in value than the previous session's objects. Change treats frequently and continue increasing the value of the treat. Continue at this step until the dog immediately drops what you give him and waits for a treat, regardless of what he's given. Don't forget to practice with things the dog commonly picks up such as socks, underwear and tissues!

CLICK TRICKS

Don't worry if you later want to teach the dog to hold onto an item (say for a retrieve). We're going to give this behavior a name, thereby giving you control over it. Any behavior you have practiced enough to name is "on cue" – you can ask for it when you want it.

---

4.   Pick 10 items that vary in interest for the dog (but would be safe for him if he chose to eat them), including some that are very high such as tissue, and some that are really low, such as an old bone. Give a low value item to the dog and immediately leave the room for 30 seconds. Come back into the room and approach the dog with your hand out (as

if you were going to reach for the item). Stop far enough away that the dog could not bite if he decided to, and wait with your arm held out. When the dog drops the item, click, drop a treat at your feet for the dog to come get, and leave the room again. Repeat 3 times at the same distance, then go one step closer to the dog when you return. Repeat 3 times. Continue to build one step closer, staying at each distance at least 3 repetitions. End the session when the dog has had 30 treats. At the next session, start at the last distance and continue to get closer. Continue until you can put your hand on the item (whether the dog still has it or not), then change to a higher value item and repeat the whole process, until you have completed this step with each of the 10 items. Each time you are clicking when the dog takes his mouth off the object. Don't take it away from the dog just yet.

CLICK TRICKS

Watch your dog carefully during this step. Does he freeze or stiffen, stare at you, stop chewing on the item but remain near it, or give you any other indications that he's worried about your approach? If so, discontinue work by yourself and seek the advice of a trainer. If he gets up from the item and comes over to you, that's a good sign you're making progress. In our group classes, we use pig's ears in step 1 to test the dog's reaction to giving up something for a treat, before starting to let go of the item. This can give you an indication of how serious a problem you are starting with.

---

5. Give the dog something of medium value (an object that you've already used to work on this behavior) and leave the room for 30 seconds. Return and go up to the dog, watching carefully to be sure he's not stressed about your approach (turning away from you with the item, body stiffening). Reach for the item and put your hand on it, click and treat when the dog drops the item (regardless of when that happens while you are reaching for it). The first few times he drops the item, make a big deal about it, telling him what a spectacular dog he is and giving multiple treats (only one click is necessary). Leave the room again and repeat the process 5 times. If the dog drops the item and comes to you as soon as you enter the room, click and give multiple treats (Jackpot!). Repeat with 5 additional items of medium to high value to the dog. Continue until your entry into the room causes

185

the dog to spit out the item, or he lets go immediately when you put your hand on it. Discontinue and consult with an experienced trainer if you see any of the following:

> the dog leaves the room with the item;
> the dog comes back to the item and tries to pick it up while your hand is on it;
> the dog stiffens or growls or snaps at you.

6. Can you predict that the dog will drop the item (either as soon as you enter the room, or when you put your hand on it)? Time to add a command. Give the dog a new object, say your command as you reach for the object, click and treat when he lets go of it, then give it back to the dog. Repeat 50 to 60 times, using different objects and working in different places, including outside. Be sure to practice with very high value items such as pig's ears, as well as low value items such as an old tennis ball.

Work on variability:

7. Pull the object toward you, look at it briefly, click/treat, and return it to the dog.

8. Gradually increase the distance the dog will come away from something he has. If the dog brings the item with him, that's okay too. Make a big fuss about him when he brings it (don't immediately take it), and trade him for something good.

9. Practice saying "give me that!" or "what have you got!" in a mock serious tone of voice before you give your command to drop the item. It never hurts to practice how the real world is — someone might react just this way before they try to snatch something from your dog.

10. Play tug with a tug toy and have the dog let go of the item. To get the dog to let go intially, you will need to stop moving as soon as you say Drop (or whatever verbal cue you have chosen) — you become a statue so the dog doesn't get rewarded for continuing to tug by having you tug back. Set up rules for play —

> 1) Don't leave tug toys around
> 2) The dog can only tug when you give the okay
> 3) The dog has to stop when you say to
> 4) The game ends immediately if the dog puts his teeth on you.

Be clear what you expect from the dog, and play by the rules, and you can play tug safely with most dogs. (We know you're doing it anyway, so you might as well set up some rules!)

11. Lean over the dog when he has something and take it from him to examine it. Gradually practice more threatening body posture.
12. Have other people practice taking things from your dog. Be VERY CAREFUL with this step, as your dog may not react the same with them as he does with you. Work through from step 1 with another person if you have any doubts.
13. Tie the dog to a doorknob and practice taking things away (the behavior is different when the dog is restricted in movement!)

Early Steps: If the dog won't take his mouth off the item, it means the value of your object is too high and the value of the treats is too low. Adjust both accordingly. Click and treat the jaw relaxing as the first step if the dog won't let go (you'll feel it through the item) and drop a yummy treat on the floor. If your dog has already growled at you for taking things away, or has been punished in the past for "stealing" you need to work with a behaviorist on this exercise. You are at very high risk for a bite.

Problem-Solving Tips:
The dog runs away with the item when I let go of it in step 2.
- Lower the value of the item (use something even more boring).
- Put the dog on leash and step on the leash.
- Sit on the floor to ensure you're not leaning over the dog.

The dog gets something while we're working on this behavior and I can't get it away from him but it's dangerous.
- Ring the doorbell, knock on the door, pick up the leash, call the kitty, or jingle your car keys. Whatever you do, DON'T CHASE THE DOG!

The dog looks for items to bring to me, so he can get a treat.
- Cover trash cans or close doors so he can't get items he shouldn't.
- Stop rewarding with treats, use lower value rewards only occasionally.
- Only reward the dog if you ask him to drop the item, don't reward if he brings it to you. (Use your clicker to refine what you expect from the dog.)

Suggested Commands: Drop it, Give, Thank you, Mine, Let me see

Variations: Have the dog bring the item to you to get his treat. That way you know what the dog is getting into. Teach the dog to pick up items dropped around the house and help you keep it clean. If you have multiple dogs living with you, teach each dog to take a toy from you only when he is indicated by name. Teach the dog to come and push his neck into your hand when you reach your hand out for something (he'll have to leave the item to do this, then can be rewarded for it).

CONFIDENCE-BUILDING EXERCISES – GETTING OVER FEARS

Whole books have been written on how to deal with fear in dogs. You can find suggestions for further reading in the Resources section at the end of the book. We are only going to touch on some specific behaviors you can teach your dog to help him work through his problem areas.

You may find that your dog has an overall fear of life, or his fears may be very specifically categorized in terms of people, places, things or noises. In other words, noises may bother him but he's not afraid of people. Fearful behavior often results from a lack of positive experiences (or no experience at all) with the feared object, but traumatic events can also create fear problems. Fears are usually generalized quite easily by the dog, so that a bad experience with one person can generalize into a fear of all men, or a fear of people in a particular environment (such as your house) very quickly.

What's in it for the Dog? The dog gets many rewards for his fearful behavior — barking and lunging makes the scary thing go away, or you react by coddling, picking up and cooing at the dog to soothe him, or you encourage barking because you think the dog is being "protective."

Let's be clear about this "protection" idea — it is NOT okay for your dog to protect you, your family, or your household from what the <u>dog</u> perceives as a threat. The problem with allowing the dog to decide is that very often the threat involves people the dog doesn't know rather than people who are actually threatening. The pack's job is to let us know that something is amiss, then it's up to us to take care of the problem. We don't want the dogs taking matters into their own paws. Usually, what owners think is "protective" behavior — barking, lunging, growling -- is fear. In 15 years of teaching, we've yet to see a dog whose aggression wasn't fear-based, despite what the owner thinks. A truly macho dog has no need for the outlandish threat displays that fearful dogs engage in.

Fear also makes good survival sense for the dog (and most other animals, including humans!). Animals that don't proceed with caution when encountering new things frequently end up dead, which prevents them from passing on those fearless genes. With dogs, we've complicated the issue by breeding out or otherwise modifying their fears to fit our specific needs. Dogs that are sensitive to sounds and suspicious of people make good watch dogs, for example, but terrible hunting dogs, where loud noise and strangers are prevalent.

Taken to the extreme, dog fears can create tremendous problems for us as dog owners, causing us to modify our life to prevent the dog from "getting spooked" and limiting our contact with other people. From the dog's perspective, he can't be healthy or happy when he lives his life in constant fear of every new thing. A dog in panic mode is physically and mentally stressed. He has a greatly diminished quality of life. And if you choose to ignore the dog's indication that he's afraid, you could be setting someone up for a bite.

The good news is that early intervention often can have a significant impact. The younger the dog, and the sooner you start, the better the prognosis. Each new thing the dog encounters in a positive way gives him a history to draw from. If all new things are fun and result in treats, then it makes it easier to accept the next new thing.

Clicker training is ideal for these problems, since no punishment will be associated with the new thing. Another very helpful thing you can do for your dog is walk him -- to socialize him and expose him to the sights and sounds of life. Even if you have to start by walking down your front walk and returning to the house because the dog is nervous. Remember that you need to stay calm also. If you get hysterical or go into mother mode because your dog is frightened, it's going to seriously impact his behavior (in a bad way).

Please note that when you're dealing with any type of fear problem, it's important that you proceed slowly, so that the dog is always working at his comfort level.

CREATING INTEREST IN TOYS – LIFE IS FUN!

The Final Picture: The dog will play with a tug toy that he was previously uninterested in.

Uses: Once your dog is interested in playing with toys, you have those available as another form of reward besides food and petting. Dogs who see life as filled with play opportunities instead of scary things will be more confident.

Preparation and Props: Dog, treats, clicker, a tug toy.

The Steps Along the Way:
(Do only one or two steps at each session, and aim for many daily sessions to help keep the dog's interest high.)
1. Starting in a low-stress environment, show the dog the toy, click and treat when he looks at it. Repeat 3 times, putting the toy behind your back in between each repetition.
2. Click and treat if he sniffs it. Repeat 3 times, hiding the toy between each repetition.
3. Click and treat when he touches it. Repeat 3 times, hiding the toy between each repetition.
4. Click and treat when he opens his mouth when near the toy. Repeat 3 times, hiding the toy between each repetition.
5. Click and treat when his teeth touch the toy. Repeat 3 times, hiding the toy between each repetition.
6. Change locations to another low-stress area, and repeat step 5.
7. Click and treat when the dog closes his mouth on the toy. Be very careful to time your click with the mouth closing, not as it is opening. Repeat 3 times, hiding the toy between each repetition.
8. Click and treat when the dog closes his mouth on the toy, and keeps it on for up to one second. Continue to add time, bouncing around (see chapter 7) until the dog will put his mouth on the toy for at least 3 seconds and up to 10 seconds. Repeat at each new average bounce at least 3-5 times.
9. When the dog closes his mouth on the toy, pull slightly. Click and treat the dog for holding on as you pull. Be VERY careful to click holding on -- if you're too slow with your click, you'll be clicking for letting go! Repeat 5 times.
10. Continue to add a stronger pull, selecting the strongest 3 out of 5 pulls to click. Click the dog for holding on and resisting against your pull.
11. Build time pulling using the bounce around method.
12. Name it when it looks the way you want: the dog grabs the toy when offered, and pulls against you for an extended time.

13. Continue to change locations as you practice this tugging behavior. Remember that sensitive dogs will need to have changes made very gradually to the environment. It's tough to concentrate on having fun if there are stressful things going on around you!
14. Add other toys to the dog's fun play, using the steps outlined above.
15. Work on other dimensions of the tug, such as a head shake, stronger tugging or adding play growling.
16. Don't forget to teach the Drop behavior outlined in this chapter!

Early Steps: If the dog shows no interest in the toy, try pulling it along the ground, even attaching it to a string so you're not close to it. You can also find toys that are designed to have treats kept in a pocket inside (see Resources) or use an old sock with one end knotted. Dogs will be more interested in sniffing, following and putting their teeth on these if you stuff them with smelly treats.

Suggested Commands: Tug, Let's Play, Get it

SLICK CLICKS
TRAINING JUST FOR FUN
Kathy Sdao, proprietor of Bright Spot Dog Training

While I trained dolphins for the U.S. Navy in Hawaii, I also decided to train a "wild" puffer fish – Barney, I named him – to spit at people's rear ends when they leaned over the dolphin cages! Barney hung around the dolphin cages each morning attempting to grab some of the fish scraps the dolphins were missing. Some of us realized what a willing student this fish was – he'd do just about anything for food. So we were able to capture this spitting behavior by whistling and throwing a fish-bit whenever Barney spit at us to get our attention. I also trained him to swim through a small hoop, though he nearly broke my finger in the process. Puffer fish have crushing mouth plates, and I think he didn't see so well and mistook my index finger for a smelt. But he was one cool fish, and I actually miss him!

OBJECT FEARS – APPROACH AND TOUCH OBJECT

The Final Picture: The dog will approach and touch something new with his nose when you indicate for him to do so.

Preparation and Props: You need a very solid response to the Touch stick, your clicker, SUPER treats, and your dog, plus a variety of old things he's not afraid of and new things he is. Object fears can be very specific -- wheeled objects or things that are metal — or may be more general — any new thing. Make a list of as many things as you can think of that your dog is afraid of. What do they have in common? For example, Mandy's golden is afraid of things that move on their own (balloons, flags, doors blown in the wind) and metal objects such as wheelchairs, bikes, and exercise pens. Mandy doesn't know why, but knowing WHAT has helped her help the dog get over a lot of these fears. It's important that the dog not be spooked during the training of this behavior. Proceed slowly to prevent that from happening.

The Steps Along the Way:
1. Work on the Touch stick behavior from Chapter 3 until your dog is a touching fool, manuevering to try to touch the stick even when it's not easily accessible.
2. Now take an object that your dog is familiar and comfortable with, place the end of the touch stick on the object, and tell the dog Touch (or whatever your command is for this behavior). Click when he touches the touch stick. Repeat 3 times. Now hold the touch stick a little off to the side, still touching the object, so that it would be easier for the dog to touch the item than the stick, say Touch, and click and treat for touching the item (or close to it). Repeat 3 times. Continue shaping a touch on the object, as you move the touch stick a small amount farther away from the object with each step. Stay at each step no more than 3 repetitions. Continue until the dog will move forward to touch the object indicated, even with the touch stick 1-2 feet away. End the session. At the next session, choose another familiar object and work through all the steps until the dog is clearly touching the object and not the touch stick. At each new session, change to another familiar object. Continue at this step until you have done it with at least 10 objects.
2b. When you can predict that the dog will quickly move forward to touch a new object, add a command if you like by saying new command,

Touch, dog touches object, click and treat. Drop the Touch as the dog begins to move forward on the new cue. (You can continue to just use Touch, if you prefer.)

3. Now choose an item that is familiar to the dog, but has some quality that would normally cause your dog to be hesitant. In our example, we would use a door that the dog passes through daily in the house. Repeat the entire sequence from step 2 with the slightly scary object. (Use your new command at the outset, if you have introduced one). Do only one object per session, but get the touch very strong on that object. Choose at least 10 objects to work with (in our example, that would be all the doors in the house).

4. Gradually fade the touch stick, and substitute pointing at the object with your finger (see Chapter 7 for hints on how to fade the touch stick).

5. Pick 10 new objects that have no qualities that produce fear in your dog - as an example, we would use a new toy, a plastic bowl, a pad of paper, and so on. Point at the object (or say your command), then click and treat when the dog touches it. Repeat 3 times, then change objects.

6. Pick 10 objects that you know create some amount of fear for the dog. Try not to start with the scariest one! Repeat step 5 with all the new items. In our example, we would use doors in someone else's house, but shut the doors so they didn't move.

7. Now go back to those same 10 slightly scary objects and change the quality such that they are a little scarier, for example, letting the doors be open a bit. The idea is to gradually make items more and more scary, until the dog has had so many experiences with slightly scary objects that are positive, that a new scary object is less so.

8. At this point, the dog should move forward to touch an object that initially frightens him when cued to do so. Continue to practice having the dog touch a variety of items for clicks and treats when you are out and about to keep this behavior very strong.

Early Steps: If at any point you lose the behavior, or the dog will not approach something, go back to the previous step and put more "layers of scariness" in before coming back to that object. Keep in mind that your success will depend on how old the dog is, how severe his fears are, how long he has had them, and what his previous experiences have been.

Suggested Commands: What is it?, What's that?, Touch

Variations: You could shape "calm, relaxed" behavior (yawning, stretching, relaxed body or shaking as if shaking off water, not trembling with fear - see below) when the dog is confronted with something scary or new. Practice clicking relaxation as your first step, then shape the specific behavior you want. Be sure to time your click so that dog is relaxed when he hears the actual click. (See the Resources for more books/videos on body language in dogs.)

NOISE FEARS

Noise fears present a special problem for dog owners. The most common ones are fear of thunder and fireworks. Generally noise fears are the MOST difficult type of fear to treat successfully. There may be components to the noise such as vibration and air pressure changes that you won't be able to duplicate. Plus you can't control storms or fireworks, so that means your dog may be exposed to them while you're working on a fear program. This can seriously impact your training progress.

The Final Picture: The dog is calm and relaxed when he hears a sound that previously stressed him.

Preparation and Props: Audio tape of fear-producing noise (you can buy pre-made tapes, see Resources for information), clicker, SUPER treats, your dog. You'll need to carefully set up the program so that the dog is not exposed to a sound not under your control during the time you are working on this, which could be a period of several months. For example, having a jackhammer going next door while you're at work is likely to throw your training into a tailspin.

The Steps Along the Way:
1. Desensitize the dog to the sound first, by playing the tape over and over (continuously throughout the day) at a level that is not noticeable to the dog (not you). You'll find this level by turning up the volume until the dog reacts to the sound, then starting your program at least 3 levels BELOW that. Do not associate any food, play, interaction or

clicking with playing the tape yet. Otherwise the dog becomes sensitive to treats predicting the "bad" sound and won't eat the treats. He may also generalize your presence or other environmental cues that are associated with the sound. Once a week, turn up the volume one level (assuming you are playing the tape on a daily basis for several hours a day). Pay attention to any signs of stress as the volume increases. You'll want to stay at a level below that for as long as necessary for the dog. As you increase the volume, the dog should have a ho-hum attitude about it. If not, it's too loud to work as a desensitization process.

2. Meanwhile, when you aren't playing the tape, you will be clicking the dog for relaxed behavior. Decide what this is going to look like for your dog. Physically doing something such as stretching or yawning or shaking his body can actually create relaxation for the dog – it's hard to be tense when you're yawning. To get these behaviors, you'll probably have to capture them. Be prepared with a clicker and treats during a time when you think the dog might do the behavior, then click and treat as soon as he does the behavior. You may only get one opportunity to click during the early stages, but as the dog starts to pay attention more, he'll try to figure out why you're clicking, and the behavior will happen more often. If you don't have a clicker handy, bridge and treat, so you don't miss an opportunity to reward what you're looking for. As the behavior gets more solid, and you can start to predict when the dog is going to do it, give it a name. Once the dog can do the behavior on command, ask for it in many different places, under many different circumstances. Reward heavily! Don't forget to vary the duration of the behavior using the bounce around technique discussed earlier in the book and again in Chapter 7.

3. Introduce the dog to massage. One of the best techniques is TTouch. There are tapes and seminars available (see Resources for more information). Any calm, slow stroking movement will probably work, with very gentle pressure. Remember to breathe slowly while you massage — play relaxing music if it helps you be more relaxed (we don't think it will do anything for the dog.)

4. As the dog starts to become accustomed to the sounds he is hearing, you are going to ask for his relaxed behavior while the sound is playing. Start the sound tape at a level that is one level below where the dog is comfortable. Have the dog do several stretches, yawns, or

shakes (whatever his behavior is), clicking and treating them each time. Then do a short 1 minute massage, release the dog and turn off the tape. At the next session, repeat the Relax behaviors and massage at the first sound level, then turn up the sound one notch, get the Relax behavior several times and give the dog a short massage. At the next session, repeat the first two levels, then turn up the sound, get the Relax behavior several times and give the dog another short massage. At each new session, you will start at the lowest level of sound, work through all your previous levels, and add one more, getting your Relax behavior and giving a short massage at each level of sound. Continue at this step until the sound is at a normal volume as it would be in real life.

5. Take the whole thing on the road. You'll need to practice having the dog relax while he listens to the sound in a variety of different environments, not just your house. This will help the dog generalize the Relax behavior and be useful when you can't control the real sound in real life. You may find that the dog doesn't generalize well and still reacts to the sound in real life. If so, go back to step 4 and repeat until you can take it on the road. Understand that this may also be the best you can get as far as mitigating the dog's fear.

Early Steps: If you aren't able to desensitize the dog to the tape at a level that is audible (in other words, the dog always reacts when the tape is loud enough for him to hear) you'll need to work with a behaviorist on this problem. Look for someone who has experience dealing with fear problems, and with sound fears especially.

Suggested Commands: Relax, Stretch, Yawn, Shake, Wiggle

Variations: Teach a variety of relaxation behaviors so you can have the dog go through them rapid fire when a stresser occurs. Instead of having him think about what he's afraid of, he'll be thinking about what he needs to do to get those tasty treats! You could even create a story about a dog waking up or a bored dog and have him act it out for an audience.

PEOPLE AND PHYSICAL CONTACT FEARS – PET ME!

The Final Picture: The dog will slide his head underneath an outstretched hand so that he can be "petted."

This is another behavior that requires close physical proximity to the dog. If you have any doubts about how your dog might react, please discuss your concerns with a trainer experienced in dealing with aggression toward people.

Uses: Even if your dog isn't worried about petting or strangers touching him, this is a worthwhile behavior to teach, because 99.999% of the people petting a dog will do it in a threatening way, directly over the top of the dog's head. This is a lower stress way for your dog to be petted.

Preparation and Props: Clicker, treats, dog, a few helpful friends. This is a variation on the hand touch we taught in Chapter 2.

<u>*The Steps Along the Way:*</u>
1.   Hold one hand out flat, parallel to the floor, with your palm facing downward (your "petting hand"), but not moving. Put a tasty treat in the other hand (your "treat" hand), and hold it directly underneath the petting hand's wrist about 5 inches below the wrist, so that the dog has to stretch forward with his head flat to reach the treat. The fingers of your petting hand are pointing at the dog, so he has to come under the hand to get the treat.   Bridge and treat when the dog brings his head under your petting hand. Repeat 3-5 times, then move your treat hand an inch or two closer horizontally to your petting hand. Continue until the dog touches the petting hand with the top of his head when he stretches for the treat, repeating 3-5 times at each step.

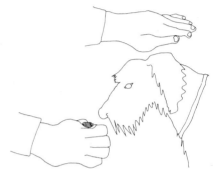

2.   Switch hands and repeat step 1.
3.   Hold your petting hand out, and put the clicker in your other hand. Place the clicker hand in the same place you previously were holding the treat. Click and treat when the dog touches your petting hand with the top of his head. Repeat 3 times.
4.   Hold your petting hand out, and move the clicker hand back a bit, closer to your body. Click when the dog touches the palm of your petting hand with his head. If he stretches for the clicker hand without making contact with your petting hand, just wait. When he pulls back, he will accidentally bump the petting hand as his neck returns to a more natural angle. (If he doesn't, adjust your clicker hand so he will the next time.) Click and treat the contact. Repeat 3-5 times. Continue to move the clicker hand closer to your body, so it is less of a cue for the dog, until it is hanging comfortably by your side, staying at each step no longer than 3 repetitions.
5.   Continue to shape a harder head bump on your palm, by clicking only the 3 most intentional head bumps out of every group of 5. Take a short 10-second break after every 5 tries. When the dog is banging his head against your hand most of the time, give it a name. Say your cue, offer your petting hand, dog butts hand, click and treat. Repeat this pairing 50-60 times, changing locations frequently, working both indoors and out. For a dog who intensely dislikes or is fearful of

physical contact, this may be as far as you go with him. Be sure that at least all family members can touch the dog, and instruct strangers not to touch him. If you would like to continue beyond this level with a dog like this, seek help from a trainer.

6. Get a friend the dog knows and is comfortable with, say your cue, then have them offer their hand, then you click and treat when the dog bumps it with his head. The friend should stand quietly, and avoid looking at the dog, with his hand held out, palm down. Repeat 10 times with each friend you can rustle up that the dog already knows, changing locations frequently. (Note that you are saying the command and clicking and treating, not the person greeting the dog.)

CLICK TRICKS

Continue as long as you do not see any behaviors of concern (such as body stiffening, growling, hard stare, avoiding the person, panting, dilated pupils, pacing) from the dog. If you see any of these or anything else that concerns you, please DO NOT continue with this exercise without the help of a qualified behaviorist. The chances are high that someone will be bitten if you force the dog past his comfort level. If you're unable to have the dog off leash around strangers, you shouldn't even be considering working alone on this problem!

---

7. Go back to an area the dog is comfortable in, and take the dog off leash. This allows the dog to decide to make contact or avoid it if he chooses to. Working with a friend the dog doesn't know, say your cue and have them put their hand out, looking away from the dog (eye contact and staring can be very threatening). When the dog bumps their hand, click and treat. Make sure these treats are way better than anything they've gotten to date for this behavior. Do not allow the "stranger" to have any other contact with the dog — it's very important that the dog not get spooked at this step. It's a good idea to have them turn their back on the dog and stand quietly until you're ready to repeat the behavior. Repeat 10 times, then try with another friend.

8. Teach the dog to come forward as soon as the hand is lifted so the behavior looks more natural to an observer.

9. Add an up and down patting motion with the hand.

10. Add a stare, lean, crouch, or verbalizations. (First with familiar people, then with unfamiliar).

11.   Have people of different ages offer their hand.

Early Steps: If your dog is very shy or worried about a hand over his head, start with the treat hand held under your wrist, but far (at least one foot, more may be necessary) below the petting hand. Shape the dog first to reach for the treat, VERY gradually moving your treat hand closer and closer to the flat "petting" hand, or start with the treat held in front of the fingertips of the petting hand and gradually work it back toward the wrist of that hand.

Suggested Commands: Pet, Hello, Go say hi, Buddy

Variations: You could teach the dog to kiss the hand as a variation. Be aware not everyone thinks dog slobber is as wonderful as you do! (But we swear it's the secret to our youthful good looks!) Teach the dog to push his neck against your hand so you could easily grab onto his collar.

MODIFYING DOG-TO-DOG INTERACTIONS

The Final Picture: The dog can sit quietly on leash around another dog.

Uses: You'll need this if you want to walk your dog in the neighborhood, go into pet stores with him, or be at dog shows, picnic grounds or other areas where dogs might be.

Preparation and Props: Teach Sit and Watch first. You'll need your clicker, SUPER treats, and your dog, and eventually, other dogs. A strong response to Come will be handy if your dog slips off leash, as will a nice walk on leash. Keep the dog away from other dogs when you can't control their approach, so he can't practice being naughty.
        Figure out what creates problems for you — How far away is the other dog when yours reacts? Is it with all dogs, or just certain ones? What's the determining factor (age, sex, size, breed or even color)? Has the dog had a previous traumatic experience that you can point to? Does it happen in certain places but not in others? Are there other prey-type behaviors that your dog has that might be contributing? Have a friend walk your dog to see if you might be part of the problem for him – does he react the same way? Make a hierarchy of things that set your dog off. For example:

Younger more likely than older dogs
Labs usually but shelties hardly ever
Always in dog class but never at home
Dogs on leash okay at 50 feet or greater
Dogs on leash okay, but dogs off leash not
Running dogs worse than walking dogs

So the lowest problem dog would be an older Sheltie, walking in front of your house, on leash, about 50 feet away. The highest would be a 6 month old Labrador with the owner on a bicycle, running toward you and your dog as you get out of the car to go to training class.

What's in it for the Dog? Most dogs are aggressive or reactive toward other dogs because they are fearful, under-, or unsocialized. It's also commonly seen in unneutered animals. (If you really want to impact that, neuter your dog early — late neutering has little impact on dog aggression.) Sometimes dogs who have been allowed to play rough or bully other dogs as a puppy don't know how to play appropriately when they're older. Your dog may not know how to give good body language, which may be interpreted as aggression by other dogs. If your dog is overly submissive, he may invite aggression from other dogs. You might be rewarding aggression by paying attention to it; over-reacting to it and correcting the dog (making the approach of another dog an indicator for your dog that you're about to wig out); or, if YOU are afraid of other dogs you've probably helped your dog learn this as well.

The Steps Along the Way:
1. Start working in a safe environment such as your living room. Put the dog on leash and start walking forward. Stop, turn to look at the dog beside you and tell him Sit, click and treat when he sits. Repeat until the dog sits automatically when you stop moving. Change locations in the house every 10 repetitions, gradually building up to more distracting locations.
2. Add the Watch behavior. Start back in your living room with the dog on leash. Begin walking forward, stop, turn and look at the dog, and click/ treat when he looks up at you (he should sit automatically, if not, go back to step 1 until he does.) Repeat 10 times, clicking after the dog looks at you for varying amounts of time at each repetition.

Remember, you've already taught this behavior, so this is just a variation for the dog. Change locations every 10 repetitions, gradually building up to more distracting locations.

3.   Enlist the aid of a friend to walk their dog while you work on this. Choose someone who has a dog that won't push any of your dog's buttons (in our example, an older Sheltie). Have them start walking toward you, starting at least twice as far away as needed so that your dog is not paying any attention. In our example, the approaching dog starts 100 ft away (2x50ft). As soon as your helper and her dog begin moving toward you and your dog, move forward 5 steps, stop and feed your dog treats rapid-fire (2 treats per second). He will, of course, be already sitting and looking up at you when you start feeding, since you worked on that in step 1 and 2, and the other dog is far enough away to not be of interest. If you need to, adjust your distance accordingly. Continue rapidly feeding until the approaching dog reaches 50 feet, then stop. At the same time, have the other person stop moving forward, turn, and walk away. We're trying to teach your dog that the approach of the other dog is what inspires you to feed so many treats so quickly, so when you stop feeding, the other dog disappears. Repeat the whole process 5 times, then end the session. At the next session, put your marker at 40 feet away and repeat the entire sequence with the same dog as a distraction. At each successive session, decrease the distance by 5-10 feet (you may find as the other dog gets closer, you have to make your change in distance smaller.) Continue at this step until the approaching dog reaches you and your dog and passes by within 10 feet without any reaction from your dog. As soon as the dog passes you and your dog, stop feeding (dog leaving means the treat bar is closed).

CLICK TRICKS
Mark the spot on the ground where you want your friend to stop so you both practice excellent timing.

4.   Select another dog to work with that has one quality that disturbs your dog, for example, a younger Sheltie, or an older dog of a different breed. Continue as in step 3 with the new dog. At the next session, pick another dog, with a different quality that is a problem for your dog and continue as in step 3. If at any time you lose your dog (he stops

eating or reacts fearfully or aggressively toward the other dog) it means that you have taken too large a step. Go back and work on smaller changes or at a greater distance until your dog is not reacting. Continue until you have worked with a variety of dogs and your dog is starting to think a dog approaching is a unique opportunity to chow down.

5. Practice moving forward toward the other dog and stopping about 25 feet away, then clicking and feeding for sitting next to you with attention. Vary how long he has to hold the attention to get clicked. Gradually make the stopping distance closer and closer, until you could actually stop and have a conversation with someone else who was walking their dog.

6. As you walk around your neighborhood, carry treats with you. When you come to a house with a barking dog, sit your dog, wait for attention, then click and feed periodically for one minute or so. Continue on to the next house. Pretty soon the sound of a barking dog will be an indicator to your dog that he's about to score some major treats. You could even toss a few treats over the fence to teach the barking dog that your approach with your dog is a wonderful thing as well. (Keep in mind that not everyone will appreciate you helping them train their dog in such a way.)

7. Click and treat your dog for allowing another dog to come up and sniff him without reacting (remember to start far away, and gradually work closer). You can select attention, a sit, or just relaxed body posture as the behavior you are marking.

8. Click solicitation and play behaviors such as pawing, play bows, lowered body, or "bouncing" the front end, or call your dog away from another dog and click and treat that response.

Early Steps: If the dog comes around to face you in step 1 for the sit, use a hand touch to show him where he needs to be or work against a wall to prevent him from turning in front of you.

Variations: Teach the dog to offer a play bow on command (or use the appearance of another dog as the cue) -- other dogs will interpret it as a friendly sign and you might avert a problem. Teach the dog to do some other calming signal on command such as yawning, turning their head away, or sniffing the ground. Teach your dog that not erupting is what makes the other dog go away. In other words, being calm results in the other dog leaving. So your dog gets two rewards, one directly from you, and one from the "pressure" being taken off when the other dog leaves.

If your dog isn't worried about other dogs, teach him to sit when they approach as a "please may I" behavior before releasing him to sniff and play. That prevents other dogs from becoming a major distraction (which would disrupt other training, such as your Walk on leash) and also allows you time to ask the other owner if the dog is friendly and likes to play.

CHAPTER 7
Go Forth
and Click

In this final chapter, we'll revisit and expand on some of the technicalities of clicker training, plus introduce some odds and ends you might be interested in knowing! We'll go through some Q&A from actual dog owners, and add in whatever we think we might have left out up till now.

Though we have avoided technical terms as much as possible in this book, if you want to read much further, you may soon find yourself floundering in a sea of unfamiliar language. So, if this is as far as you plan to read about clicker training, skip this first section with a light heart. But if you're hooked and will be seeking further wisdom, read on for an introduction to the scientific language of clicker training.

THE LINGO IF YOU WANT TO READ THE SCIENTIFIC STUFF

First, you're likely to see or hear the whole concept referred to as operant conditioning. Sounds very forbidding and lab-rat-science-inclined, we know, but all it really means is this — modifying (conditioning) behavior by reinforcing the desired response (operant, or operating on).

But it quickly becomes less easily explained and more full of a jumble of abbreviations. One of the stickiest bits concerns reinforcement and its opposite, punishment. This is presented in four parts: positive reinforcement, negative reinforcement, positive punishment and negative punishment. You may see them written in shorthand as R+ (positive reinforcement), R- (negative reinforcement), P+ (positive punishment) and P- (negative punishment). A "punisher" may also be referred to as an aversive — it's anything the dog will seek to avoid. When you chart it out, it looks like this:

	Behavior Increases	Behavior Decreases
Add	+R Add something dog likes, behavior increases	+P Add something dog dislikes, behavior decreases
Subtract	-R Take away something dog dislikes, behavior increases	-P Take away something dog likes, behavior decreases

Though positive reinforcement makes good intuitive sense, positive punishment sounds a bit contradictory. That's because, in this scientific usage, "positive" and "negative" do not mean "good" and "bad." Instead, think of them in arithmetic terms — "positive" means to add and "negative" means to subtract. Scientists do not use the term punishment in the same way we do, either. Whether consequences are reinforcing or punishing is actually defined by their effect on behavior. Something that increases behavior (makes the animal do it more) is called "reinforcing" and something that decreases behavior (makes the animal do it less) is termed "punishing." So . . .

Positive reinforcement means you ADD something the animal likes, which makes him do the behavior again. You give him a cookie or produce his favorite toy and he sits more. It has to be something the dog likes and will work to get.

Negative reinforcement means you SUBTRACT something the animal dislikes, which makes him do the behavior again. You stop yanking up on the choke chain when the dog sits, or turn off the electronic shock collar and he sits more – it has to be something the dog doesn't like and will work to avoid.

Positive punishment means you ADD something the dog finds disagreeable, which makes him stop doing the behavior. You yell at him or yank on a choke collar and he stops barking.

206

Negative punishment means you SUBTRACT something the dog likes, which decreases the amount of the behavior. You put away the cookie you were going to give the dog or you turn your back on him (taking away your interaction with him) and he stops barking.

Another sticky piece of this puzzle is that you can look at a lot of behavior from both a decreasing and increasing perspective. For example, if a dog sits instead of jumping, his sitting behavior is increasing and his jumping behavior is decreasing. Whether you are using reinforcement or punishment depends on whether you are applying consequences after the sitting or the jumping. If the consequences come after sitting, they are reinforcing, if they come after jumping, they are punishing. Did you turn your back when the dog jumped? That's negative punishment (you took away something the dog wanted — your attention — which decreased the jumping behavior). Did you give him a cookie when he sat? That's positive reinforcement — you gave the dog something he wanted which increased the sitting behavior. If the dog doesn't want the cookie, and therefore doesn't sit more, then it's NOT positive reinforcement.

Confused? Now you know why we chose to stay away from all of this up to this point. Where all this information becomes important is when you run into problems – you think you are "reinforcing" sit but the dog is sitting less often. You may be reinforcing some other behavior or even punishing the sit without being aware of it. Here's something a little easier, the ABCs of operant conditioning.

A = Antecedent, anything that comes before a behavior. This is what your hand signals and verbal commands (as well as anything else the dog notices) are.
B = Behavior, whatever the dog does.
C = Consequence, the after effects of behavior, which could be reinforcing or punishing. Consequences drive behavior. If a dog learns that by begging at the table he will sometimes get tasty tidbits, he will put great effort into begging, even if he doesn't succeed every time.

You may also see shaping referred to as successive approximation. We briefly described shaping at the beginning of the book. It simply means building a behavior bit by bit, getting ever closer to the desired final picture. You gradually raise the criteria – rewarding better and better approximations, the effort the dog must make, the correctness of the action — until you get to the final behavior.

REINFORCERS AND HOW TO USE THEM

Okay, we've given your brain a little break — time to get back to reinforcers (abbreviated as RF). Clicker training is actually a subset of operant conditioning, whereby you are using a marker (a secondary RF, which is classically conditioned to a primary RF) to shape behaviors. Clicker training uses primarily two parts of the quadrant: R+ and P-.

A primary RF is something the dog inherently values and desires, that he will work to get or keep, such as food, water, freedom, play, touch, sleep, or sexual interaction. Primary RF may vary somewhat from dog to dog — some are chow hounds while others are toy nuts — but you should be able to discover several for your dog. Primary RF are very generally defined as something the animal needs for survival. (There is some debate about whether such things as play, social interaction and touch are "necessary for survival" for dogs. There are certainly dogs who live without them, and others who work very hard to get them. The only thing that really matters is whether YOUR dog will work for them!)

A secondary RF, also known as a conditioned RF or a bridge, gains value by being associated with a primary RF. So when you click and then treat, or smile and then pet your dog, you are "conditioning" the click or the smile to be a secondary RF. These secondary RF allow you to reward behavior precisely, even at a distance from the dog. A pleasant side effect of using secondary RF is that they can sometimes be conditioned to the extent that the dog will work for the secondary RF and skip the primary RF when it's offered.

There are also rates of reinforcement and schedules of reinforcement, two different things. The rate of reinforcement is simply how frequently you are delivering a reward. We've cautioned you throughout the book that your rate must be high or your dog may lose interest — learning requires a lot of effort and must be abundantly rewarded.

There are two basic schedules of reinforcement, continuous and variable. Continuous means that every time the dog performs the behavior, he gets a reward. However, once the behavior is established, a continuous schedule of reinforcement may mean that if the circumstances don't allow for the behavior to be rewarded every time, the dog may give up and stop offering the behavior (called extinction). If you expect that every time you put a dollar in a soda machine, a soda will come out, and it doesn't, you stop putting dollars in that machine. If it happens with other machines, you will stop buying sodas from machines altogether. Continuously RF behavior is very resistant to extinction initially. If the animal goes without a reward long enough, however, the behavior quickly drops off.

A variable schedule of reinforcement simply means that the reward is not given every time the dog offers the behavior. Sometimes three behaviors in a row may be rewarded, but sometimes five behaviors may be necessary before a reward is forthcoming. Catching a fish and getting a payoff from a slot machine are both examples of variable reinforcement activities. And think how obsessed people can become with pulling that lever or casting that line. Variable schedules of reinforcement encourage the player, be they fisherman or dog, not to give up, to keep trying. In other words, it's very resistant to extinction, since even an occasional reward can maintain the behavior. The rewards have to come often enough that continuing to play is worthwhile, though. If you dump $100 into a slot machine without getting so much as a dollar back, you very likely will quit playing that machine (although you're unlikely to swear off slots altogether!).

There is some controversy among dog trainers about continuous versus variable reinforcement. While many insist that you must switch to a variable schedule or risk losing the behavior, long-time trainers Bob and Marian Bailey maintain that they use continuous schedules of reinforcement and have rarely encountered a problem. Perhaps the answer lies in the complex behaviors trained by the Baileys, where even a "continuous" schedule of reinforcement may mean one reward in ten minutes or far more. Since they have actually been using this stuff with a variety of mammals, birds and invertebrates, and making a living at it, we have to assume they know what they are talking about! In the context of a competition dog, they will be in the ring for anywhere from 30 seconds (a jumper's run in agility) to 15 minutes (a normal performance in the obedience ring) so a behavior which has been continuously RF will easily hold up during that short amount of time. Plus, you're going to have other RF at your disposal besides a cookie, such as praise, petting and encouragement in most cases!

We suggest that you do add some variability to your training, in a couple of different ways. While you are shaping behaviors, you are putting them on a type of variable schedule, where only certain responses are clicked and treated — that is, the ones closer to your end behavior. Once you have a behavior solid, vary your reinforcement somewhat, asking for two or three behaviors before offering a reward, asking for longer and shorter durations of behaviors. We encourage you to use a variety of rewards, some of which will be better (more reinforcing) than others. The more interesting and unpredictable and rewarding you can make yourself, the more attention your dog is apt to pay, waiting to see what else you've got up your sleeve.

But for the purposes of training your pet, it really doesn't matter all that much. The reality is, humans aren't very good at paying attention well enough to continuously reward behavior once it's established. So the behavior automatically gets put on a variable schedule. You'll only need to worry about it when you see behavior deteriorating — it may be that you have switched abruptly to a variable schedule (either intentionally or unintentionally) after a long period of continuous RF or there may be something else going on, but it's worth looking at how often the dog is being rewarded for the behavior to see if the problem lies there.

Reinforcers can also be impacted by the Premack principle, which says that you can use a high probability behavior (something the dog gets a lot of RF for or intrinsically enjoys) to reinforce low probability behaviors (something that isn't rewarded often, or doesn't have intrinsic value to the dog.) That is, play with another dog (an enjoyable, high probability behavior) can be used as a reward for look at me (a not-so-interesting, low probability behavior). You can use this principle to add a variety of rewards to a dog's repertoire. For example, if the dog loves food, but isn't very interested in chasing a ball, you could shape the behavior of ball chasing using a clicker and treats. With enough pairing of "chase a ball, click, get a cookie," chasing a ball comes to have value to the dog because it predicts the click, which predicts the cookie. Eventually it becomes rewarding enough that you no longer have to give a cookie for ball chasing. We call high-probability behaviors the dog likes to engage in "life rewards." They are things that the dog values because he is a dog. You have control of a lot of the things a dog wants, because you're a human (with opposable thumbs and the ability to reason!) We referred to some of them in Chapter 6. If you can figure out what kinds of things your dog likes just because he likes them, you can use them to reward the dog for doing behaviors YOU want him to do.

Here are some other life rewards your dog might be interested in, and some suggestions for how they might be used to get what you want from the dog. Create your own list for your dog by observing the types of things he likes to do.

- Visit to another person or dog to reward attention
- Running loose to reward coming when called
- Play to reward sitting quietly

- Moving forward to reward walking beside you
- Access to a distraction to reward any behavior
- Access to a swim to reward waiting for permission to get into the water

Introduce "life rewards" by asking the dog to Sit or Down, click/treat, say "Release" or "Get it" and point to the reward, encouraging the dog to engage in the activity or grab the item. (Hint: Many of the items on your table of doggie distractions are "life rewards"!) Give the dog a few moments to enjoy the reward, then lead or call the dog back to you. Click, treat, then release to get the "life reward" again. You are conditioning the dog to understand he must wait for permission to get the life reward, which will improve his attention around distractions. If you need to, start with the dog on leash, so he can't get to the reward without your permission. Using life rewards is just like using food treats, the dog must understand when he can have access in order for the process to have the desired effect on behavior. As the dog begins to get the idea, vary how long he has to remain with you before he gets released to the reward.

DIFFERENTIAL REINFORCEMENT

Two other terms you may see in the scientific literature are DRA and DRI. These mean "Differential Reinforcement of an Alternative behavior" and "Differential Reinforcement of an Incompatible behavior," respectively. If your dog has some behavior you'd rather not see — say, jumping up on guests as they come in your door — you can reward the dog for instead running to get a toy and bring it back (an alternative behavior) or for sitting to accept a greeting (an incompatible behavior, since the dog can't jump up and sit at the same time).

SUPERSTITIOUS BEHAVIOR

Superstitious behavior usually involves accidental or coincidental learning of some irrelevant behavior along with the desired one. If you used your "emergency" $2 bill to buy your weekly lottery ticket because you forgot to go to the bank and get cash, and the ticket won a $1,000 prize, you might only buy tickets with $2 bills after that, even though it really had nothing to do with winning. It's also the source of all those "lucky shirts," "lucky socks," or whatever that bowlers, ballplayers, and other sportspeople are so fond of. Dogs and other animals pay attention to other things in their environment that may be occurring while they are learning. If you are teaching speak and the dog happens to back up before barking and you reward the bark, backing up could become a superstitious behavior. It's part of the behavior of "speak," as far as the dog is concerned, since it was paired with a reward, but totally irrelevant as far as you are concerned. If you then wanted to get rid of backing up, you would carefully have to click only speaking that didn't involve backing up. This is much more difficult than avoiding training in extra behaviors at the outset.

PUNISHERS AND HOW TO USE THEM

PUNISHMENT is applying something unpleasant (a squirt bottle for barking) or removing something pleasant (your presence when the puppy bites too hard), which decreases a behavior. The effectiveness of any form of punishment depends on how quickly it follows a behavior and how consistently it is applied. In order to work, punishment must
1) Be IMMEDIATE;
2) Follow EVERY INSTANCE of the behavior you are trying to change;
3) Be startling enough to impact the behavior;
4) Be associated only with that behavior;
Physical types of punishment may have unpleasant side effects – dogs often associate punishment with very specific circumstances, creating fearful or aggressive responses toward a particular person or in a particular environment. They can also learn to discriminate. They may cease doing a behavior, but only when you're around. A human example of this is driving slowly when a cop is visible, then returning to your previous speed when he exits the freeway. Dogs (like humans) are very good at discriminating in this way.

Clicker training, by its very nature, encourages a dog to experiment, to try things out. If you sometimes respond to experimentation by doing something nasty (positive punishment) to the dog because you don't like what he's doing, and sometimes respond by clicking (because you DO like it), your dog is going to be very confused. He's also going to be a lot less likely to try new things. This is a common problem with crossover dogs — those who initially learned a different way to figure out what is expected from them, and now are being encouraged to try new things on their own. If the worst thing that happens to your dog when he tries something new is that he doesn't get clicked, he is going to keep on experimenting (and believe us when we say, for a sensitive dog, not getting clicked can be very distressing!!) For more information on how to work with crossover dogs, see the section later in this chapter.

When you are clicker training with your dog, you are in a partnership. Both partners are working hard and, we hope, enjoying the process. You may need to apply a mild negative punishment if the dog becomes overexcited and barks instead of working, or is distracted by other things in the environment (you'll also need to change the environment for the next session!) You can interrupt the session, rather than shouting at or correcting the dog. If you're training outdoors on your own, this can be as simple as turning your back on the dog. If you're with other people or at home, you can be more sophisticated, by pretending to take a phone call or talk to someone else. Sitting down and chatting on the phone (or even pretending to) takes your attention away from the dog, offering no chance for a reward. Turning to talk to another family member or training buddy can have the same effect, showing your back to the dog and focusing your attention elsewhere. (But don't let your training buddy ignore her own dog while you're doing that!) This is a brief time out from training, less than 30 seconds. Beyond that, you're really not helping the dog to understand anything.

Also be careful about what you choose to "punish" in this way. NEVER punish your dog for lack of understanding, or for taking a break by going to get a drink or lying down in the midst of a session. Learning is tiring and the dog must be allowed to take a break. Negative punishment is most effective when it is used sparingly, and offers specific information for the dog, rather than causing him to shut down completely. You can gauge the effectiveness by seeing if it had the impact you wanted — did the dog settle down and get back to work? Or did he do more barking? In that case, review your training — it means your shaping plan needs modification to make the dog more successful.

Turning your back on the dog briefly is akin to a form of negative punishment commonly used by marine mammal trainers called the Least Reinforcing Stimulus. These trainers can't just walk out of the arena if their dolphins start misbehaving in the middle of a performance in front of a few hundred paying customers. Instead, the trainer will stand still and not look at the offending animal for several seconds. No movement means no cues and no eye contact means no chance for a fish reward — the trainer has become as uninteresting ("least reinforcing") as possible without actually removing herself.

EXTINCTION

Extinction is the cessation of a behavior because it's no longer being rewarded. But before it goes away, it may actually increase in frequency and intensity. This is called an extinction burst. It's an effort to regain the reward that has previously been associated with the behavior. For example, if your dog has been getting attention for jumping on you, and you decide to just stand still and completely ignore the dog (don't look at, touch, or talk to him) he will jump higher, harder or faster to gain your attention. In the past it has always worked, so he expects that it will work this time too, if he just tries harder. If the extinction burst goes unrewarded, the behavior will eventually stop. Remember, however, that not all rewards come from you, and also that what you see as punishment (yelling at the dog, say) could actually be reinforcement. If your dog dislikes being left alone or ignored, and you give him attention by yelling at him for jumping on you, you may actually be rewarding the jumping.

Some behaviors are impossible to extinguish, because they are inherently reinforcing for the dog. Many dogs enjoy the process of barking, or the stress relief it brings. With these dogs, barking problems will be difficult to resolve. Other behaviors which are difficult to extinguish include car chasing or getting into the garbage. Careful management of the environment will help, and having an alternative behavior you can ask for will at least give him something else he can be rewarded for.

We actually use the process of extinction when we are shaping new behaviors. If a behavior that previously worked no longer does, the dog tries harder. For example, if a paw movement at the old level is not clicked, the dog pushes harder, and then is clicked for the new level of paw movement.

Another way to use extinction to your advantage is to put a behavior on cue, reinforce it every single time, then stop asking for the behavior. For example, if your dog jumps on you, teach him to jump and attach the name Hug to it. Reinforce every single time you ask for the Hug (a continuous RF schedule). Give the dog something else he can do instead to be RF, like Sit, which is incompatible with jumping. Alternate Sit with Hug, and only reward what you ask for. Unrewarded hugs will drop off. You now have control of the behavior. You could also put jumping on a continuous RF schedule, then stop reinforcing it. After a short extinction burst the behavior will quickly drop off because it was previously put on a continuous schedule. Compare that to the situation now, where jumping is reinforced totally randomly - some of your friends don't mind, some don't know what to do, and some unintentionally reinforce it. Trying to extinguish a behavior that is randomly reinforced is much more difficult, and will take longer. The dog knows if he's persistent enough, eventually he'll get a reward.

CHAINING

Chaining involves teaching each part of a behavior separately until it looks the way you want, then bringing all the parts together, or combining a series of behaviors in sequence to create a more complex behavior. For example, an obedience recall is a chain of behaviors — you have the dog sit and stay, walk away, turn and call, and the dog has to sit straight in front of you after running to you. You can work on each part of the chain separately to make them strong when they are linked together — such as teaching "sitting straight" separate from "running fast to me."

    Back chaining (or backward chaining) is doing the same thing starting with the last piece of the chain and working backward. The theory is that learning is made easier by working from the new piece of behavior to already learned pieces of behavior, and the whole chain is made progressively stronger. Many people teach the retrieve this way, starting with having the dog hold and release the dumbbell; then reach for it, hold, and give; then pick it up off the ground, hold, and give; then pick it up, take a step while holding, and give; and so on. You'd keep working backward until you had the entire

behavior of running to the dumbbell, picking it up, bringing it back, and giving it to you. Because the dog is rewarded so often for giving the dumbbell to you while working on the backward chain, that is the strongest piece of the behavior. In effect, giving the dumbbell up becomes a secondary RF because it's paired with a primary reward often enough. That behavior then ends up reinforcing the behavior prior to it, which ends up reinforcing the behavior prior to THAT, and so on. This is another example of the Premack principle discussed earlier.

OVERSHADOWING

Overshadowing is a not-often-discussed but relatively frequent occurrence. It simply means that the most important detail in the environment — this is from the animal's point of view, not yours — can effectively blot out other details present. So, with a toy-crazed dog, waving a toy around as a lure may result in the dog focusing so strongly on the toy that he doesn't realize you are giving him a verbal cue as well, and the training you think you're doing may actually not be registering with the dog.

COUNTER-CONDITIONING

Counter-conditioning is teaching the dog to have a different physical response to a cue or antecedent. It's most commonly used with problem behaviors such as fear and aggression. Essentially, by pairing a strong reinforcer with the appearance of a cue, the animal comes to associate the cue with the reinforcer. This is really classical conditioning, which is the experimental area that Pavlov worked on. In other words, if every time a child appears, the dog gets a piece of steak, eventually the dog will salivate when the child appears. The child is a cue to the dog that he is going to get a tasty tidbit. One concern with counter conditioning is that it can sometimes work differently than you want it to. If not done carefully, instead of the dog thinking children predict steak bits, he learns that whenever steak appears, a child is lurking nearby. If the fear of children is stronger than the desire for steak, you will actually teach the dog to be afraid of steak! When working with counter-conditioning, it's important not to use a novel food (which could easily be assumed by the dog to predict something since he's never had it before) AND to work at a level where the dog is not traumatized by the cue (the child is far enough away) AND the order is correct — child predicts steak, not steak predicts child.

DESENSITIZATION

Desensitization is often used with counter-conditioning to deal with fear problems. It involves making a hiearchy of fear-producing events, and working gradually through them while practicing being relaxed. For example, if you are afraid of spiders, you might start with imagining a spider out in the woods (a low level) while practicing deep breathing. When the thought of a spider in the woods no longer bothers you, you would go to the next level, such as imagining a spider closer to you and so on until you could actually pick up a live spider. How far you (or the dog) are able to progress depends on how strong your fear is, how good you are at using relaxation techniques, and how slowly you move through the hiearchy so that you aren't traumatized during the process. With dogs, we can't ask them to list a hierarchy, we have to guess at it. We also aren't as good at producing relaxation on their behalf, and we frequently move too quickly, in a hurry to get the dog past the problem. All of these impact the success of a desensitization program.

CLICK TRICKS — Laws of Learning

The acquisition of behavior for all animals (humans included) is guided by these main principles of learning, sometimes called the "Laws of Learning:"

If a behavior is rewarded, it is likely to increase

If a behavior is not rewarded, it is likely to decrease

Once learned, if a behavior is randomly rewarded, it increases rapidly and can become obsessive

If a behavior is associated with a disagreeable experience, it decreases rapidly and can be extinguished

Dogs Do What Works!!!

SHAPING Q AND A

Q: The dog has done the behavior before, so I have upped the ante and required him to do more to get the treat. Then all of a sudden he just walks away and appears disinterested. Should I start from the beginning when he comes back or still require the higher level response to get the treat?

A: The dog is disinterested because he can't win. The training sessions are too long. Barking, walking away, etc. indicate the steps are too big and too difficult for the dog. If he leaves, reevaluate the step and break it down into smaller pieces. But don't go back to the very beginning. "Doing the behavior before" does not mean you should up the ante. At the start of each training session (lasting only 1 minute or 10 treats), decide what you are going to click. Anything AT THAT LEVEL OR ABOVE gets clicked through the entire step — you don't up the ante in the middle of the step. As a general rule of thumb, stay at each step until the dog has repeated the step at least 3 times, and up to 10 times if the dog is easily discouraged or new to clicker training. Again, during any 1 minute step, you are staying at one level of behavior, moving up to the next level of criteria at the next step.

Q: When working on the same behavior over a multiple-day period, do I start from step 1 on each new day, so he knows the behavior I am asking for (if it doesn't have a name yet), or do I require the higher response that we achieved the previous day in order to get a treat?

A: Do not start at step 1 each day. Keep notes on where you left off so you can start at that level for the next session and continue moving on. If the dog is new to clicker training, you might do a short (30-second) review at the last step you were at when you start a new session on a new day, but most dogs will soon learn to jump right in.

Q: What is a realistic (#/day and days/week) amount of training?

A: We work about 5-10 sessions per day depending on what we are working on and how much time we have. In other words, about 10 min a day spread out through the day. Some behaviors you can get in a day, some take weeks or months, it depends on how complicated the shaping is. As soon as the dog is to the point where you can predict he will do it, give it a name so that you can work on another behavior.

MODIFYING THE DIMENSIONS OF BEHAVIOR

As you become an expert on the use of the clicker, you'll find that you want to modify different pieces of a behavior, or maybe even go back and fix some behaviors that don't look quite the way you need them to. How a behavior looks is called the "topography" of a behavior. For example, how high a dog reaches with his paw when he waves, as well as how fast he moves his paw, is part of the topography of the wave. The duration of a behavior is how long the animal does it, such as how long the dog holds his nose on your hand when he touches. The latency or speed of response is how quickly the animal begins the performance after getting his cue, such as beginning the process of sitting immediately upon hearing the word Sit.

You can change the dimensions of a behavior easily with a clicker. There are a couple of things to keep in mind as you work through the process, however. First, change only one dimension at a time. If you want the dog to respond more quickly when you say Sit, don't try to change how the sit looks during the same session. Think of each dimension as a corner of a rubber band stretched into a triangle shape. As you make changes to one corner, the other corners have to give a bit. When you have one piece looking the way you want, work on another piece. You will gradually improve all three "corners" bit by bit, over several sessions (see more on Fluency below).

Second, break apart any chain of behavior to work on the piece you need to fix separately. If you are trying to get the dog to sit straight in front of you, don't leave the dog, call him to you, then try to get a straight sit. Instead, work on your sit with the dog directly in front of you until it looks the way you want it to. Then add it back into your chain bit by bit. Have the dog come to you from gradually increasing distances to a straight sit, until you have the distance you need. Then leave the dog, call him, and get your straight sit.

VARYING AROUND AN AVERAGE TO ADD DURATION

Duration is one of the more difficult aspects of a behavior to modify. It requires excellent timing with your clicker, as well as a clear idea of what you will be clicking. In some cases, you will be clicking an incremental change in the length of time the animal is doing something (maybe not even a second longer). This is where being adept at the bouncing around method we've mentioned earlier will come in handy.

If you've been working through the training in this book, you should be an old hand at "bouncing around." But you might have been wondering why we've been having you do it. It's because humans are such predictable stick-in-the-muds. If we didn't give you a specific way to vary how long you asked for a behavior, you'd be very likely to unconsciously fall into a rhythm. And if you always, however unconsciously, ask for the same duration, you will train the dog that that's as long as he ever needs to do it. You'll have trouble later if you need to extend duration.

So, to review. . .

While you are training a new behavior that needs to be done for an extended amount of time, delay the click and treat for one second. This is the first step in extending the behavior. After a step at a one-second delay — 3 to 5 repetitions — you extend the delay to two seconds. Work up a second at a time this way, until you can delay the click and treat for about five seconds, then begin your "bouncing." Back off a second or two from your maximum — so if your highest count was 5, your average would be 3. Now vary each time how long the dog has to maintain the behavior before you click, staying around your average of 3. A step in your session might go like this —

dog holds behavior for count of 2, click, treat

dog holds behavior for count of 5, click, treat

dog holds behavior for count of 3, click, treat

dog holds behavior for count of 1, click, treat

dog holds behavior for count of 4, click, treat

dog holds behavior for count of 3, click, treat

So for 6 repetitions, the dog held the count an average of 3 (18 total count divided by 6). If it helps you, by all means, write down how long you are going to count on each repetition. In fact, we encourage you to do this in the beginning so you don't fall into a pattern. As your next step, you are going to up the average by 1 or 2 counts. So your average will now be 4. Figure out how many repetitions you will do (no more than 10) and what the count will be at each repetition. If the dog stops the behavior before you get to the number you were counting to for that repetition, reset the count — don't click for less than what you planned on initially. If you find as you increase the average count that the dog is less successful (he's not getting clicked at least 80% of the time because he stops the behavior before you get to your count), just stay at a lower average for another step or two and build up your average more slowly. Here's where the artful part of training comes in, figuring out how much to move up so that you don't lose the dog, but are still adding time to your count! This way, the dog never knows for how long he may be asked to continue a behavior. You will find it much easier to accomplish whatever duration you may need.

WORKING AT A DISTANCE

The clicker is an excellent tool for building behaviors at a distance from you. It allows you to mark, with precision, exactly what you want without having to be directly next to the dog to provide your reward. If you've trained a behavior in close proximity and want to build distance from the dog, shape it the way you would any other criteria. Start close to the animal and add a few steps distance away every three or four repetitions. A solid Wait (Chapter 2) will help the dog understand he is not to follow you as you move away. Being able to have the dog catch a tossed treat will also encourage him to stay put. You can also work the dog on a mat (Chapter 3) or a platform to define for him the area he will remain in.

To teach the dog to catch, start with the dog in a sit in front of you. Hold a treat about one foot over the dog's head and say "catch" as you drop it. (Popcorn is a good choice for teaching catch since it's highly visible and "floats" a bit when you toss it.) If the dog has never done this before the treat will probably bounce off his head. Keep trying! Young pups may have difficulty at first, because their coordination isn't very good. Eventually he will start to open his mouth when you say "catch," in anticipation that you will drop the treat. Once he is catching well one foot from his nose, add more distance, one foot at a time. As he starts to get good at it, don't let him get the treat if it hits the floor. Try alternating with treats and favorite toys. (Do be careful that it's safe for your dog to catch, however. Hard bones and Kong™ toys should not be tossed at the dog. Tennis balls can be lodged in the throat of larger dogs.)

FLUENCY

Fluency is what makes us say "Gee, that is a WELL-trained dog!" It means that the dog performs the behavior with precision and speed immediately when given the cue (and only when cued). The behavior has been added to his repertoire of behaviors. When behaviors are fluent, the dog can perform them regardless of what else is going on (they are distraction proof) and will do them with a minimum of reward (they are extinction proof) in any environment (they are generalized). It's similar to learning to speak another language. We can understand a lot of Spanish, but we're not fluent in it because we don't speak it easily — it's not second nature for us. Training to fluency means the animal has mastered the behavior — he can "speak the language." The drills we suggest below will help your dog master fluency of a behavior. Remember when training to fluency that you can only modify one criteria at a time. As the dog becomes more fluent, all of the different aspects of the behavior will improve.

Once you have a behavior on cue, you need to generalize the behavior. Generalization means that skills or performance of a behavior are easilytransferred from one environment to another. For instance, our behavior of driving a van transfers over to driving a compact car. The skills of turning the steering wheel, using a brake and the gas pedal are consistent from vehicle to vehicle. Traditional training refers to this as "proofing for distractions." Unfortunately, this tends to encourage people to look at the dog as an adversary, a creature who is resisting training instead of participating in it. We prefer to look at it as a way to teach the dog that the behavior is done exactly the same regardless of when, where, or what else changes. Keep it interesting and build in the kinds of things that might encourage your dog to go off track, such as throwing a ball and either calling him to you or sending him to get the ball. The dog doesn't know initially which behavior he will be asked to do, but he gets rewarded either way, so there is always a payoff for doing what is asked.

Dogs do not generalize very well at all. That's why one of the most oft-heard handler laments is "But he always does it at home!" To help your dog generalize, be aware of:

- Your body postures — practice while you are sitting, standing, crouching and even lying down on the couch or ground.
- Your orientation (or how you are facing the dog) — try facing the wall, standing behind him, standing on the left or right side of him and every angle in between.

- The dog's orientation (or the direction the dog is facing) – change where the dog is facing in the room or approaching the prop.
- Your location in the room — move to a different part of room further away from TV, closer to bed, next to table, etc.
- Changing rooms — practice in different rooms and go through all of the above once you change rooms.
- Time of day — don't train at exactly the same time of day once you have the behavior if you want to generalize it.
- Other items in the environment — things that your dog finds rewarding are going to draw him into other behaviors. Use this to your advantage by offering the distraction for performance of a specific behavior you asked for. Now the presence of a "distraction" will inspire your dog to work harder to get it, instead of to go off track. Initially, you'll have to have control of the distraction, so that the dog can't self-reward even if he doesn't do the requested behavior.
- Changing locations — take it on the road to increasingly more distracting environments. Rank the environments so you gradually increase distractions. For most dogs the least to the most distracting would be: back yard, front yard, in front of next door neighbor's house, on the way to the park, at the edge of the park, in the park, etc.

GAMES TO PLAY TO IMPROVE PERFORMANCE

Improving Latency

Latency is the time it takes a dog to respond to a given cue (as opposed to the time it takes for him to complete the behavior). A dog that has a very short latency to cues is well on his way to being fluent.

Do three repetitions of a behavior that your dog knows well, clicking and treating after each repetition. Note the dog's average response time from when you give the cue to the beginning of his response to it. (This is likely to be a very short amount of time, so it might be handy to have a helper time his response for you.) Set your maximum response time to the longest of the three repetitions. This time will be your "limited hold" — it means that after this amount of time, the treat is no longer available even if the dog does respond.

Now cue the behavior 10 times, but click and treat only the 5 faster responses to your cue. You'll have to do this with a bit of intuition, since you won't be able to ask your helper and still click in a timely manner. Some of your clicks might be wrong, but don't worry about it too much. You're looking for an overall pattern of faster responses to your cue. If the dog does not respond within maximum time alloted, turn away and eat his treat (or just pretend to!) Then turn back and re-cue him. If the dog has an unusually fast response to your cue, remember to JACKPOT him with treats as well as heaping on verbal praise and petting.

Remember, you are clicking and treating for starting his response to your cue, not for completing the behavior. You will find that the behavior itself deteriorates a bit. That is, if you're clicking the dog for a fast response to Down, he will be clicked when he starts to perform it, but before he actually completes the down. At other sessions, work on fast completion of the down so you don't lose the behavior (see below).

Speed Drills

Remember those drills you did in order to become faster when you learned to type? The object was to maintain precision while building speed, gradually getting faster and faster with each repetition. Before you start speed drills, the behaviors you are working on should look the way you want them to and be on a random schedule of reinforcement. In other words, you're not clicking and treating every single response.

Start with 1 behavior. Using a manual counter (one that doesn't make noise) or having a helper count, cue the behavior over and over, noting how many times the dog does it during your set time frame (we'll start with a short amount of time, 10-15 seconds). Let's say you decide to start with Sit. Cue Sit, then Release, Sit, Release, for 15 seconds (an egg-timer to count down the seconds will be very helpful). How many times did the dog Sit during that time? Write it down. This is your baseline. For the next set of trials, click and treat the fastest completed sits during the 15 second time, dropping the treat on the floor to get the dog up and reset for the next repetition. For this drill, remember we are clicking the fast <u>completion</u> of a sit, not the response to your cue as before(although how fast the dog responds will also impact how many behaviors he does in a given time frame.) In other words, you're clicking him for getting his butt on the floor quickly.

Try to increase the number of sits for each 15 second session, gradually building up to the maximum number the dog is physically capable of doing. Take a break between sessions. If your dog makes an error or doesn't respond to the cue, wait a moment, and then re-cue it. If this happens repeatedly, or if the behavior deteriorates and doesn't look the way you want it to, stop working speed trials and go back and solidify the behavior.

Keep track of your progress. For example, say the first time you do this, you are able to get 6 behaviors in 15 seconds. Try for 8 behaviors in that time frame, then 11, and so on. When you get to the maximum you think your dog can do in 15 seconds, up the time to 20 seconds. Continue to build rapid-fire responses for longer periods of time, up to one minute.

Add another command such as Down (you'll be cueing Sit, Down, Sit, Down in rapid succession), starting with a 15 second block and building to faster repetitions before adding more time. When you add a third command, cue the behaviors randomly. Continue to intersperse more commands as the dog becomes speedier with his responses. Don't forget to write down what behaviors you're working on and how fast the dog is performing them! Over time, your speed will build to the point that you can give rapid-fire cues that the dog completes instantly. You can maintain proficiency with very little practice — once a week or so work on speed trials just for fun. You'll have a dog that not only understands and listens for the cue but also responds instantly and eagerly, on his way to being fluent!

Variability Card Game

This game encourages your dog to experiment and give you a wide variety of responses. You'll notice your dog tries new behaviors and variations of the one you're working on. As you vary rewards on a Down, for example, he may experiment by going down really fast or agonizingly slow, to see what is paying off. Since different things are paying off randomly, he will offer a number of responses. It also causes you to be more animated and experimental in your rewards, which the dog will enjoy. Play with these ideas and watch what happens with your dog's behavior.

Take a deck of cards and mark them with different instructions such as:

Click/Treat
Click/Jackpot
Bridge/Treat
Bridge/Play
Bridge/Jackpot

Click/Pet/Treat
Click/Praise/Pet/Treat
Click/Throw toy
Bridge/Throw toy
Click/Throw treat
Bridge/Throw treat
Throw toy, run and grab it
Run away with toy
Praise only
Praise/Pet only
Bridge/Praise/Treat
Click/Play
Click/Run/Chase
Use anything else that may be a reward for your dog

It's helpful to have someone read the card to you before you cue the behavior, so you are ready to respond appropriately when the dog does the behavior. To start the game, cue a behavior and give a 5-treat jackpot (handed to the dog one at a time or dropped on the floor in a pile). From that point on, follow the card drawn. If the behavior disappears, reward each of the next three repetitions, then return to the deck.

The Listening Game

This exercise teaches your dog to listen for the verbal cue (otherwise known as stimulus control). Pick two behaviors that your dog has on cue and knows well, such as Sit and Down. Give the cue, then click and treat if the dog does the correct behavior. If he does the wrong behavior, or offers a behavior without being cued, move away to a different spot to reset the dog, and give the cue again. If he does the correct behavior on the second cue, praise but do not click. He needs to do the correct behavior on the first cue in order to earn the click.

SIGNS, SIGNALS, CUES, AND COMMANDS

Signs can be considered anything in the environment that gives information to the dog about what is about to happen. Getting out the clicker and your treats is a sign to the dog that he's about to start working, the click means he's going to get a treat, putting on your tennis shoes in the morning tells the dog you're about to go for a walk. The dog may perform some behavior in response to this sign. If the behavior is then rewarded, the next time he sees the sign, he is more likely to do the same behavior (now the sign is a cue for the dog). Our dogs, for instance, start doing stuff when we pick up the clicker, and they stay very close when we put our tennies on, hoping that we'll head toward the front door and give them the next sign, picking up the leashes.

A cue is anything which tells the dog to do a behavior. A command is a verbal cue, whereas a signal is a visual cue. Cues are unique to a specific behavior. The cue "Sit" means to put your butt on the ground, but shouldn't have any other meaning. On the other hand, behaviors can have more than one cue, so that you could have both a hand signal and a command which mean "put your butt on the ground." Here's the tricky part — dogs pay attention to all kinds of things.

There may be cues in the environment or your body language or intonation of your voice that you're not even aware of. If you're not careful, you could be training in cues that you don't intend to. It's common for dogs to

learn that reaching for food means they are about to get a reward — causing them to totally ignore the clicker, since it is no longer relevant for them. (To solve this, make sure you always click before reaching for food.) That's why dogs sometimes appear to not understand cues in a different context, or when they're given by a different person — or as we so often hear "the dog won't do it without food." When we watch them give the cue with and without food, they are vastly different cues! Of course the dog won't do it when he's learned something else altogether is the cue. Something as simple as sitting and waiting for his bowl to be put down can be impacted by the presence of another person or dog, or changing rooms. We suggest you start your training in a boring environment, and also suggest that you have a "training" room where you start new behaviors. The dog will learn that the cues that are specific to that environment aren't relevant (or salient) to what he should be paying attention to.

The second thing that will trip you up about cues is that many people don't think carefully enough about them or make them distinct for the dog.

Then they blame the dog when he doesn't do what they asked him to. A really common example of this is when someone tells the dog Down, but they mean "don't jump," not "lay down on the ground." If the dog doesn't jump and gets rewarded, the meaning of Down for Lie down is muddied. Pretty soon when you mean for the dog to lie down, he doesn't — and people always blame the dog. Another common example is to add a body signal unintentionally when you are teaching the dog something, such as leaning forward and facing the dog when you say Come. Then when you try to call the dog and your back is to him, he has no idea what to do. It's no wonder, half of the signals he depends on for this behavior are missing! Have someone watch you to make sure you aren't adding cues that you don't intend to, or videotape yourself.

Command or Signal or Both?

You may have wondered when you might use a verbal versus a visual cue or whether you need to teach both. Well, you could choose only one or the other, and you'd get by. But having both at your disposal will give you more options. For example, there might be a time when you are in noisy surroundings and would have to shout to be heard, or you might be some distance from the dog and don't want to yell. You can use hand signals in this case. For older dogs losing their hearing or deaf dogs, hand signals are invaluable, and the only option you have. But there could also be times when your arms are full of grocery bags (or otherwise occupied!) but you need to direct the dog to do something. Having behaviors under control of verbal cues would be very useful in this case. In competitive events such as obedience, you'll be restricted to whether you can use a verbal or a visual cue for the performance of each behavior. In competitive events such as agility (where you and the dog complete an obstacle course in as little time as possible) you'll find that the dog most often is relying on body cues — having verbal cues in addition will give you more control over the dog.

A visual signal is generally a more obvious cue for the dog, and something they naturally pay attention to. Canines are marvelous students of body language, and watch their humans carefully for any clues about good things to come for dogs. So it's easier for them to recognize hand and body movements as having meaning than it is to learn words which are totally foreign to them. Some behaviors we've included in our instructions easily lend themselves to including a hand signal from the outset, because of the use of targeting or food to lure the behavior.

You have to do a little additional work to teach both, as you might have noticed from our continued instruction to pair the verbal cue with the behavior for at least 50 repetitions. But it's only a little extra work, and well worth it. Just be sure that once you have the dog doing a behavior with both a verbal cue and a visual cue that you don't always pair them together, otherwise you won't be able to use them separately. Also, if you use both a hand signal and a verbal cue consistently to ask for behavior, the dog may focus on the signal and ignore the verbal cue. If you do this often enough, you may actually wipe out the meaning of your verbal cue over time.

Adding Commands or Signals

We've mentioned many times in the instructions that you add a command at the point that the dog is doing the behavior reliably — about 80% of the time. You may be wondering why we picked this number. Actually, it's because the Baileys say to do it then! (And they've done this many more times than you or we will ever do in our lifetime.) And they have a good reason for it, as Bob Bailey explains:

> "Marian and I teach the 80% rule. If you are training a behavior that will be cued, you get the behavior to the point that about 80% of the time it is given it is just what you want. That is when the cue goes on. Most trainers wait not long enough (behavior too weak or imperfect) and they lose behavior, or too long (behavior is virtually 100% for a while) and there is a lot of extinction required, slowing down the installation of the cue. Certainly, what you don't want to do is train a behavior to the point of fluency before the cue is started. By the way, there is nothing magical about 80%. 73% is pretty good too, as is 84%. What you don't want is to be adding cues when the behavior is at 50-60% (too soon) or at 95-100% (too late).
> "By the way, the Brelands came up with the 80% rule in the late '40s. Much later, the laboratory types discovered that, lo and behold, a lab rat fully trained is slower to adapt to a new signal than a less well trained rat - suprise! Just another example of how early field work with animals was often far ahead of the much more restricted applications in the lab."

If you wait until the animal is doing the behavior 100% of the time, then something else is providing the cue for the behavior. Let's say, for example, that you are teaching the dog to wave. You could practice this behavior over and over, in different environments until it was 100% reliable. Something, though, is telling the dog to lift his paw in all those different environments, since you haven't given this behavior a name or a signal (you think). Perhaps it's that you tilt your head and look expectantly at his paw. It's probably something you're not even aware that you're doing that the dog pays attention to. Something has become the most salient thing for the dog – it has become a cue. It is the one thing that never changes when other variables change. Now let's say you want to call this Wave. You don't know what the dog is cueing to, but you start to say Wave just before he lifts his paw. You repeat the pairing over and over, thinking that the dog is learning to Wave because you say it. But the dog doesn't need to pay attention to what you're saying, something else already tells him to lift his paw. When that something else is gone, the dog won't lift the paw. When someone else tells him to Wave, he doesn't do it, because they don't cock their head in that cute way that you do when you want the dog to wave.

The other risk of waiting too long to add the cue is that the dog might begin to think it is the only behavior he should do, so he offers it first no matter where he is. It makes it difficult to work on other behaviors. (By the way, it's not impossible to add a cue even if you've worked a long time with a different one or even without one — it's just not a very efficient way to train!)

At the start, all you're doing is pairing your cue with the performance of the behavior, so that it occurs just before the behavior. The dog will start to realize that something comes just before he does the behavior. It becomes relevent for the dog when it discriminates for him when he will get the treat and when he won't. So when you give the cue, click and treat when the dog does the behavior. (You are actually shaping a different aspect of the behavior, by the way, "wave when I say this word.") Don't click and treat if you haven't given the cue. Now the dog starts to discriminate that your verbalization has to be there in order for him to get clicked. Initially, you want to do a lot more pairings of *cue - behavior - click/treat* than *no cue - no behavior - no click/treat*. You don't want to lose your new behavior while you're trying to add the cue! It's also important to continue to click and treat the correct response at this point. If you suddenly stop rewarding because you think the dog's "got it," he won't know that your cue is important to tell him WHEN he should do the behavior. As the dog starts to get the idea, you will gradually give your cue earlier and earlier, until it actually causes the dog to perform the behavior even if he was doing something else. At that point, you can put the rewards on a random schedule if you want and work on stimulus control — giving other commands interspersed with this behavior.

Fading or Changing Cues

At some point in working on a behavior, you may find that you need to get rid of a cue for the dog. Either because you unintentionally created it, because you need to change it to something else or because you no longer want it to be part of the cue. Getting rid of a cue is called "fading." The process involves making the cue less and less obvious to the dog, so that it gradually fades away. A good illustration of this is with the touch stick. In our instructions, we sometimes have the dog touching the stick, using the stick to get some other behavior. You can fade the stick in a couple of ways, either by making it gradually smaller and less obvious, or by putting it gradually farther away from the target object. If you were using a disk, you could cut the disk a little bit at a time until it disappears completely. For a hand signal, you would make the signal less obvious over a period of sessions. Let's say you started with a signal that involved putting your arm up pointing to the sky. To fade this signal, you would put the arm up slightly less far after each couple of repetitions, until you were no longer putting the arm up at all.

To change a cue, you need to fade the old cue and replace it with a new one. The best way to do this is to pair the new cue with the old in the same way that you pair a command with a behavior to name a behavior. The order is ALWAYS new cue - old cue - behavior - click/treat. (Remember it's alphabetical — N - O!) The dog will start to anticipate that the new cue predicts that you will give the old cue — he begins to anticipate that you will give the old cue. This is one case where anticipation works to your advantage! So he starts to do the behavior as soon as he sees or hears the new cue, in a hurry to get his click/treat. The old cue no longer is important to him, so it can be quickly faded at that point. Keep in mind that this pairing can also work against you, where the dog sees something that predicts your cue and does the behavior before he is cued. If you don't want that to happen, make sure there is nothing to indicate to the dog you are about to give the cue, and don't reward a behavior that's already on cue if you haven't yet given the cue. Again, here's where a training partner or videotape of your session can help you problem-solve.

What Is the Dog Trying to Tell YOU?

In addition to paying attention to what you're doing to help him understand what is expected, the dog will give you information about what's going on with him — is he enjoying himself or not? Some of what you see may be behavior that indicates the dog is stressed. Remember that we said that learning is stressful — for both you and the dog. You don't want it to be so stressful that the dog is unable to learn at all. To prevent getting to this point, you have to be paying attention to what your dog is trying to tell you — you have to learn to speak dog. For us, this is THE most important thing we've learned with clicker training. We have a confession to make - prior to clicker training, we ascribed all kinds of motivation to what the dog was doing. Part of our early learning in dog training involved such motivations as "the dog's blowing you off" "he's doing it intentionally" "he doesn't want to work." Mandy even had someone suggest to her that she get rid of a dog (after she had complained endlessly about how difficult the dog was to work with and motivate).

We're here to tell you that dogs don't have any underlying plot to make your life difficult. They do what works — they do what works — they do what works. You'll find that once you embrace this mantra, you'll be free to actually FIX all those "distraction" problems you're having. Become a student of the dog — what's in it for them? How does the behavior they are doing pay off? How can you make what YOU want them to do pay off for them? WHY doesn't he want to work? How does your dog exhibit stress? The behaviors that people say are "blowing you off" are stress behaviors — avoidance, pacing, sniffing the ground, doing something else like scratching, leaving the area, turning away from you, jumping on you, acting "silly." An excellent resource on stress behaviors is Turid Rugaas' book "On Talking Terms with Dogs: Calming Signals." Watch dogs play, watch dogs when they're yelled at, watch dogs when they're corrected. You'll see many different ways that dogs try to give information to other animals, including humans.

If your dog behaves like an idiot or seems to do odd things when you start to train, treat it as a learning experience and figure out why the dog is behaving that way. A very wise friend once commented "every dog teaches you something."

CUES Q AND A

Q: What happens when I am not working with him and he is doing the behavior I have been trying to get him to do? I'm assuming I should initiate the lesson, so I haven't been responding, but then I am worried he will only do the behaviors when he sees me ready with the clicker and it won't generalize to everyday situations. Any suggestions?

A: The behaviors have to be under stimulus control (done on cue, but not when not cued) eventually. I wouldn't react at all to anything he offers when you're not training for something specific. He's already shown you that he will do the behaviors without having the clicker around, so you don't need to worry about that.

Q: If you are trying to teach him to do nothing (sit or lie quietly) how do you get him to stop going through every sequence of behaviors he has ever done before in order to get a treat? (or do I just need to wait forever, let him bark, get aggravated etc). Will he learn that these other things don't work anymore? (I don't want that to happen).

A: Reward doing nothing. In other words, give treats for lying quietly (you don't have to use the clicker for this). Gradually reduce the frequency of the treats. If you are working with him in a training situation, you want him to be offering all kinds of behaviors. The dog is experimenting. If he doesn't experiment with how to make clicks happen then you can't shape behaviors. He will learn that only specific things get clicked. That's another reason why you need cues. If he is offering stuff willy nilly, those behaviors are not under cue. That's also why it's helpful to start behaviors in a "training area" so it's clear to the dog he should be doing something.
Also, if he is going through his whole repertoire, I suspect you are taking TOO BIG OF A STEP for the beginnings of the behavior you are working on. He's trying to get clicked, you're not offering any clicks, he's getting frustrated and trying things, then being reduced to barking because nothing is working. Try the exercises from the first chapter, and the Variable Card Game in this chapter, to teach him to offer different behaviors.

Q: Once he does the behavior consistently (usually after 10 min for easy things) do I start naming it then?

233

A: Would you bet money that he will do it? Is he doing it 80% of the time? "Consistently" and "after 10 min" may be mutually exclusive. Consistently implies he will perform the same behavior over a number of days in a number of environments.

Q: I'm getting confused about how he should figure out what I want him to do if these commands don't have a name yet - he goes through a routine of things that worked in the past.

A: He's confused too. He doesn't know what you want him to do without there being a cue attached to the behavior. If he is offering multiple behaviors:
        1) the OTHER behaviors are not on cue;
        2) You are working on too many new things at one time;
        3) You are taking steps that are too big, forcing him to run through his repertoire where he hopes something will be clicked.

        As an example, if we start a behavior in the living room (where we start most new stuff), we don't start another behavior in that same room until the first one has been named or put on some kind of cue. Sometimes that cue is visual (a piece of equipment the dog should be interacting with), sometimes verbal. We only work on one behavior during a group of sessions. There has to be SOMETHING to indicate to the dog that you are looking for a different behavior, a separation of time, a cue, a different location.

Q   Getting him to perform the behavior is good, but what I really want is getting the behavior, when I want the behavior, which is what I am having trouble with — now he waves at me all the time trying to get a treat.

A: Yes, because for xxx days, waving at you HAS gotten the treat. Now put it on command. Start another behavior by clicking "not waving" — any behavior which does not involve a foot movement. Break your behaviors down into smaller steps so he can get clicked for something that doesn't resemble waving.

Q: How do I mark the end of working on one command and beginning a new one? Once he gets something down pat I move on.

A: I'm concerned that your definition of "down pat" and the dog's don't match. It sounds like you're in way too much of a hurry to "move on."

234

Have you worked that behavior in different environments, with various distractions? Have you named it? Will he offer it only when cued and not when it's not cued? If not, it's not "down pat." Also, be sure to separate your sessions. Don't work on two different behaviors during the same session.

Q: But then it's like he doesn't think the other behavior is worthwhile any more and at first he goes through an extinction period where he tries the once successful behavior, but gets nothing. Eventually he moves on to a new behavior, but how do I maintain all of the behaviors he is learning, without extinguishing one with the next?

A: Put the old behaviors on cue, and continue to reward them when you ask for them. He will learn that only behaviors that are asked for get reinforced. You have to practice a behavior until it is 80% reliable, then do at least 50 repetitions to put it on cue before you can consider it in place. Then you can mix it with other commands the dog knows and reward only correct responses to cues.

GETTING RID OF THE CLICKER AND TREATS

To get rid of the clicker you need to have the following in place: 1) The behavior "looks" the way you want it to (done in the shaping process); 2) The behavior is on cue (he does it when asked and doesn't do it if not requested); and 3) The behavior is generalized. Once you have completed these steps, you don't have to click EVERY performance of the behavior. Sometimes you click and throw a toy, sometimes you praise without clicking, sometimes you bridge and treat, sometimes you ask for two behaviors, etc. (See the Variability Card Game for more ideas.) As the dog's performance gets more reliable, his rewards get more variable and unpredictable. This keeps the dog guessing, which keeps him interested in working. You can get rid of the click/treat for the behavior, but you never "get rid of" motivation. You wouldn't expect to go to work without being paid and the dog shouldn't either.

You won't actually stop using the clicker, even though you may not be using it for already learned behaviors. When you teach new behaviors, start them with the clicker. When the behavior looks the way you want it to and is on cue, give the cue, then reward the behavior. The clicker is no longer needed as a secondary reinforcer at that point. It doesn't really have to be "weaned off" because the dog is rewarded for performing the behavior on cue. But it won't hurt if you want to continue to click the behavior once you have it all put together (it's just one more thing you have to have in your hand). You can also reintroduce the clicker if you need to fine tune a behavior or change an aspect of it, say speed up the performance or increase the duration or change the final look of the behavior.

For dogs who are highly motivated by food, you'll need to teach them to like other things if you want to use them instead of or in addition to food as rewards. See the information earlier in the chapter on the Premack principle for the steps to do this. Not all dogs are motivated by food, however. Kibble is only valuable if the dog wants it — he won't work for it if he doesn't. You can hand feed the dog to increase his desire, decrease the amount of overall food he is getting (even skipping meals), or use a different kibble to improve his interest. We find that the interest level for not-so-exciting food treats improves as the dog gains experience in the game of clicking, but if you need to boost your dog's interest in food treats, try some of the following:

Brand Name Bite-size Treats:	Human Food Treats:	Dog Treats You Can Break Into Bits:
Liver Biscotti	Cheese tortellini	Rollover
Clean Run Crunchies	Hot dog cut into bits	Bowser's Best Buffalo Bites
Wildside Salmon	Bits of cheese	Any brand beef jerky
Tia Bits	Leftovers - steak, chicken	Pupperoni
OMH Bitz, Meaties	turkey, pork, fish	Snausages
Rollover Mini Bites	Grapes, raisins	Canine Carry Outs
Great Bait	Cheerios or other cereal	Chicken Grillers
Redi freeze dried liver	Popcorn	Alpo steak treats
Plain beef or turkey jerky	Ostrich jerky	

Remember to count the food you're using when you click as part of the dog's daily ration. If you're feeding his normal amount, and doing several training sessions per day, you will very quickly end up with a tubby puppy. We mix a variety of treats (and a bit of kibble) into one container so the dog is getting a different treat on every click, but you can set it up in whatever way works best for you and the dog.

Toys are effectively used when you want to increase the speed or intensity of a behavior. If the dog's reward for running quickly to you is that he gets to chase a toy, he will add speed much more quickly than if you stopped his movement by handing out a treat (or you could always fling the treat, so he gets to chase it!) The one thing you have to be very careful about is not letting the dog know that the toy will be thrown until AFTER you get a behavior that is clicked. Don't use the toy as a lure to speed him up, dangling it in front of him. It will be very difficult to fade. Have someone else throw the toy after you click if you have a tendency to "show your hand" before you actually get the behavior you're looking for. You could even leave the toy on the ground, then click and race the dog to the toy as his reward (he'll always beat you but it's much more fun this way!) Conversely, if you wanted the dog to remain in one spot, flinging a toy would not be your best choice for a reward, but food treats or gentle petting might work perfectly.

We mentioned before that the click sometimes interrupts behavior, because the dog has to collect his reward. If you bring the reward to the dog, this won't be an issue when you want a behavior that requires the dog to stay put. Rest assured that either way the dog will learn, it will just take longer to get where you're going. Having a variety of options for rewarding your dog will be very handy as you work on different behaviors.

With any type of reward that you are using, keep in mind that if the dog has free access to it, it will be less valuable to him. So if he gets petting whenever he nudges you, it won't be as valuable as it would if he had to work for a rousing session. The more creative you are about using different rewards with your dog, the more useful and interesting they will be for him.

BUILDING THE BRIDGE
(when you don't have a clicker available)

A bridge can be a sound (a click or word), or a sight (a light turning on). In your dog's life, there are many varieties of secondary reinforcers which are "natural" bridges. The sound of a baggie rustling, a can opener, car keys, etc. all tell the dog something good is about to happen. Sight cues might include picking up the leash, or putting on your tennis shoes. You can use a verbal bridge to substitute for a clicker when you don't have one handy. Note that the verbal bridge is much less precise than a clicker, so it is less effective for shaping behaviors. You can also use a visual bridge (such as a flashlight turned on and off quickly) instead of a clicker for dogs that don't have hearing. Condition the bridge the same way you did the clicker, by pairing the bridge with food. A bridge word needs to be short, distinct and enthusiastic. Suggestions are: YES, RIGHT, WOW, BINK, GREAT, YEAH. Avoid using

GOOD, since it is frequently used to praise the dog and is not distinct enough. Be sure to present the bridge first (say the word or flash the light) then immediately follow with the food treat — they don't occur at the same time.

KEEPING RECORDS

One of the most important things we've learned while training chickens with Bob and Marian Bailey is to keep records. When you work with multiple dogs, it's sometimes difficult to remember what you're doing with each dog (sometimes it's hard to remember even when you're only working with ONE dog!) Records allow you to set a baseline of a behavior — how will you know if there's improvement if you don't know where you started? They also allow you to modify your training program if your dog didn't follow along with the book! Records will help you break behavior into smaller bits when needed, and move ahead when you can. Plus it's fun to go back and realize that you really haven't been working on this behavior all that long and be encouraged by your success! You can make records as detailed or brief as you like, but at a minimum you want to include:

- The date
- The session number
- The success rate of the behavior — whether the dog got to the criteria you set out originally, or whether he's repeating the behavior often enough that you could add a cue. One way to determine the success rate of the behavior as well as the length of the session is to count out 10 treats and set your egg timer for one minute. During that time, you might note how many treats the dog got, or how many times the behavior was repeated correctly. Or you could time how long it took you to get rid of 10 treats. If the dog is getting faster, you'll know the behavior is moving along well.
- A baseline if you're trying to change something specific about the behavior (for example, how often will the dog do it in a given period of time – 10 seconds or so — without treats?) When you start to click and treat the behavior, that will change. If it's not improving, you'll know something needs to be changed in your program.
- How long you worked — by session or repetitions.
- What your plan is for the next session — what will your criteria change be, can you change criteria or do you need to split the behavior finer? If you tried something different, did it work? How will you build on it?

- You might also want to include environmental information (where you are working, with who or with what), types of rewards, an overall impression of how the dog is working, or the time of day. What you include is totally up to you, your needs and your willingness to write things down. Even very minimal records will help you improve your shaping skills and work effectively with the dog.

CLICK TRICKS
Bob Bailey

"I find most dog trainers to be in a great hurry all of the time. Why? Where are they going? Take your time and make sure you have what you want pretty good before you move on. One successful trial does not a behavior make! By the same token, one unsuccessful trial does not a behavior break!...Don't be discouraged when things don't go exactly as planned. Keep gathering data and learning from each experience. There will be a strong and natural tendency to want to abandon the systematic approach and go with what is expedient. Memory is fickle. Memory is very short. Those that rely on memory are doomed to repeat many mistakes because they think they remember, and they don't."

CROSSOVER DOGS AND CROSSOVER TRAINERS

In the world of clicker training and clicker trainers, someone who learned to train in a traditional way (whether using food to lure behaviors or with a choke chain and leash) and now uses a clicker is called a crossover trainer. Crossover trainers generally run into problems in clicker training in these areas –

- They find it difficult to let go of the control of the behavior (that is, letting the dog figure it out is difficult for them).
- They have a tendency to fall back on what worked in the past when things aren't going well (resorting to luring or corrections if the dog isn't figuring out the behavior).

- They don't trust that the dog will figure it out (they want to help the dog by luring or showing the dog what to do).
- They tend to assign motivation to the dog's behavior ("he's blowing me off").

Crossover dogs are those that have learned some behaviors in a traditional way. Crossover dogs don't tend to offer behaviors in the absence of lures, cues, or prompts. They aren't good at doing a lot of different things – they wait to be told what to do. There is nothing derisive about either term, mind you. It just means that you used to do something one way, and now you do it another way. Both of your authors are crossover trainers, as are most of the people you'll meet who use clicker training. We find that adopting clicker training as an exclusive method follows a pretty predictable pattern, so we thought we'd lay it out for you here.

One of the most fascinating things for us about clicker training is that it has an application for anyone of any skill level. It can be used very simply as a marker for correct behavior by someone with no interest in developing skills beyond that, or someone whose timing isn't the best. It can be used to shape simple behaviors by someone with minimal skills. It can be used to create and build complex behavioral chains by someone with good timing who is willing to practice and experiment a bit. Or it can be used with great skill to teach phenomenal things and actually communicate with the animal — any animal. You get to decide how you're going to use it.

The first step in learning about clicker training is generally experimental. You either use it to mark completed behaviors or you shape one or two behaviors, finding that it works very nicely, in which case you add it to your "toolbox" and try it with other behaviors. Or you may find that you run into significant problems using it with your dog. Generally those problems fall into a couple of categories, either with the dog not wanting the food offered, being unwilling to work for it, being afraid of the clicker or unable to understand what he's supposed to be doing. We suppose that if you had problems at the beginning, you probably didn't make it all the way to the last section of the last chapter, but if you did — Click! — here's your reward.

If the issue is fear of the clicker, we gave suggestions for that in Chapter 1. Don't be afraid to use something else as a marker. Eventually you could (if you wanted) use another secondary reinforcer to teach the dog not to be afraid of the clicker. If the dog isn't interested in food, we gave you some tips in the last section. If your dog isn't willing to work for food, you have to make the food more important to him by giving him less of it and then making him work for it. Start with something simple like having him sit to get his water bowl put down and build up to making him sit to get every single piece of kibble he gets during the day. It will take a couple of weeks, but in the end it will be worth it. We can guarantee that if you're having problems with the dog in this area, you're having them in others. Clicker training will give you access to solving other problems if you put the work in to teach the dog how to learn and how to work for what he wants in life.

If the dog is confused about what's expected from him, you'll have to teach him how to learn differently. Your dog can learn how to learn. Really, trust us, he can. Right now he's waiting for you to show him what to do. That's what you've been doing his whole life up to this point. He doesn't know how to learn any other way. The most difficult step for him will be learning to offer behaviors. The best exercises we can recommend are the Warm up exercises in the first chapter and the Variability Card Game in this chapter. Do them over and over until your dog starts doing lots of silly things when you pick up the clicker. Don't be concerned about it, don't panic — that's exactly what you want. The clicker gives you the power to take that silly stuff and mold it to what you want. Don't clicker train anything important in the meantime, anything you'll really need — you'll both just end up frustrated. Teach tricks and silly stuff you won't care about, play with it. One of our dogs learned to put one foot on one stair – totally useless, but fun nevertheless to shape. Keep in mind that your dog has been taught NOT to offer stuff. Anything other than what you were looking for has been corrected before this point, experimentation has been discouraged. It may take him a while to feel safe experimenting again. A correction means, anything but what I want you to do is wrong; the clicker means, keep trying different things until you figure out what I want. They really are mutually exclusive ways to learn. Here's where you come to the next stage in your development as a clicker trainer.

As you see what the potential is for clicker training, you will take the skills and concepts, and lay them over the top of your usual training method. It won't work (you'll just have to trust us on this) but you're going to do it anyway. It's part of the progression of changing methods. Some behaviors you'll do in the tried and true method you've been using, whatever that is. Some you'll teach with the clicker. Sometimes you'll try to take a behavior that you used to teach, and add in the clicker (usually using it as a marker, rather than shaping behavior). You'll experiment with ways of getting behaviors that involve luring, for the most part. You'll get more creative about how you lure things, and get more complicated training tools, like folding touch sticks. It's okay. It's part of YOUR learning process. You may never move beyond this point. That's okay too! Remember, above all, that this is a partnership with your dog, it's supposed to be a fun game. No one ever died because they weren't able to teach their dog to wave (not that we know of, anyway!)

At some point, though, you may start to notice a change in how you view things. Every task will start with asking "What's in it for the dog?", "How can I change what's in it for the dog and make him work for me?" You'll want to teach complicated stuff, just because you can. You may have an epiphany with your own dog about how he reacts to corrections. You'll start to look at things in terms of "what do I want the dog to do and how could I teach that?" With this comes a real understanding of the dog as a dog — what motivates them and how they communicate, why they do what they do. Now you'll look at your old method and say "how could I do this differently, more quickly, easier, with less stress on the dog?" Shaping will become second nature to you. You've been converted — you'll speak in "clicker," you'll recognize other clicker-ers You'll have clickers all over the house, you'll travel with them so you can introduce clicker training to others (well, maybe that's just us!) Just remember when you get to this stage, that others may not be there yet. Don't denigrate other trainers for not using "your" method. Show them, instead, how wonderful it is and let them make their own choices. Reward what you like, and ignore what you don't. The principles are the same for clicker training your dog — only the motivation to work is different for humans!

We hope you enjoy clicker training as much as we have enjoyed bringing it to you and teaching it to our own dogs! Good luck with your training, and remember, it's supposed to be fun!

Resources

WEBSITES:

www.APDT.org (finding a trainer who uses positive, treat-based training)
www.cleanrun.com (treats and supplies)
www.clickandtreat.com (Gary Wilkes' site - books, videos, supplies including touch sticks and contact trainers, training information)
www.clickersolutions.com/clickersolutions/cshome.htm (A clicker list)
www.clickertraining.com (Karen Pryor's website – books, videos, supplies including touch sticks, training information)
www.click-l.com/faqs.html (A clicker list)
www.doggonegood.com (treats and supplies)
www.dogpatch.org/obed/obpage4.cfm (Competition information for agilityand obedience)
www.dogwise.com (books, videos and toys)
www.hsnp.com/behavior/ (the Baileys' site)
www.inch.com/~dogs/clicker.html (American Dog Trainer Network clicker trainer link)
www.legacybymail.com (supplies, books, videos, clickers)
www.legacycanine.com (conferences and seminars on dogs, training information)
www.puppyworks.com (conferences and seminars on dogs)
www.sitstay.com (supplies and treats)
www.suesternberg.com (books and videos for shelter dogs)
www.wazoo.com (finding a trainer who specializes in clicker training)
www.writedog.com (Cheryl Smith's website, where you can find articles about training and information on new books)

RECOMMENDED READING:

Don't Shoot the Dog, Karen Pryor — The "bible" of clicker training
Clicker Training For Obedience, Morgan Spector — Designed for obedience competitors
Clicker Journal - order at www.clickertrain.com (Includes articles on training other species)

Behavior Modification, What it is and how to do it, Garry Martin and Joseph Pear — All the scientific details in an easy to understand book
Choose to Heel, Dawn Jecs — Training easily accommodates using a clicker

DEALING WITH FEAR AND AGGRESSION (MENTIONED IN THE BOOK):

Culture Clash, Jean Donaldson — Behavior problems, general dog behavior, desensitization and counter-conditioning programs
anything by John Rogerson (or go see him in person if he comes to your area!)
Help for Your Shy Dog, Deborah Wood

BODY LANGUAGE IN DOGS (MENTIONED IN THE BOOK):

On Talking Terms with Dogs: Calming Signals, Turid Rugaas
Speak! Real Communication Between You and Your Dog, Cheryl S. Smith (available Winter 2001/02), The Crossing Press
Canine Behavior: Body Postures and Evaluating Behavioral Health, Sue Sternberg, Animal Care Training (video) www.4ACT.com or 1-800-357-3182

ORDERING BOOKS AND SUPPLIES:

Legacy By Mail – www.legacybymail.com
Dogwise – www.dogwise.com
SitStay.com – www.sitstay.com

TOYS DESIGNED TO HAVE TREATS KEPT IN A POCKET (MENTIONED IN THE BOOK):

Jackpot Trainer, available in chicken, chipmunk and other forms, from Legacy by Mail, Dogwise

DESENSITIZATION TAPES (MENTIONED IN THE BOOK):

Terry Ryan's from Legacy by Mail
K-9 Counterconditioning - thunder, crowds, fireworks, gunfire, traffic, sirens, baby crying available from Steve Boyer, 1-800-952-6517
Virtual Competition dog show noise tape - available from Positive Power Productions 1-410-295-7415
Ttouch tapes/videos on relaxation and massage - available from Thone Marketing International, 1-800-797-PETS

Index of Behaviors

Behavior	Chapter/Page	Description	See also
Buddy	6 (People and physical contact)	Dog will slide his head under someone's outstretched hand	
By me	3 (Walk off leash)	Dog walks beside you with no leash	Walk on leash, ch 2
Check in	3	Dog will come and work with you regardless of what's happening in the environment	
Chill out	4 (Go to your place)	Dog goes to place indicated and lies down	Look there, ch 3
Close, close walking	3 (Walk off leash)	Dog walks beside you with no leash	Walk on leash, ch 2
Come	2	Dog comes directly to you when requested	
Compass	4 (Turn around)	Dog turns 180 degrees from the direction he was facing	
Confidence building	6	Various exercises to help build confidence in the dog	
Crash	2	Dog lies flat on ground	Down, ch 2
Dance	5 (Put 'em up/ dance	Dog dances around on his hind legs	
Dead dog	5 (Play dead)	Dog falls on side on ground	

Behavior	Chapter/Page	Description	See also
Desensitization	6 (Noise fears)	Desensitizing the dog to noises	Ch 7
Dog-a-Polt	3 (Paw touch)	Dog touches target with paw	
Doggie distractions table	6 (Calming excitable dogs)	List of all the things that distract your dog	
Dog-to-dog interactions	6	Dog will sit quietly on leash while another dog approaches	
Dog's name	2	Dog comes directly to you when requested	Come, ch 2
"Doggy Zen"	1 (Attention)	"To get the treat, you must give up the treat"	
Don't touch	2	Dog removes his nose/ teeth/paws from whatever he is touching	
Down	2	Dog lies flat on the ground	
Drop	2	Dog lies flat on the ground	
Drop	3 (Check in)	Dog comes and works with you no matter what else is going on	
Drop it	6 (Possession problems)	Dog willingly gives up anything he has	

Behavior	Chapter/Page	Description	See also
Duration	3 (Watch) 7 (Varying around an average)	Building up the amount the dog does a behavior	
Easy	1	Dog takes treat from fingertips without injuring you, using his tongue	Take a treat gently, ch 2
Easy	2 (Walk on leash)	Dog walks on leash without pulling	Off leash walking, ch 3
Excitable dogs (focus, focus, focus)	6	Dog looks first to you for permission if he wants something	Watch, ch 2; Touch, ch 3
Find me	5	The dog waits until told to find a person or item	
Fluency	7	Games to play to improve performance	
Freeze	4 (Stand still)	Dog stands quietly while you bathe or groom him	
Front	4 (Turn around)	Dog turns 180 degrees from the direction he was facing	
Gentle	1	Dog takes treat from fingertips without injuring you, using his tongue	Take a treat gently, ch 2
Get back	3 (Back up)	Dog backs away from you in a straight line	

Behavior	Chapter/Page	Description	See also
Get it	6 (Confidence building)	Creating interest in toys	
Gimme five	5 (Wave/high five)	Dog brings paw to palm of person	Paw (touch), ch 3
Give	6 (Possession problems)	Dog willingly gives up anything he has	
Go say hi	6 (People and physical contact)	Dog will slide his head under someone's outstretched hand	
Go to your place and settle	4	Dog goes to place indicated and lies down	Look there, ch 3
Head down	5	Dog lies down with his chin resting on the floor	
Heel	3 (Walk off leash)	Dog walks beside you with no leash	Walk on leash, ch 2
Hello	6 (People and physical contact)	Dog will slide his head under someone's outstretched hand	
Here	2	Dog comes directly to you when requested	Come, ch 2
High	5 (Put 'em up/ dance)	Dog stands up on his hind legs	
High five	5 (Wave/high five)	Dog brings paw to palm of person	Paw (touch), ch 3

Behavior	Chapter/Page	Description	See also
Hold still	4 (Relax for vet. exams)	Dog lies quietly on his side while you examine his body	Play dead, ch 5
Hold still	4 (Toenail clipping)	Dog allows you to clip his nails without moving	
Hold up	2 (Wait)	Dog remains behind a doorway or threshold	
Launch	2 (Paw touch)	Dog touches target with paw	
Leave it	3 (Check in)	Dog will come and work with you regardless of what's happening in the environment	
Left	3 (Walk off leash)	Dog walks beside you with no leash	Walk on leash, ch 2
Left	4 (Turn around)	Dog turns 180 degrees from the direction he was facing	
Let me see	6 (Possession problems)	Dog willingly gives up anything he has	
Let's go	3 (Walk off leash)	Dog walks beside you with no leash	Walk on leash, ch 2
Let's go, Let's walk	2 (Walk on leash)	Dog walks on leash without pulling	Off leash walking, ch 3
Let's play	6 (Confidence building)	Creating interest in toys	

Behavior	Chapter/Page	Description	See also
Look	3 (Watch)	Dog looks at you when requested	Attention, ch 1; Check in, ch 3 Excitable dogs, ch 6
Look ashamed	5 (Head down)	Dog lies down with his chin resting on the floor	
Look there	3	Dog looks away from you, in direction indicated	
Mark	3 (Look there)	Dog looks away from you, in direction indicated	
Mine	6 (Possession problems)	Dog willingly gives up anything he has	
Nice	1	Dog takes treat from fingertips without injuring you, using his tongue	Take a treat gently, ch 2
Nighty night	5 (Head down)	Dog lies down with his chin resting on the floor	
Noise fears	6	Desensitizing the dog to noises	
Nose	3 (Touch w/nose)	Dog touches hand with nose	
Object fears	6 (Confidence building)	Approach and touch object	
Off	2 (Don't touch)	Dog removes his nose/ teeth/paws from whatever he is touching	Check in, ch 3

Behavior	Chapter/Page	Description	See also
Off-leash walking	3	Dog walks beside you with no leash	Walk on leash, ch 2
Okay	2 (Release)	Dog no longer has to do the command	Sit, ch 2
On your mat	4 (Go to your place)	Dog goes to place indicated and lies down	Look there, ch 3
Open	4 (Take medication)	Dog allows you to open his mouth without struggling	
Park it	2	Dog puts butt on ground	Sit, ch 2
Park it	4 (Go to your place)	Dog goes to place indicated and lies down	Look there, ch 3
Pause	2 (Wait)	Dog remains behind a doorway or threshold	
Paw touch	3	Dog touches target with paw	
People and physical contact	6	Dog will slide his head under someone's outstretched hand	
Pet, Petting problems	6 (People and physical contact)	Dog will slide his head under someone's outstretched hand	
Place	4 (Go to your place)	Dog goes to place indicated and lies down	Look there, ch 3
Play dead	5	Dog falls on side on ground	

Behavior	Chapter/Page	Description	See also
Plotz	2	Dog lies flat on ground	Down, ch 2
Possession problems	6	Dog willingly gives up anything he has	
Punch	3 (Paw touch)	Dog touches target with paw	
Push	3 (Paw touch)	Dog touches target with paw	
Put 'em up	5	Dog stands up on his hind legs	
Quiet	5 (Speak)	Dog stops barking when told to	
Ready	3 (Watch)	Dog looks at you when requested	Attention, ch 1; Check in, ch 3; Excitable dogs, ch 6
Relax	4 (Go to your place)	Dog goes to place indicated and lies down	Look there, ch 3
Relax (for vet. exams)	4	Dog lies quietly on his side while you examine his body	Play dead, ch 5
Release	2	Dog no longer has to do the command	Sit, ch 2
Resource guarding	6 (Possession problems)	Dog willingly gives up anything he has	
Ride	5 (Skateboarding)	Dog rides a skateboard	

Behavior	Chapter/Page	Description	See also
Right	3 (Walk off leash)	Dog walks beside you with no leash	Walk on leash, ch 2
Right	4 (Turn around)	Dog turns 180 degrees from the direction he was facing	
Sad puppy	5 (Head down)	Dog lies down with his chin resting on the floor	
Say Ahhh!	4 (Take medication)	Dog allows you to open his mouth without struggling	
Say bye	5 (Wave/high five)	Dog picks up leg and paws at the air in "waving" motion	Paw (touch), ch 3
Search	5 (Find me)	Dog waits until told to find a person or item	
Seek	5 (Find me)	Dog waits until told to find a person or item	
Settle	4 (Go to your place)	Dog goes to place indicated and lies down	Look there, ch 3
Settle	4 (Relax for vet. exams)	Dog lies quietly on his side while you examine his body	Play dead, ch 5
Shush	5 (Speak)	Dog stops barking when told to	
Side	3 (Walk off leash)	Dog walks beside you with no leash	Walk on leash, ch 2

Behavior	Chapter/Page	Description	See also
Sit	2	Dog puts butt on ground	
Sit/stay (while greeting)	4	Dog sits while you let someone into the house or greet someone on the street	
Skateboarding	5	Dog rides a skateboard	
Sleep	5 (Play dead)	Dog falls on side on ground	
Sound off	5 (Speak)	Dog barks on command and keeps barking until told to stop	
Speak	5	Dog barks on command and keeps barking until told to stop	
Splat	5 (Head down)	Dog lies down with his chin resting on the floor	
Stand, Stand still for bathing and grooming	4	Dog stands quietly while you bathe or groom him	
Stay	4 (Sit/stay for greeting) 4 (Stand still)	Dog remains in position until released	Sit, ch 2
Stomp	3 (Paw touch)	Dog touches target with paw	

Behavior	Chapter/Page	Description	See also
Take a treat gently	2	Dog takes treat from fingertips without injuring you, using his tongue	Don't touch, ch 2; Give me that!, ch 6
Take medication (Say AHH!)	4	Dog allows you to open his mouth without struggling	
Thank you	6 (Possession problems)	Dog willingly gives up anything he has	
Tired puppy	5 (Head down)	Dog lies down with his chin resting on the floor	
Toenail clipping, Toesies	4	Dog allows you to clip his nails	
Touch	4 (Turn around)	Dog turns 180 degrees from the direction he was facing	
Touch object	6 (Object fears)	Approach and touch object	
Touch stick	3 (Touch w/nose)	Dog touches end of stick with nose	
Touch with nose	3	Dog touches hand with nose	
Touch with paw	3 (Paw touch)	Dog touches target with paw	
Tug games	6 (Confidence building)	Creating interest in toys	

Behavior	Chapter/Page	Description	See also
Turn	4 (Turn around)	Dog turns 180 degrees from the direction he was facing	
Turn around	4	Dog turns 180 degrees from the direction he was facing	
Varying around an average	3 (Watch)	Building up the amount of time the dog does a behavior	
Wait at the door	2	Dog remains behind a doorway or threshold	
Walk off leash	3	Dog walks beside you with no leash	Walk on leash, ch 2
Walk on leash, Walkies	2	Dog walks on leash without pulling	Off leash walking, ch 3
Watch me	3	Dog looks at you when requested	Attention, ch 1; Check in, ch 3; Excitable dogs, ch 6
Wave	5	Dog picks up leg and paws at the air in "waving" motion	Paw (touch), ch 3
What is it, What's that	6 (Object fears)	Approach and touch object	
Where's (....)	5 (Find me)	Dog waits until told to find a person or item	

Behavior	Chapter/Page	Description	See also
Who's there	5 (Speak)	Dog barks on command and keeps barking until told to stop	

Mandy Book has been training dogs professionally for 16 years and previously owned and operated her own California-based training business for 10 years. In that time, she trained over 6000 dogs and their owners, including service dogs-in-training. As a volunteer at the Humane Society, she socializes and trains dogs of all ages, giving her a wide variety of experience with many breeds and temperaments. With a BA in psychology from San Jose State and ongoing seminar work in behavior with other industry experts such as Susan Garrett, Jean Donaldson, Sue Sternberg, Terry Ryan, and others, Ms. Book is widely considered a leader in the field of dog training. She currently teaches pet classes for Sirius Puppy Training, competes in agility, and does Bite-Free presentations to area schools with her boxer. She has been clicker training for 6 years.

Cheryl S. Smith is one of the "founding 500" of the Association of Pet Dog Trainers, as well as a long-time member of the Dog Writers Association of America and Cat Writers Association. She has won several awards for her writing on dogs. She frequently attends both training and veterinary conferences as a representative of the pet press, and has lectured at the Tufts Expo and Nutrition and Regulatory Conference. **Quick Clicks** is her ninth book on dogs, and others are in production. Ms. Smith has competed in many dog sports with a variety of purebreds and mixed breeds, and is currently practicing agility, herding, and tracking. She is still a crossover trainer, but learning more every day.